T0305311

MARKETING SCIENCE FICTIONS

An Ethnography of Marketing Analytics, Consumer Insight, and Data Science

Robert Cluley

BRISTOL
UNIVERSITY
PRESS

First published in Great Britain in 2025 by

Bristol University Press
University of Bristol
1–9 Old Park Hill
Bristol
BS2 8BB
UK
t: +44 (0)117 374 6645
e: bup-info@bristol.ac.uk

Details of international sales and distribution partners are available at bristoluniversitypress.co.uk

British Library Cataloguing in Publication Data
A catalogue record for this book is available from the British Library

ISBN 978-1-5292-3336-0 hardcover
ISBN 978-1-5292-3338-4 ePub
ISBN 978-1-5292-3339-1 ePdf

Cover design: Qube Design
Front cover image: Shutterstock/Normform
Bristol University Press uses environmentally responsible print partners.
Printed and bound in Great Britain by CPI Group (UK) Ltd, Croydon, CR0 4YY

FSC
www.fsc.org
MIX
Paper | Supporting
responsible forestry
FSC® C013604

Contents

List of Figures and Tables

Figures

Tables

Acknowledgements

I would like to thank my family, Victoria, Lana, and Wren, for supporting me during my ethnographic observations and for putting up with me as I completed this book.

I would also like to thank: Dr Campbell Jones for making my career as an academic possible and for being an inspirational and principled scholar; Dr Stephen Dunne for his insights on marketing theory, humour, and friendship; Professors Martin Parker and Gibson Burrell for teaching me everything I know about organization theory and for being tremendous gossips; Professor Alan Bryman for promoting ethnography; and Professor Steve Brown for his sage advice and his unrivalled intellect.

I met these academics, among many others, at the University of Leicester – an institution which, for about 20 years, was a bastion of innovative organizational scholarship. We thought that organizations, markets, and management were too important not to think about, critique, and study. The school attracted some of the best minds in social theory, philosophy, and politics. Sadly, it now stands in ruins – dismantled in the name of 'business'.

The research underpinning this book was enabled by Professor Andrew Smith at the University of Nottingham. The team he has assembled at N/LAB taught me much about data science and this was invaluable in this project. At the University of Nottingham, I was fortunate enough to be mentored by Professors Scott McCabe and Marek Korczynski and to learn from the brilliant Drs Linda Peters and Elizabeth Nixon. The research was supported by Nottingham University Business School and the British Academy (SG161403).

The ideas developed in the book have presented during research visits to the Universities of London, Edinburgh, Durham, Sussex, Birmingham, and Università della Svizzera italiana. Participants in these events are too numerous to name individually but the comments, questions, and criticisms they offered have been invaluable. Bristol University Press have been amazing, and I am very grateful to Paul Stevens and Isobel Green for their support. Finally, I would like to thank Bronwen Barradell for her beautiful line drawings.

1

Introduction

This book is about a unique type of organization: a marketing company. Although most people know what marketing is – or, at least, think they know – we know surprising little about these organizations, how they work, and the experiences of people in them. According to Svensson, a leading scholar of marketing in the real world, there is even 'little agreement as to what should be included in the notion of marketing work' (2019: 156). Marketing is, in this sense, an example of the kind of black box that keeps society ticking over (Latour, 1994). It is something which we all know exists but rarely stop to consider how it works.

Ask someone on the street and they will probably tell you that marketing involves selling products and creating brands. They may complain about being bombarded with invitations to complete surveys, describe nuisance cold callers, or annoying online adverts (Cluley, 2016). They will most likely point to advertising agencies, shopping malls, call centres, and tech companies as places where marketing happens (Heath et al, 2017).

Yet, marketing organizations rarely think of themselves in these terms. They tend to speak about fulfilling consumers' dreams (Marchand, 1985). At marketing industry events and in practitioners' accounts, you hear marketers talking about how they make mundane objects magical and invest them with meaning (Hegarty, 2011; de Waal Malefyt, 2017). They talk about helping their clients to make better decisions, driving economic growth, and improving social welfare (Wilkie and Moore, 1999). They present themselves as possessing unique knowledge about consumers and markets (Alvesson, 1994).

Although people might not immediately associate these ideas with marketing, they are not completely alien to many of us. We see them in critical studies of marketing. Here, marketers are described as hidden persuaders (Packard, 1957), captains of consciousness (Ewen, 1976), and conquerors of cool (Frank, 1998). They are also reflected in popular culture. TV series such as *Mad Men* present the world of advertising agencies to us in a way that makes it seem cool, stylish, and attractive. In this show, ad agents such as Don Draper and Peggy Olsen pull inspirational ideas out of thin air as they swig glasses of whiskey in tailored suits.

In making these claims, marketing organizations, marketing theorists, and cultural producers draw on two stereotypes about marketers (Nyilasy and Reid, 2009). They sometimes speak about marketers as creative artists. At other times, they imagine them as scientists who understand the fundamental laws of the marketplace.

These two stereotypes have been locked in an ongoing battle for the hearts and minds of marketing organizations since their emergence around 100 years ago (Braverman, 1974). For example, in 1923 an advertising agent called Claude Hopkins published a book called *Scientific Advertising*. He argues that advertising could, in fact should, be a science. He emphasizes the importance of developing scientific knowledge about consumer decision-making and advocates the use of scientific studies in marketing practice. He famously champions the use of advertising tests. These are quasi-experiments in which a marketing organization studies the effectiveness of different adverts on different groups of audiences. They can then select the most successful advert for wider release.

For Hopkins, marketing organizations and marketing workers such as advertising agents have the unique ability to take wider lessons from these tests. Specializing in producing, testing, and analysing marketing, they can discover the fundamental laws of the marketplace that apply to all products, all brands, and all consumers. Based on his research, for example, Hopkins advised his clients: 'brilliant writing has no place in advertising', 'frivolity has no place in advertising', and 'do not try to compete with the stories or the news columns, with the pictures or the cartoons in their field'.

Despite being wildly popular for decades, Hopkins' ideas hit problems in reality. The 'laws' he claimed to have discovered failed to produce the results he promised. One issue that emerged was that, in encouraging marketers to use the same methods, scientific advertising meant that everyone's adverts tended to say the same thing and look the same. Instead of differentiating mass-produced goods, scientific adverts were, themselves, indistinguishable and often ignored (Fletcher, 2008).

So, in the 1950s and 1960s, a new movement developed around another famous marketing practitioner called Bill Bernbach (Tungate, 2007). It became known as creative advertising (Feldwick, 2015). It epitomizes the stereotype of the marketer as an artist. Bernbach believed:

> The truth isn't the truth until people believe you, and they can't believe you if they don't know what you're saying, and they can't know what you're saying if they don't listen to you, and they won't listen to you if you're not interesting, and you won't be interesting unless you say

things imaginatively, originally, freshly. ... To keep your ads fresh you've got to keep yourself fresh. Live in the current idiom and you will create in it. (Bernbach, 2003, np)

In Bernbach's view, marketers should cultivate good taste, not learn rules. They should take risks so that the brands and products they promote stand out from the crowd. They should find ways to get people to listen and, through this, help brands persuade their customers of *their* truths – not the facts. This could not be achieved by following numbers but by following intuitions, passions, and instincts (Wells Lawrence, 2003).

This more creative and risky approach is rarely encouraged in the large bureaucracies that employ marketing organizations. It is for this reason, advocates of creative marketing argue, that marketing organizations exist as a unique business. They offer a creative service that their clients cannot perform for themselves. To fulfil this function, they must be organized around fun, emotions, and cultural consumption as these allow marketing workers to specialize in creative practices.

Despite the success of creative advertising in marketing practice from the 1960s onwards, the idea of marketing science refused to die. In fact, while creative advertising flourished in industry, scientific ideals were embedded into marketing scholarship (Tadajewski, 2014). There has long been a belief among marketing scholars who entered the field from outside disciplines such as psychology, economics, and engineering that marketing 'should be admitted into the category of a science' (Hutchinson, 1952: 286). This led, in the 1950s, to much soul-searching as marketing scholars questioned why their work 'is not more generally characterized as a science' (Bartels, 1951: 319).

It was not enough, some argued, to follow a scientific method, ape experimental logics, nor promote quantitative methods to make marketing scholarship a science. Thoughtful marketing scholars, such as Arndt (1985), turned to the sociology of science to suggest that marketing scholarship could become *more scientific* only by embracing alternative research paradigms including social constructionism, critical theory, even Marxism. However, a narrower idea developed as marketing scholars, influenced by operational research and microeconomics, branded their empiricism as 'marketing science'. According to Neslin and Winer: 'The earliest contributions to what we today call marketing science came from outside the field, usually from faculty trained in operations research/management science and residing in engineering departments, not business schools' (2014: 2). Founding contributions came from the likes of Frank Bass, who later inaugurated the Ehrenberg Bass Institute for Marketing Science – which we will see name-checked in practice in Chapter 7 – and Philip Kotler. These scholars formalized their approach in new academic journals such as *Marketing Science* and formed new associations such as the Marketing Science Institute, which was inaugurated in 1962.

As an intellectual movement, they did not bother questioning what made marketing scientific. Instead, they adapted Hopkins' (1923) experimental approach but fetishized increasingly complex statistical relationships between quantitatively measured variables that could be combined into mathematical models. As Neslin and Winer explain, 'the definition of "scientific techniques"' accepted in the marketing science movement 'was not limited to mathematical models' as the field also welcomes experimental approaches (2014: 4). But, there was an acceptance that mathematics is 'the language of science' – as an editorial in *Marketing Science* puts it (Shugan, 2002: 223). Scholars in the marketing science movement published textbooks illustrating their preferences with titles such as *Mathematical Models and Methods in Marketing* (Bass et al, 1961), *Mathematical Models and Marketing Management* (Buzzell, 1964), *Quantitative Techniques in Marketing Analysis* (Frank et al, 1962), *Marketing Models: Quantitative Applications* (Day and Parsons, 1970), and *Marketing Decision Making* (Kotler, 1971). Marketing science, as these titles indicate, came to stand for advanced statistical analysis.

The development of marketing science as an intellectual movement did 'not come about without resistance or controversy', but, as Bass writes, 'the resistance has been futile and the development of science in marketing inevitable. An old Arab saying best describes the outcome of the controversy: "The dogs bark, but the caravan passes"' (1993: 1). For evidence of its influence in academia today, we need only look at the references to 'marketing science' in the names of academic organizations, journals, and textbooks and the kinds of work they produce. The leading academic journals in the field of marketing reference marketing science and its institutions such as *Marketing Science* and the *Journal of the Academy of Marketing Science*. Contemporary best-selling textbooks are named *Data-driven Marketing* (Jeffery, 2010) and *Principles of Marketing Engineering* (Lilien et al, 2013).

The focus on quantifying the effects of variables such as pricing and product design on consumers and markets led marketing science to claim that it was more practical and business-focused than other ways of thinking about markets and consumers. A connection between science, quantitative research, and business was formed. It has become more prominent as new digital technologies have brought with them vast quantities of data and new modelling techniques. Marketing science has come to be linked with new scientific fields such as neuromarketing, marketing analytics, and data science. Each of these claims that, through the application of scientific methods and techniques, marketers can almost perfectly manage markets. They can push the 'buy button' in consumers' brains (Renvoisé and Morin, 2007), 'persuade anyone, anywhere, anytime' (Morin and Renvoisé, 2018), and predict consumers' behaviour (Smith, 2019). They can reveal inner truths that the consumers, themselves, are unaware of (Zuboff, 2019).

Yet, while opening the pages of academic journals, consultancy reports, and the business press, we might think that science has finally defeated art as the basis of marketing, when researchers have looked at scientific approaches used in marketing practice, they have found a host of non-scientific action and thinking (Zwick and Denegri Knott, 2009; Quinn et al, 2016; Zwick and Bradshaw, 2016). There is a thought that marketing science only works when people involved in marketing do not take the time to objectively, even scientifically, interrogate the tools, data, and theories they are using. The science of marketing may be a matter of blind faith more than anything else. It may be what the economic historian, Phillip Mirowski (2002), calls a 'machine dream'.

Cluley (2018), for example, asks what it means to say that a viewer has watched on online advert. He finds that many companies that sell online advertising space avoid asking this question – even though it is the foundation of their businesses. When they do, some argue that it is enough for an advert to just be loaded onto someone's computer or phone for it to count. They argue that it does not matter if the ad is instantly scrolled over by the viewer. But does this really tell us anything?

This splinter in the eye of scientific marketing is hard to avoid unless people are wilfully blind. In 2015, Randall Rothenberg, Executive Chair for the Interactive Advertising Bureau, the trade association for online and digital marketing in the United States, commented to the *Digiday* podcast: 'We've been in kind of like a ten-year craze mentality that begins with marketers who have not really inspected closely the meaning underneath the words they bandy about. So they go: "Data, data, data, data, it's all about the data, the data, the data, the data". Well, what data?' (Rothenberg, 2016). In response, there is a small but growing move to look past the hype and study 'marketing in its natural environment' (Zeithaml et al, 2020: 49).

Developing this perspective has implications outside of marketing theory and practice as, in various ways, marketing has assumed an important social role through its influence on digital technologies. The business model for most radical technologies of recent years, from Google to Facebook, Apple to Amazon, has depended on marketing (Srnicek, 2017). If we take Google as an example, it has been estimated that each web search costs around 10p. Google's consumers do not have to pay this (Berners-Lee, 2020). Rather, it is covered by advertisers who pay Google to access consumers. Companies like Google need to make technology that appeals to marketers' interests and this, consequently, shapes many of the essential tools we use in our everyday lives.

On this point, Zuboff's influential thinking on surveillance capitalism sees marketing as a key influence on contemporary social relations. Zuboff tells us that marketing has traditionally 'been a guessing game: art, relationships, and conventional wisdom, but never "science"' until the advent of digital technologies and social media (2019: 77). By collecting and analysing huge databases, these new technologies can help marketers to 'read user's minds for the purposes of matching ads to their interests' (Zuboff, 2019: 78). For Zuboff, they have fulfilled the machine dream of 'being able to deliver a particular message to a particular person at just the moment when it might have a high probability of actually influencing his or her behaviour' (Zuboff, 2019: 77–78).

But while critics such as Zuboff point the finger at marketing, they tend to reproduce the marketing science hype. They too accept the machine dream – even if they interpret it as a machine nightmare. A foundation of this book is that we cannot understand the role of marketing on society unless we actually understand marketing. Yet, we cannot understand marketing unless we study how marketing organizations actually work. Without doing so, we will swallow the Kool-Aid. We will take the promise of marketing science and digital technologies at face value. We will over-inflate the influence of marketing and the power of data science and overlook cracks in practice that could be opened up for critical interventions.

Marketing and science

To explore the relationship between marketing, science, art, and technology, this book takes inspiration from the sociology of science. In a sense, I want to take seriously the claim that marketing is a science and hold it up to the same level of scrutiny that is applied to other scientific fields. In the sociology of science, it is widely accepted that science exists separately as a cultural ideal *and* as a practice (Merton, 1973). The cultural ideal of science has a special function in society represented by 'the ethos of science' (Merton, 1938: 326). This is the idea of truthful and unmediated knowledge.

To explore how the cultural ideal of science plays out in practice, scholars have studied 'what people who claim to be doing science do' (Becker, 1996: 54–55). They have found that a scientific fact is not simply a matter of truthful or accurate knowledge as the cultural of ideal of science would have us believe. Indeed, there are plenty of wrong facts and more truth than scientific communities can recognize (Latour, 1987). A fact is, instead, better understood in terms of persuasion, rhetoric, and power relations – so-called 'extra-scientific factors' which shape what scientists, and others, accept is true (Collins and Evan, 2002: 239). In short, the practice of science does not live up to the ethos of science.

Expanding this, a branch of the sociology of science sometimes known as science studies tells us that a scientific fact is best understood as 'a product of the interaction between a large number of diverse actors' (Callon,

1990: 132). A fact must bring together a scientific community and fit into wider systems of knowledge (Kuhn, 1962). It will remain an interesting idea unless it opens up 'new acting capacities, new referential ventures and new empirical realities' (Muniesa, 2014: 93).

Callon (1984) describes these interactions as translations. Translation, he argues, is 'the mechanism by which the social and natural worlds progressively take form' and the way that actors 'define and associate the different elements by which they build and explain their world' (Callon, 1984: np). It is a four-stage process. First, a group of actors frame a situation as a problem (problematization). This attracts others to think about the issue in the same way (interessement). As a wider network is recruited, the original definition of the situation is locked in place (enrolment). Finally, a network capable of acting in concert emerges (mobilization). When they do, the fact is solidified as the basis of action and works its way into society.

Here, science studies suggests an affinity between science and marketing. It sees science as something that involves marketing. For example, Law and Williams suggest that when they disseminate their discoveries, scientists act like 'those who attempt to sell products in other areas of social life, scientists undertake a version of market research' (1982: 537). Law and Williams explain that scientists 'assess the likely value of their product to this group or that. They design the product in such a way that its value will be as clear as possible to potential users. They package and place it with the same considerations in mind' (1982: 537). Science in action, in other words, not only fails to live up to the ethos of science but may often follow the ethos of marketing.

Given this, I believe we can separate the ideals of marketing science from marketing science in action. To study marketing as a science, we need to pay special attention to the things people involved in marketing science actually do and not be misled by what they, and others, say they do. We need to understand how they translate the ideal of science and scientific practices to interest, enrol, and mobilize others to act on the basis of their facts.

Discourse and materiality

The sociology of science not only reveals the importance of marketing in scientific knowledge, it tells us that the process of translation that creates a fact from a discovery is not something that is done by humans alone. Latour and Woolgar (1979), for example, influentially illustrate how much of the work of science is delegated to measuring devices, recording equipment, and other non-human things. These are not neutral tools but shape what can be seen, known, and said. They must also be enrolled into a translation – as must other non-human things, from presentations to policy documents (Callon, 1984).

This has encouraged much debate in social theory, including marketing theory, about the ontological status of non-human actors (Fox and Allred, 2017). It has prompted new areas of social theory based on the view that society is 'the outcome of local constructions, but we are not alone at the construction site, since there we also mobilize the many nonhumans. ... To be human requires sharing with nonhumans' (Latour, 1994: 51). The key point, for me, is that we need to recognize the ways in which non-human actors shape social interactions. Here, Latour tells us that every artefact 'has its script, its "affordances", its potential to take hold of passersby and force them to play roles in its story' (1994: 31).

On this point, there is a connection between science studies and wider sociological thinking about how organizations work. It tells us that the things people work with and the spaces they work in reveal something about their activities – just as the vocabularies people develop when working together often reveal something fundamental about their activities (Deleuze, 1988). In *White Collar*, C. Wright Mills (1951) provides us with an early example of this viewpoint. For Mills, the design of offices and office buildings symbolizes a deep social change. It represents a society increasingly structured by large corporations and big business. He observes:

> As skyscrapers replace rows of small shops, so offices replace free markets. Each office within the skyscraper is a segment of the enormous file, a part of the symbol factory that produces the billion slips of paper that gear modern society into its daily shape. ... The office is the Unseen Hand become visible as a row of clerks and a set of IBM equipment, a pool of dictaphone transcribers, and sixty receptionists confronting the elevators, one above the other, on each floor. ... In the morning irregular rows of people enter the skyscraper monument to the office culture. During the day they do their little part of the business system, the government system, the war-system, the money-system, co-ordinating the machinery, commanding each other, persuading the people of other worlds, recording the activities that make up the nation's day of work. They transmit the printed culture to the next day's generation. And at night, after the people leave the skyscrapers, the streets are empty and inert, and the hand is unseen again. ... For every business enterprise, every factory, is tied to some office and, by virtue of what happens there, is linked to other businesses and to the rest of the people. Scattered throughout the political economy, each office is the peak of a pyramid of work and money and decision. (Mills, 1951: 189)

For Mills (1951), then, we can look at workspaces and the arrangement of physical objects in work settings as symbols of broad social trends. We can, in effect, see social relations in them. For Goffman (1959; 1961), in contrast, the selection of material objects in a space not only reflects wider social facts but also tells us about what type of organization occupies the space. Similar to his observations of individuals selecting their dress, manner, and language to present themselves to certain audiences, Goffman tells us that there are 'substantive implications' to the design of organizations' physical spaces (1961: 98). Organizations use material objects and spaces to symbolize their aims and values. It is part of their *impression management*.

This is particularly important in knowledge-based activities such as science and marketing. Goffman (1959) argues that organizations in these areas face a unique problem. Their 'clients cannot "see" the overhead costs of the service rendered them' – consequently, it is difficult for knowledge-based organizations to justify their costs (1959: 41). In response, such organizations tend to engage in elaborate displays and performances of their work which, literally, show the value of their efforts to their clients. Goffman writes:

> [I]t often happens that the performance serves mainly to express the characteristics of the task that is performed and not the characteristics of the performer. Thus one finds that service personnel, whether in profession, bureaucracy, business, or craft, enliven their manner with movements which express proficiency, and integrity, but, whatever this manner conveys about them, often its major purpose is to establish a favourable definition of their service or product. (Goffman, 1959: 83)

Burrell (2013), one of the most imaginative and innovative thinkers on organizations, brings these ideas together in his notion of *styles of organizing*. Whether they are involved in science, marketing, or making widgets, he argues that organizations are comprised of a constellation of cultures, identities, knowledge, communication systems, and materiality. Burrell explains: 'The architecture of our thought systems, by which we undertake the ideational organizing of ourselves, resembles in no small measure that solid material architecture in which we walk, work, and sleep.' Accordingly, Burrell calls for researchers to 'look up at the buildings that they inhabit – but to think foundationally'. If we do, we will see 'the same underlying expressions [and] intra-actions' at work in political economic systems, architecture, organization, and design (Burrell, 2013: 19).

The result is that, when we want to account for the practice of marketing science, it is not simply a matter of looking at what people involved do but also at what things, from buildings to technical artefacts, do and what they mean. We need to ask what the tools involved in marketing science tell us about what the people involved think they are doing. Material objects, the design of buildings, and the physical environment, all these things perform their own translations. They, too, do science and, we might assume, should also play a role in the practice of marketing science.

Marketing science studies

Scholars associated with and influenced by science studies have begun to apply this thinking to marketing practice (for example, Cochoy, 2007; 2008; 2009). Callon and Muniesa (2005), in particular, argue that calculation is the key translation practice in contemporary markets. Calculation, in their view, involves three translations. First, an object of measurement is agreed upon. This is a qualitative judgement in which a group of actors come to accept that something is important. Second, the actors agree on some way to measure it and, in the process, embed their understandings into the objects, technologies, and measuring devices they work with. Finally, the measurements produce new objects and acting capacities. In this process, Callon and Muniesa (2005) argue that calculation should not be equated to quantification. In fact, for Callon and Law, calculation 'has nothing to do with quantification' but everything to do with qualitative judgement about *what counts* and *who counts* (2005: 730). For Callon et al (2002), consumer markets should, accordingly, be conceived as spaces of quality rather than quantity.

But can we develop a science studies view of marketing – rather than apply concepts from science studies to marketing activities? That is, can we understand marketing science in action and develop new concepts to explain what marketing scientists do that are specific to marketing? My aim in this book is to follow Becker's guidance and develop what we can call *marketing science studies*. It starts from separating the ideal of marketing science from the practice of marketing science. It looks at what people who claim they are doing marketing science do. It asks us to find people who claim they are doing marketing science, find out *what* they do, and find out *how* they convince others that their work is valuable. It demands that we document how these marketing scientists describe their work and consider the tools, techniques, and objects they work with. It will account for discourse and materiality. It requires us to go to work with marketers.

Why ethnography?

The idea of marketing science studies calls for an ethnographic analysis of marketing. Ethnography is a research technique in which a researcher lives with their research subjects. The ethnographer might get into a music scene to understand how it works, they might join an online community or, in organizational ethnography, go to work in a specific organization. The aim is to both 'go native' – that is, learn to fit into the environment – but also maintain a position as an observer who does not accept the taken-for-granted assumptions and conventions that normally go unquestioned. Ethnographers, then, move between being participants in action and observers. They make the familiar strange.

Ethnographic research has two strengths for marketing science studies which are worth acknowledging.

First, it allows the researcher direct access to the action they are interested in. They do not have to rely on other people's accounts – as is the case with interviews, for example. While it is likely that people might be sceptical about being watched, over time, the ethnographer may be accepted as a confederate to the action. Eventually, a skilful ethnographer's role as an observer slips away as people let their guards down and stop editing their talk and behaviour. When this happens, ethnography can reveal what people do, not what people say they do. It exposes what organization theorists call theories-in-use rather than relying on practitioners espoused theories (Argyris and Schön, 1974).

Second, ethnographers have access to specific incidents and events. They do not have to rely on critical incidents, impressions, or anecdotes. To exploit this benefit, ethnographers aim to provide thick descriptions of the action they observe (Geertz, 1973). Their accounts are journalistic and detailed. They take the reader into the action.

With this in mind, in what follows, I present ethnographic observations from the work of a marketing company that is anonymized in the book as Super. I believe Super represents a setting in which people claim to be doing marketing science. I identified Super having seen their director of research present as part of an expert panel at a marketing industry workshop on data-driven discovery. He was introduced to the audience as an expert on marketing analytics, data science, and consumer insight. In short, a marketing scientist. I subsequently found out that Super had successfully convinced others about the legitimacy of its work as marketing science. It began as an idea in a bedroom but, having developed research products and marketing technologies, it had attracted government funding, venture capital, and, shortly before I saw the presentation at the industry workshop, had been bought by a Fortune 500 media conglomerate for nearly US$500 million. In publicizing these activities, Super promoted itself as a data science, advertising, and technology company operating the AdTech and MarTech spaces. These are relatively new business sectors which innovate new technologies and applications for marketing purposes of the kind that have attracted critical attention from the likes of Zuboff (2019).

To study the action at Super through a marketing science studies lens, in this book, I will think through three concepts.

Marketing action

Throughout the book I use the term 'marketing action' to refer to interactions that take place in marketing organizations such as Super. These involve productive activities that marketing workers perform, discussions between marketing workers about their work, and social relationships that develop within marketing organizations. Marketing action also includes the ways that marketing organizations relate to their clients, technology, culture, and wider society. In short, marketing action is what happens when people do marketing. As we will see, some aspects of marketing action are studied in some depth in the existing literature. But they are typically studied separately and are rarely combined into holistic accounts. I hope to overcome this limitation. Marketing action at Super was observed for 14 months, including a six-month participant observation ethnography in Super's European-based head office.

Marketing organizations

The book is about a unique kind of organization: the marketing organization. These are social spaces where marketing action occurs as the primary activity. They serve other organizations which, while possibly including some marketing activities, do other things as well. Marketing organizations depend on these other organizations for their purpose and existence. The structure of the relationship between them shapes marketing action in marketing organizations. It helps us to explain the strange and curious action that we see in marketing organizations. This book concentrates on a single marketing organization: Super.

Marketing workers

Marketing workers are the people who act within marketing organizations. I use the moniker 'marketing workers' here, as opposed to marketers or practitioners, because I want to acknowledge the fact that people in marketing organizations are at work. Their action is shaped by the employment relationship (Svensson, 2019). Marketing workers labour to earn a living. As such, they generate surplus value for the organization that employs them by entering into an organized labour process (Rosen, 1985). Without recognizing this, it is impossible to explain much marketing action (Brown, 2007). The marketing workers described in this book primarily work in the research team at Super. This is a department that has responsibility for designing, executing, and reporting marketing research conducted at Super. Put simply, the research team at Super perform scientific marketing for Super's clients. Reflecting the name of the research team, in what follows, I tend to refer to them as marketing researchers rather than marketing scientists.

Marketing science fiction

Based on my experiences in the research team at Super, I argue that both the stereotypes of marketers as scientists and artists are wrong. Marketing is neither an art nor a science. It is both. Marketing is a science fiction. That is, marketing is the art of using scientific knowledge, discourses, and artefacts in creative ways to help organizational decision-makers take actions in the face of otherwise overwhelming uncertainty.

The key here is the notion of modelling. As we have seen, marketing science is oriented around producing models. Academic marketing scientists think these have value because they use the language of science – mathematics. This is their mistake. Models are important because they simplify the world for organizational decisions. It does not matter if they do this through numbers or words. Indeed, as we will see, in marketing action, words have some significant advantages over numbers. When they work together with numbers, they are even more powerful. I describe this as marketing science fiction.

Marketing science fiction displayed at Super has three distinguishing features.

First, it is built from a particular view of the service marketing organizations offer their clients. Marketing organizations act on the basis that their clients are organizational decision-makers who need help so they can make decisions. They do not view them as being myopic, cowardly, or stupid partners who rely on marketing organizations to tell them which decision to make – as others in the ethnographic study of marketing argue. Rather, they are attuned to the problem of uncertainty as a core motivation for marketing action (Braverman, 1974). Marketing organizations perform a function organizational theorists call uncertainty absorption for their clients. This is an idea developed by Herbert Simon (Simon, 1945; March and Simon, 1958). Interestingly, marketing science as an academic discipline is in rooted in Simon's work. Following Simon's belief that decision makers operate through models, the founders of marketing science originally thought of themselves as marketing modellers not mathematicians (see Bass, 2001). Yet, Simon's theory of modelling in practice has alluded them. By providing trusted but simplified models and explanations that align with their clients' interests, needs, and expectations, marketing organizations help their clients to make decisions. They treat science as a tool, not an objective.

Second, marketing science fiction enrols discourses and artefacts that represent science to non-scientists. Scientism, or the aping of scientific methods, language, and objects, ironically organized by creative artists, lends marketing organizations an air of authority and certainty. Following

Goffman (1959), scientific resources symbolize the type of knowledge marketing organizations offer. At Super, these references can be distinguished into *general scientism* and *specific scientism*. The former refers to a wide range of scientific practices without noting differences between them. The latter references computational sciences through appeals to big data, algorithms, and computational technologies.

Computational methods, though, produce both too much data and not enough information. The size of big datasets and the fine-grained analysis that computers afford creates what I call surplus research and, at the same time, produces many empty signifiers that marketing researchers must fill with meaning. This forces marketing workers to engage in the final stage of marketing science fiction. I call it artistic qualification. This begins with the practice I label marketing outsight. Here, marketing workers both hide, ignore, and reframe much of the data they gather. They do so to construct simplified models and explanations for their clients. They then bring new interpretations to the data based on their imaginations and intuition.

The result of these three features of marketing science fiction is that the supposed victory of marketing science marks the reinforcement of creative practices in marketing action. Ironically, this occurs under the guise of science. Recognizing this helps us to put the ideal of marketing science into perspective. It has implications for marketing theorists, practitioners, and educators. It shows that marketing is far more complex than the ideal of science suggests. In many ways, marketing action would be much easier – but also less valuable – if it genuinely lived up to the ethos of science. If all marketing workers had to do was communicate findings about consumers in a disinterested and objective way, their work would be straightforward. But, as the sociology of science tells us, if this were the case, marketing action would be less scientific.

Understanding marketing science fiction also prompts caution concerning some of the most stringent critiques of marketing and its influence on contemporary society, such as the idea that marketing is driving the automation of social life by embedding surveillance technologies and feedback loops into our everyday experiences (Turow, 2012; Srnicek, 2017; Zuboff, 2019). These accounts focus on the technical, computation, and mathematical infrastructure of the digital technologies that marketers use (O'Neil, 2017). They rarely explore them in use. Like the advocates of marketing science in industry, they fetishize the technology. But these infrastructures bring with them a machine dream, or machine nightmare, that is not borne out on the ground in marketing organizations. They are far from perfect. They require much more human action to make them work than the critics suggest and, at the same time, offer more opportunities for critical reflections and interventions.

Overview of book

By way of overview, the book opens with three chapters looking at existing ethnographic studies of marketing. This work is done to demonstrate both the value of ethnographic understandings of marketing and the limits of existing studies. Chapter 2 offers a detailed account of three classic ethnographic studies to set a theoretical basis for the book. It suggests that marketing has traditionally been theorized in this tradition through a structural functionalist paradigm. Chapter 3 develops the discourses of Marketing Art and Marketing Science in more depth. Chapter 4 engages with methodological issues. These chapters form an academic foundation for the book. Readers who want to get straight into the marketing action might want to start on Chapter 5 and return to these chapters as needed.

In these background chapters, I engage in some unusual academic writing practices. In particular, I conduct what I call 'ethnographic quoting'. Put simply, this involves detailed expositions of ethnographic studies that include lengthy direct quotations. This practice contradicts the conventions of normal academic publishing with its focus on 8,000-word journal articles. But, recognizing the important link between ethnographic observation, analysis, and writing, the so-called ethnography-as-text perspective, I have included lengthy quotes from original studies to reflect their authors' accounts. Without doing so, I believe it is impossible to exploit the benefit of ethnographic studies. It is hard for thick descriptions to travel to other texts without the use of direct quotations.

Having set the background to the book, Chapter 5 introduces the case study organization – a large marketing company anonymized as Super. It offers an account of the everyday action at Super and gives a sense of what life is like working in the organization in general and within the research team specifically.

Chapter 6 asks what kind of service market researchers at Super think they are offering their clients. Focusing on a meeting in which members of the research team discuss how to analyse a dataset, I argue that marketing researchers at Super assume their clients are organizational decision-makers who face complex questions, act in information-rich environments, and have to balance competing demands. In short, they imagine their clients are people who need to make decisions but struggle to do so because there is too much uncertainty about what they should do. Instead of offering them instructions on the best course of action, market researchers absorb uncertainty so that their clients can act. To understand this, I provide a review of classic organization theory associated with the thinking of Herbert Simon.

Chapter 7 builds on this understanding. It describes the ways that scientific ideas, methods, and images are presented to clients at Super. I argue that Super projects a general image of its activities as being scientific to encourage its clients to put their faith in Super's research. But Super also emphasizes what I call the 'computationality' of its work by materializing the immateriality of computer code. This also builds clients' confidence in Super and facilitates the process of uncertainty absorption.

Chapter 8 looks at the ways that computational methods call for creative work. Analysing the technical infrastructure behind one of Super's most computational research products, I show how it leads to the practice of 'marketing outsights'. Here, we see how the wealth of data that can be analysed by computers and the fine-grain nature of their analysis produces surplus research. While granting marketing work an air of science, computational methods create problems that can only be solved by researchers using their imaginations and intuitions to push much of the surplus research out of sight.

Chapter 9 explores the practice of interpretation in more detail. Analysing a single meeting, it shows how market researchers think about their data using the analytic tools of 'the stat' and 'the headline'. The stat is a single number – often a percentage. The headline is a short statement about a stat that has a matter-of-fact quality to it. Together the stat and headline summarize the key findings of a research study. In the language of Simon's organization theory, they are simple models that absorb uncertainty. We will see how these two analytic tools allow market researchers to engage in a process of 'artistic qualification', in which they iterate between what they want to say, what the data allows them to say, what they think their clients want to hear, and what they think people will believe.

Chapter 10 shows how these more creative practices are materialized in space and in the objects on display at Super. It describes a presentation of a research project to a client audience and shows how this is staged as a theatrical event to encourage conversation, prompt social interactions, and increase the empathy between the presenters and the audience. Returning to science studies, I argue that these effects enrol the audience into the research process. They transform cold, objective, scientific research into the basis for organizational action taken by humans by encouraging sociality between marketing researchers and their clients. In the final chapter, I offer reflections on my experiences as an ethnographer in a marketing organization.

2

The Ethnographic Classics

Is there a unique ethnographic theory of marketing? Or, put otherwise, if we study marketing through ethnography can we develop new ways of understanding it? According to Wang, an ethnographer who observed marketing action in the Beijing office of one of the world's most successful creative advertising companies, 'theory is inextricably linked to methodology' (2010: 305). Ethnographic studies should, in other words, support a specific theory of marketing. Here, I want to focus on the things we have learned about marketing action by looking through an ethnographic lens.

To do so, I describe what I consider to be the three classic ethnographic studies which, despite their different empirical contexts and concerns, set the foundation for an ethnographic theory of marketing action. These are studies reported by Rosen (1985), Moeran (2005; 2006; 2007; 2009), and Alvesson (1994; 1998; 2001). Collectively, they look at marketing from the peculiar, surprising, and unexpected action witnessed in marketing organizations – not academic definitions and industry hype. They show us that, alongside doing their actual jobs, marketing organizations and individual marketing workers spend much of their time trying to 'convince themselves, as well as customers, that they have something to offer' (Alvesson, 1994: 544). These are actions that are so ingrained in marketing that many marketing workers take them for granted. Perhaps because of this, they are almost completely ignored by most academic marketing theory too. The experiences of the people doing marketing 'have been given poor attention both in research and marketing textbooks' (T. Nilsson, 2019: 233).

To explain these peculiarities, the classic ethnographic studies draw on a range of sociological traditions. Rosen (1985) emphasizes the discursive and ideological nature of marketing action, Moeran (2005; 2006; 2007; 2009) emphasizes the theatrics of self-promotion, and Alvesson (1994; 1998; 2001) emphasizes power and organizational politics. However, on closer inspection, there is a structural-functionalist view of marketing action implicit in this body of thinking (see Burrell and Morgan [1979] for a detailed overview of this research paradigm). As we will see at the end of the chapter, although this paradigm is not often linked with ethnographic research, nor the theory explicitly discussed in the classic ethnographies of marketing, each of the classic ethnographies explains marketing action through the uncertain nature of marketing work and its implications for the relationships between marketing organizations, their clients, and marketing workers. To establish this, in this chapter, I will take a deep-dive into the classic ethnographic accounts of marketing action, workers, and organizations.

Things don't just happen

As discussed in Chapter 1, ethnography is a method for making the everyday and mundane seem extraordinary. Ethnographers work to reveal elements of experience that are taken for granted by the people involved but are fundamental to those experiences. In this regard, where the ethnographic lens focuses on marketing, it has looked past the kinds of marketing activities one finds discussed in Marketing 101 textbooks, such as writing advertising copy, managing distribution channels, listening to customers, and so forth. Instead, ethnographers have concentrated on what social theorists call 'impression management' (Goffman, 1959). This refers to the ways that marketing organizations and marketing workers display themselves as competent and professional partners to each other and their clients. Such action is not necessarily about doing marketing but, rather, presenting it.

This is illustrated beautifully in Rosen's (1985) early ethnographic study of an annual social event held by an American advertising agency. It is worth reviewing this study at length both because it develops key themes discussed later in the ethnographic tradition and because of the ethnographic detail reported by Rosen (1985).

The organization Rosen (1985) describes, Spiro and Associates, is a leading advertising agency based in Philadelphia in the United States. It employs over 100 people. Every year, after the Labor Day holiday, Spiro and Associates hold an 'Agency breakfast' at a local luxury hotel. All employees are required to attend. The event's importance leads Rosen to develop what he calls a 'Breakfast analysis' (1985: 32). This is a detailed description and interpretation of the event as an attempt by senior leaders to 'influence the practice of members' of the company using the same 'manipulation of ideas' that the advertisers working at Spiro's normally use to influence consumers (Rosen, 1985: 32).

Breakfast at Spiro's

The breakfast is held in a ballroom. Twelve circular tables are set with fine tableware. Attendees arrive promptly. Men are in business suits and women

18

wear business suits or dresses. Breakfast is served, silver-service style, by formally suited waiters in synchronization at exactly 8:30am. It begins with Eggs Benedict.

At 9am, Walter Spiro, chairman of the company, takes to a stage at the front of the ballroom. A 59-year-old man of about five feet, seven inches, 'with a balding head and a face soft and creased with years of evident well living', Walter Spiro appears to Rosen as 'a Bronx boy in fine clothes' (Rosen, 1985: 32). He delivers a speech that celebrates the company's performance over the last year, highlights the challenges they have encountered, and hints at storms looming on the horizon.

Commenting on the staging of the event, Rosen argues that the breakfast seems designed to increase the 'commensality' in the company (1985: 33). That is, it is a way of bringing together employees who, in their day-to-day activities, are stratified by seniority and function such that they experience very different realities at the agency. Rosen writes:

> That the members of Spiro and Associates all sit and eat together in one room as one body transforms formally unifunctional, contractual relationships to one another and to the agency into an arena for multifunctional relations of communion and amity. At the same time, group identity and exclusiveness is signified by the body 'breaking bread together'. Those inside the ballroom are Spiro and Associates. Those outside are not. (Rosen, 1985: 33)

An important way in which the event increases the sense of community and social ties among the Spiro's employees is by removing the divisions that structure their normal interactions – notably, the divisions between creative and business personnel and between those inside the power structure, such as senior executives and team directors, and those on the outside, such as clerical workers. These divisions are symbolized in everyday activities at Spiro's through the dress code. Rosen writes:

> The primary bifurcation in a 'typical' advertising agency, both socially and culturally, is between the creative and business roles. In general, the dress norms governing each of these roles are different. This is also the case at Spiro and Associates, where there is an explicit dress code for those performing business functions, but none for those performing creative functions. The dress code, in fact addressed only to business males, states that suits (of appropriate color, tailoring, and fabric – not polyester, for example) must be worn at work, and so on. Female business clothing norms have yet to be formally codified. Though expected to dress in a fashion paralleling the requirements for men, more leeway exists for women for variations on the theme

of formality, such as wearing dresses. … The difference in dress norms between roles in the agency correspond to its power hierarchy. The clerical workers and, by and large the creative people, are not in the main contest for wealth, influence, and power, and are hence not as socially constricted in their behavior. By contrast, the behavior of those vying for the larger rewards of power, the business people, is highly circumscribed. Clothing, hair styles, expressed values and goals, friendships, verbal patterns, social club memberships, and other presumed ideational expressions are more closely restricted. Through these closures the borders of the powerful are in part maintained. (Rosen, 1985: 34)

At the breakfast, these sartorial divisions are removed. All employees, from those on the lowest rung of the organizational hierarchy to those on the top tier, wear the same attire. Indeed, they sit at the same tables, eating the same meal, served to them by the same waiters at the same time. In Rosen's words, these features of the breakfast are 'used to camouflage distinct intra-organizational role identity, and hence power and status differences, in order to create a communion among disparate groups' (Rosen, 1985: 34).

Normal divisions within the agency are not only overcome by the arrangement of the breakfast but also its style. Just as the dress code undermines functional divisions that exist at Spiro's between creative and business departments, the quality of the meal and the luxury of the surroundings symbolically removes distinctions based on seniority and power. The breakfast is a moment where all members of the organization share an experience of economic success. Rosen writes:

The techniques of using the opulent hotel, ballroom, china, food, and so on also serve an additional function. On the basis of their salaries the majority members cannot normally afford such aspects of high culture, the attaining of which is a goal dictated by capitalist logic. The fine surrounding reinvests this goal with meaning, saying that at least by association members can now afford part of 'the good life'. If the members continue participation more will be theirs in the future. (Rosen, 1985: 34)

But, even though these arrangements bring the organization together symbolically for the duration of the breakfast, the divisions exist. Indeed, for Rosen, the image of community symbolized by the staging of the breakfast may actually be intended to sustain divisions. Here, Rosen compares the sense of community symbolized in the breakfast with the content of Walter Spiro's speech.

Walter Spiro opens his presentation by highlighting the company's strong economic performance. He emphasizes that they have seen an 18 per cent increase in revenue compared to the previous year. He then honours individual employees who have given outstanding service to the company. He offers gifts to employees who have been with the company for at least five years and commands the attendees to show their appreciation of these colleagues by leading a round of applause for each recipient. After this, he discusses the state of the business and invites representatives from each department to present their view of the last year. For Rosen, they enter into a social drama in which each departments seeks to legitimize its version of events and to reify – or make real – its version of the company's reality.

Walter Spiro returns to discuss the company's policy on pay, bonuses, and 'profit sharing' (Rosen, 1985: 42). That is, the distribution of economic rewards between the company, its owners, and its employees. Rosen tells us that, prior to the breakfast, the senior leaders at Spiro's had decided to postpone all increases in pay.

This is a contentious issue. Justifying it in his speech, Walter Spiro explains that the management team have decided to pause pay rises for all employees so that they have more time to understand the economic situation. Despite the strong revenue growth he had highlighted earlier in his speech, Walter Spiro now explains that senior leaders have agreed they need to be more confident before they can decide the acceptable level of retained profit. This, in turn, is dependent on continued strong performance inside the company and good fortune when it comes to external factors beyond anyone's control such as turbulence in the wider economy.

In his next breath, Walter Spiro emphasizes the munificence of the company towards its employees. He tells them that 'while other companies may put away money for retained earnings for a rainy day … we've decided to give our money in the most generous possible way' by offering more significant bonus payments (Rosen, 1985: 42). This claim, combined with the opulence they are experiencing, may give attendees a strong impression that they are all sharing equally in the economic successes of the previous year and, by implication, all suffering equally from the pain inflicted by the pay freeze. Walter Spiro makes a point of emphasizing that the decision to pause pay increases also affects senior managers, including him.

However, in conversation with the agency's finance officer and executive vice president after Walter Spiro's speech, Rosen hears a different side of the story. The finance officer tells Rosen that Spiro and Associates is well-known in the industry for its poor rates of pay. The bonuses that the company awards typically only bring its employees' compensation to the industry average. In the finance officer's view, 'top management is primarily depriving general members of realizable income here through bonuses' (Rosen, 1985: 43).

The finance officer explains that the use of bonuses in place of wages pushes financial risks from the company to the workers. In lean years, in fact even in successful years, senior leaders, headed by Walter Spiro, can legitimately withhold bonus payments on the basis that the company's financial performance has tied their hands. At the same time, the company can operate with lower staff costs than its competitors. This maximizes the profitability of the company and its value for its owners. So, the use of bonuses rather than basic pay offers a direct financial benefit to the company's owners, primarily Walter Spiro, at the expense of the workers.

On this point, the finance officer also informs Rosen that Spiro and Associates typically retains a higher proportion of its earnings than similar companies and that, given the ownership structure of the company, these are essentially payments to the senior leadership team. Seen through this lens, 'Walter's discussion obscures the securing of profit by capital' (Rosen, 1985: 44). He presents an interpretation of economic relations at Spiro's which differentiates pay, stock dividends, bonuses, and retained earnings. As the finance officer argues, this interpretation is open to challenge as, ultimately, each of these payments is really 'a related distribution' of the company's income (Rosen, 1985: 44).

Yet, Rosen tells us, 'although many members expressed discomfort concerning the freeze, no one with whom I talked proposed any relation between it and these extra-wage returns to capital' (1985: 45). In other words, by the end of the breakfast, Walter Spiro's economic 'reality is reified to the extent that the assumptions upon which it is based are reified' (1985: 44). Put simply, the audience accepts the separation of pay, bonuses, and retained profits and the securing of profit by the owners of the company as a natural part of life in a marketing organization.

So, Rosen concludes, while it appears to focus on communality, the breakfast is really a way of selling economic inequality within Spiro and Associates. It is staged and scripted in two, seemingly contradictory, ways that fit together in an act of persuasion. The arrangement of the breakfast strengthens social bonds within the organization. The workers in different departments and at different levels in the power structure share an aspirational experience of economic success. At the same time, Walter Spiro's speech convinces members of the organization of a particular version of their economic relationships that sustains economic inequality in the organization.

For Rosen, these two different dramatic effects work together like the acts of a play. The contradiction between the techniques that promote community and those which reify the social and economic division in the organization give the event a dramatic tension. Summarizing the performance, Rosen suggests a sleight of hand: 'Where munificence is declared, appropriation exists, clouded against a background of familial caring for the "we-ness" that is proposed as Spiro and Associates' (1985: 44).

Social drama

To make sense of this event, Rosen (1985) frames the action he observes as a performance. In fact, Rosen's description of the ways that the leadership team at Spiro's seeks 'to influence ideas, thus shaping action, thus shaping experience, consequently shaping ideas' has been applied widely outside of studies of marketing to understand the cultural and symbolic elements of bureaucracies (1985: 33). His report is probably more influential outside of marketing studies thanks to his contribution to organizational dramaturgy. This is a field of study which assumes that 'many aspects of life in organizations and elsewhere may be seen as being staged' (Mangham, 2005: 943). In this regard, Rosen explains:

> [T]he style of dress affected, the particular hotel and room chosen for the event, the time of day it is held, the technique of commensuality, the type of food eaten, the manner in which the food is presented and served, the general technique of rhetoric and the specific message verbally communicated all combine to communicate a particular message, to objectify and reify a particular social structure with ramifications for the maintenance of a particular order. (Rosen, 1985: 33)

Nevertheless, the particular social order that Rosen observes is a marketing organization. His study is an ethnography of marketing action. The breakfast is an elaborately staged performance by senior leaders in a marketing organization. This context is important. It shows us that marketing organizations must convince marketing workers that their compensation is fair, that any extra rewards accrued by senior leaders are justified, and that any losses of spending power incurred by the workers are not up for discussion. It demonstrates that marketing workers, ultimately, work for others and that marketing action is organized to create a profit from their work.

In this sense, Rosen's ethnography shows us how the leaders of marketing organizations convince their workers of the value of their work. In so doing, Rosen's (1985) account not only illustrates that marketing organizations can be spaces of economic inequality but also that these relations are sustained by the same persuasive techniques marketing organizations use to influence consumers. In other words, Rosen (1985) shows us that marketing is a technique that influences relations in the office as well as the market.

On the surface the breakfast might appear frivolous and unconnected with the real activities involved in marketing. Yet, Rosen's (1985) analysis suggests it is incredibly functional for a marketing organization. The breakfast reifies senior leaders' views and legitimizes the distribution of economic rewards in their favour. It is an episode in which symbolic resources are used to facilitate economic inequality. In short, as much as the breakfast illustrates the importance of symbolic action in sustaining organizational relationships, it also tells us about the social and economic relations within a marketing organization. Even here, value comes from exploiting workers and recruiting them to support their own exploitation.

Bringing this together, we can say that Rosen's (1985) ethnography provides us with a foundational proposition for an ethnographic theory of marketing. Marketing is not simply a matter of advertising, distribution, branding, consumer research, and so on. It involves significant symbolic interactions. These are staged to valorize economic relations within a marketing organization.

Tricks of the trade

While Rosen's (1985) account focuses on the ways that marketing organizations stage performances to shape internal relations between workers, managers, and owners, the second classic ethnographic study of marketing I want to discuss describes the ways marketing organizations influence their clients' perceptions using similar dramatic techniques. Moeran's (2005; 2006; 2007; 2009) studies of the creative processes at an advertising agency explore these actions in depth. He describes his experiences at Asatsu, a large Japanese advertising agency, and details a particular event in which the agency pitches creative concepts to a Japanese electronics brand called Frontier.

As with Rosen's (1985) account, the action Moeran observes is intended to secure an economic advantage for a marketing organization. It too involves the translation of symbolic resources into economic rewards. However, Moeran focuses on the ways marketing organizations make this translation in their relations with potential clients. Moeran explains:

> It is an advertising agency's job to persuade an advertiser that it is better suited than its competitors to take on a particular account. This it does by actively soliciting a prospective client, with the aim of being asked to participate in a competitive presentation or 'pitch' in which, together with other agencies, it will propose marketing and creative strategies on the basis of the client's orientation of its needs. (Moeran, 2005: 904)

The preparation of a pitch is, then, for Moeran, a moment when a marketing organization brings to the fore fundamental elements of its relationships with its clients. A pitch involves 'a number of carefully staged phases' that come together in 'a rite of persuasion' (Moeran, 2005: 912). Similar to Rosen's (1985) observation of Walter Spiro staging a compelling presentation of a partial account of reality to encourage his audience to reify it as an objective fact, Moeran's ethnography witnesses marketing workers using symbolic resources to convince their client of the value of their work so they can win an account.

Preparations

Frontier, a large Japanese consumer electronic brand, has asked its current creative agency, J&M, to prepare an advertising campaign to strengthen its brand image in Germany and the United States. Simultaneously, it invites Asatsu to prepare a campaign for consideration as well. Asatsu already handles some of Frontier's domestic accounts and, as key decision-makers at Frontier's International Division are not satisfied with J&M's work, Frontier wants to see what Asatsu can offer. Asatsu and J&M enter a competitive pitch for the account that will culminate in an in-person presentation to Frontier (see Cluley [2017] on pitching).

The prospect of winning a prestigious, 'blue chip' account like Frontier's International Division is strategically important for Asatsu. These accounts make it easier for an agency to win new business. As Moeran puts it:

> Accounts are not simply sums of money. Like art objects, they bring with them certain values that are not purely economic, but derive from their ownership (or provenance), history and association (with previous agencies, for example). In advertising industries all over the world, therefore, agencies gain prestige from the clients whose accounts they are contracted to handle. (Moeran, 2006: 32)

Reflecting this importance, after being contacted by Frontier, Asatsu sets up an unusually large account team to develop creative concepts based on data supplied by Frontier and to deliver the final pitch to Frontier. The team is led by an account manager called Ueda, and includes two other account managers, one of whom had previously worked on a Frontier account. The team works with Asatsu's marketing team, media buyers, and creative team. Initially, they decide to pitch aspirational adverts that emphasize the quality of Frontier's products, the brand's reputation for innovation, and the role of entertainment in consumers' lives. The creative team produce six possible campaigns that fit this brief.

Now, they recruit Moeran, who was visiting Asatsu as an academic observer, to support their work. Answering a telephone call at home late in the evening, the team ask him if, as an anthropologist and European, he could check the English in the adverts and give his assessment of the six potential ads that the creative team has prepared. Moeran describes his reaction at being invited into this normally hidden space of marketing work: 'Me? Help? Doing my best to hold down my excitement, I reassured [the contact from Asatsu] that I was still very much awake and asked what I could do to help' (2006: 7).

The next morning, Moeran enters a small, windowless meeting room in Asatsu's office and is introduced to half a dozen men who are 'all smoking and gazing at several large placards on the tables in front of them' (2006: 7). The walls of the room are adorned with adverts by Frontier's rivals. Ueda asks Moeran to assess the six campaigns developed by Asatsu's creative team and explains that the account team will present them to Frontier's managers that afternoon in a 'pre-presentation' (Moeran, 2005: 907). This is a meeting that occurs before the final pitch and gives the account team a chance to get feedback.

The pre-presentation lasts two hours. Three members of Frontier's International Division are joined by a large delegation from Asatsu in a cramped meeting room in Asatsu's offices. Ueda talks through the overall approach and faces 'some sharp questions' from Frontier's team (Moeran, 2006: 9). They question the choice of colours and taglines in the mocked-up campaign adverts and probe the details of Asatsu's media plans. Troublingly, the most senior Frontier executive asks if Asatsu is going to 'recommend a particular approach' in the pitch or is it 'going to leave Frontier to fumble around on its own?' (Moeran, 2006: 9). As well as pushing Asatsu's team for concrete plans, they emphasize the importance of market research into 'American and German cultural differences' to Frontier's head office (Moeran, 2009: 10). It needs 'back-up reasoning to persuade its staff that whatever choices it made were right' (Moeran, 2005: 909).

Following the pre-presentation meeting, the account team hold a 'post-mortem' meeting to discuss this feedback (Moeran, 2005: 909). This is a separate meeting among themselves in which they discuss the events in the pre-presentation. Here, the account team decides that the presentation was too fragmented and that the final pitch should be delivered by a single presenter. They predict that J&M will 'certainly take along at least one foreigner to its presentation' to establish their credibility in handling international accounts (Moeran, 2006: 10). So, while they had already 'co-opted' Moeran 'as a "real" Westerner to conceptualize' their creative ideas, the team now ask if he will also attend their final pitch (2005: 915).

In the post-mortem, the account team agree that they must find out who the 'target man' is at Frontier (Moeran, 2006: 10). This is the key decision-maker at Frontier who is most likely to decide the result of the pitch. One of the account team offers to use his social network to talk informally to contacts at Frontier. They say they will find out who the target man is, investigate which campaign the target man is 'likely to approve or disapprove of', and try to make the target man 'better predisposed to select Asatsu' (Moeran, 2006: 11). Having found out in the pre-presentation that J&M would pitch before them, the account team also agree to postpone their final decisions about which campaign to pitch until they have 'heard what had gone on there' (Moeran, 2006: 11). This means that they will have even tighter deadlines and will have to deal with much more uncertainty.

As luck would have it, as the account team discuss the demand to include research on American and German culture, they discover 'half a dozen forty-year-old American men with artificial suntans' in Asatsu's building auditioning for a role in a TV commercial (Moeran, 2005: 910). They recruit them as a focus group and ask them to evaluate six mocked-up campaign ads. However, this proves unsuccessful and the focus group does not reveal anything interesting. So, later that evening, Moeran talks through the taglines developed by Asatsu's creative team with his international friends. Based on their feedback, he calls Ueda that evening and suggests his own tagline. He recommends that the presentation team explain that they designed a concept that 'did not have any associations with those of rival companies' (Moeran, 2005: 911).

On the call, Moeran offers a Saussurian justification for the campaigns. He reports that 'Ueda listened politely, but did not sound particularly enthusiastic. I had the distinct impression that he had a sound grasp of both the theory and practice of structural linguistics and had already done this kind of reasoning for himself' (Moeran, 2006: 13). Nevertheless, with a final deadline looming, the account team is occupied with sorting out last-minute issues, compiling statistics, and calculating media costs, Moeran's justification may be the best they have.

The pitch

The pitch takes place in Frontier's head office. Asatsu's account team travels there by train, carrying projectors, slides, print-outs, and storyboards with them. Once they arrive, they are shown to a meeting room on the top floor of the building. They learn that it is normally reserved for meetings of the company's board of directors. This space includes an 'anteroom for the performers to prepare in and retire to' (Moeran, 2006: 14).

They set up the materials they brought with them. Then Asatsu's delegation sit down at one side of a large oval conference table in the centre of the room. Two dozen executives from Frontier take their places opposite them.

The spatial division between the presenters and the audience is augmented by other distinctions in the room. Within the account team from Asatsu, there is a sartorial division between creative and account staff, similar to that noted by Rosen (1985). The creatives 'sport eye-catching accessories (silver bracelets, gold rings, tinted glasses) and dress in flamboyant shirts without ties', while the account executives wear 'the sober dark suit, white shirt and innocuous tie expected of "humdrum" office personnel' (Moeran, 2006: 72). The latter offer a point of alignment between Frontier's staff, who largely wear formal business attire, and Asatsu's account team. Moeran explains that the account team 'neatly combines through manner and appearance the two requirements sought after by a client in search of an advertising agency: "creativity" ... and a business-like approach to everyday matters of importance to the client' (Moeran, 2006: 71–72).

Before starting, the 'most senior person present' from Frontier, who has also abandoned the 'standard "salaryman"' uniform, in preference for shirt sleeves, announces his presence 'with the throwaway line: "You'd better keep me awake. I've only just come back from New York and am suffering from jet lag"' (Moeran, 2006: 71). Ueda then begins the presentation. He gives a general introduction that orients Frontier's relationship with Asatsu and proceeds to discuss Asatsu's proposed strategy and market analysis. He works through different taglines, including Moeran's, and explains the reasoning behind each possible appeal. Here, Ueda justifies the work 'along precisely the Saussurian lines' that Moeran had suggested (Moeran, 2006: 14). Upon finishing, Ueda, who had 'clearly given everything to the presentation', nearly collapses (Moeran, 2006: 15). His initially smart appearance is replaced by a 'dishevelled collar and tie, accompanied by beads of perspiration' (Moeran, 2006: 73). After the pitch, the account team packs up their things and returns home.

The next day the account team is asked to assemble for a formal announcement about the pitch in a meeting room in Asatsu's offices. On the way, Moeran hears rumours that Asatsu has won the account. This is confirmed in the meeting. There, the account team are told that, while the creative work was broadly acceptable to Frontier, they were convinced to choose Asatsu over J&M by the strength of the pitch. Frontier reported that they were particularly impressed by Ueda's commitment and energy.

The announcement is a special occasion. This is the reason why it takes place in a comfortable room that is 'usually reserved for presentations made by the agency on its home turf' to its clients (Moeran, 2006: 15). This room has a single window that looks out at a closed roof area that is decorated as a Japanese garden. There are no clocks or telephones in the room. The chairs are plush and its single, long conference table is 'expansive and well-polished, affording those present a sense of their own significance' (Moeran, 2006: 61). For Moeran, compared to the cramped conditions in the room the account team had worked in to create the pitch, the space has an atmosphere of '"hallowed exclusion" ... in large part because, like a church, it was not used that much, and then generally only for special purposes' (Moeran, 2006: 61).

The production of authenticity

Reflecting on his experiences, Moeran (2005) highlights the importance of impression management in marketing work. Just as Rosen describes how

Walter Spiro presents a view of the economic relations at Spiro's in a way that manifest them as the reality of the situation as far as those involved are concerned, Moeran (2005; 2006; 2007) argues that the account team's work was centred on convincing Frontier about the value of their work. The production of the six concepts used up a comparatively small amount of the account team's time. They were not revolutionary. Rather, they were obvious ideas relating to a long-established brand. Most of the account team's activities were concerned with how best to present themselves and their agency to a potential client. Moeran writes:

> When an advertising agency makes a presentation, it implicitly requests its would-be client to take seriously the impression that is fostered before it as part of its cultural performance. The client is asked to believe that the character of the agency actually possesses the attributes it appears to possess, that the task it is performing in terms of market analysis and strategic communication ideas will have the consequences implicitly claimed for it and that, in general, things are what they seem. (Moeran, 2006: 60)

This observation leads Moeran to summarize that marketing organizations are 'in the business of managing impressions of two fronts' (2005: 919). On the one hand, through marketing work, they make their clients' products and services more appealing to their customers. On the other hand, they must also sell themselves as 'a professional, legitimate, and credible partner' to their clients (Moeran, 2005: 919).

This latter display work has almost 'nothing to do with the consumers at which a client's advertising campaign is to be directed' (Moeran, 2005: 919). It takes marketing workers 'into areas well beyond the boundaries set by their technical expertise' (Moeran, 2009: 965). However, it is essential to marketing action. Unless prospective clients sign their accounts to them, a marketing organization will have nothing to do. Moreover, while the effectiveness of their sales to consumers might be harder to quantify, a marketing organization's success in winning accounts can be directly measured and managed. It brings economic rewards that can be divided within the organization.

To sell themselves to their clients, Moeran's account shows us that an advertising agency engages in a Keynesian beauty contest. This is a thought experiment Keynes (1936) develops to explain the mechanics of financial speculation and the performativity of economic value. In Keynes' beauty contest, participants are invited to select the most beautiful model from a gallery of faces published in a newspaper. If they select the one chosen by the most entrants, they will be eligible for a prize draw. In such a scenario, Keynes (1936) argues, participant's judgements will not be based on the face they find most appealing but on their prediction of the face that others are most likely to find appealing. This produces a self-fulfilling prophecy as the most popular guess about others' judgements will win. Such self-fulfilling prophecies are typical of financial markets (see Merton, 1948; MacKenzie, 2006).

Similarly, at Asatsu, Moeran observes advertising agents developing an advertising campaign that they think will most appeal to the target man at Frontier – not what they think is best. Winning the account depends on the account team 'being able to get into and find out about the closely guarded back region of its audience, the client' (Moeran, 2005: 918). The key difference is that, unlike Keynes' beauty contest, marketing workers need to justify their entry in terms of objective facts and market analysis. That is, the account team not only have to pick the most popular model, by proposing a strategy or campaign, but also produce a compelling justification for their choice.

Indeed, while we might think that creative ideas, advertising concepts, and designs develop from market analysis, Moeran shows us that marketing action can work the other way around. In Moeran's words: 'Asatsu found itself in a complex situation where the objective realities of the market tended to be confused with the subjective tastes and preferences of individual personalities, which were themselves influenced by more general stereotypes associated with "cultural imaginings" of both the West and the East' (Moeran, 2005: 905).

So, having finally settled on an advertising campaign which they thought Frontier would accept, Asatsu's presenters engage in a 'post-rationalization' to justify their choice (Moeran, 2005: 911). This action is taken for granted. As Moeran explains, in their presentations to clients, 'participants – especially the person making the pitch – know exactly what they are up to and calculate very precisely how to make an impression by means of language and other readily understood symbols' (2006: 72). The display work of a pitch uses symbolic resources and creative practices to achieve economic success. In this sense, like Rosen (1985), Moeran's study shows the importance of material and economic relations in marketing action. It, too, shows us that marketing action is a process of translating symbolic work into economic rewards.

Here, Moeran's work extends our ethnographic theory of marketing into relations between marketing organizations and their clients. It shows us how these relations shape what happens inside a marketing organization. It is only by understanding how clients distribute their accounts, or at least how marketing organizations believe they make their decisions about their accounts, that we can explain the peculiarities of marketing action. Indeed, Moeran is clear that to understand marketing action, 'we need to find out how money is circulated among the different players in that industry' (2006: 21).

In general, this is based on an uneven distribution of symbolic and economic resources possessed by marketing organizations and their clients. Marketing organizations privilege their comparative advantage when it comes to symbolic resources in order to persuade their clients to give up economic resources. However, although clients might be 'dazzled' by a marketing organization's creative skills when deciding who can service their accounts, ultimately, they value them for their economic effects (Moeran, 2009: 967). This means that there are 'structural tensions' inherent in the relations between marketing organizations and their clients (Moeran, 2007: 963). These are the focus of the final classic ethnographic study of marketing action I will review in this chapter.

Structural ambiguity

Marketing organizations want to win accounts and secure profits from their operations, but they can only achieve this by providing a service to their clients. The advertising agency, for example, wins an account by dazzling prospective clients with its creativity and commitment. But, can the client ever be certain that they will get what they pay for? Here, the final classic ethnographic account I want to focus on, Alvesson (1994; 1998; 2001), provides an important addition to our ethnographic theory. It shows us how the ambiguous nature of marketing causes further display work in marketing organizations.

Alvesson draws on ethnographic observations lasting 'a few month's duration' at 'a small advertising agency' in Sweden dubbed AD AG (1994: 540). The agency employs approximately 20 people. Alvesson's report, unlike Rosen and Moeran's, does not describe a single event. Rather, Alvesson (1994) highlights the peculiar, but regularly occurring, aspects of the action he witnesses. He argues that these cannot be understood without contextualizing the relationship between marketing organizations and their clients in terms of the nature of marketing work and its unclear methods and outcomes.

Good taste

Much of Alvesson's (1994) report centres on the issue of legitimacy. How is it, he asks, that advertisers can claim specialist knowledge when they lack the normal symbols of a profession such as formal qualifications? Indeed, in contrast to other forms of knowledge work such as engineering and accountancy, marketing does not 'operate according to a handbook of scientific methodology' and 'sophisticated knowledge' (Alvesson, 2001: 866–867). Even successful advertising agents struggle to identify exactly which techniques, theories, and methods they use. Alvesson tells us:

The advertising professionals, i.e. project manager, art director and copy writer, are well paid and often work with tasks involving large amounts of money. They supposedly have a specific competence and creative abilities. Advertising agencies are built around the competence and abilities of the personnel, which means that they can be said to be 'professional' organizations, in the broadest sense. They hardly live up to the traditional criteria of recognized professions. Advertising professionals sometimes claim that they are consultants and experts in communication, but free access to the occupation, beliefs concerning highly varying skills within the industry and the difficulties in evaluating advertising ideas and products tend to make these claims somewhat precarious. (Alvesson, 1994: 543)

The central problem for marketing organizations and marketing workers is, then, that they have no way of proving their skills and competencies. Alvesson tells us that advertising 'professionals often have difficulties in convincing customers about their "know-how"' (1994: 543). Moreover, because their work involves a translation of symbolic resources for economic rewards, their work, their products, and the results associated with them 'do not talk for themselves' (Alvesson, 1994: 544). They must be valorized through different, and competing, value systems.

On this point, Alvesson explains: 'In the absence of the existence of tangible qualities available for inspection, it is extremely important for those claiming to be knowledge-intensive to nurture an image of being so' (2001: 870). In other words, Alvesson argues that marketing organizations and workers must spend a great deal of their time trying to project an air of 'professionality' (1994: 545) or 'knowledge intensiveness' (Alvesson, 2001: 864) because otherwise clients could not value their activities.

One way marketing workers and organizations do this is by emphasizing their *good taste* as a proxy for technical skill. Such good taste is represented in the spaces marketing organizations occupy, their working practices, and in the appearance and mannerisms of marketing workers. For example, physical appearance is a key criterion for selecting the employees at AD AG. Alvesson writes:

Advertising people are usually young (or appear younger rather than older) and are physically fit. ... They are also well-dressed. During our observations at the agency we noted that almost everybody wore different clothes for every new work day and all the components matched in every detail. Sometimes males appeared unshaven, but also here it seemed to be an expression of conscious consideration. The bristles never became too long. We have been led to believe that female advertising people, in particular, should also be ... in their mid twenties, and attractive. Looks were a salient criteria in the recruitment of female employees. Being modern and fashionable was also important. (Alvesson, 1994: 546)

Here, Alvesson (1994) emphasizes that the image of 'good taste' is represented through a set of established symbols – in particular, modernism. The result is that, to prove their competence, advertising agents tend to look like other advertising agents. In other words, they engage in a Keynesian beauty contest. They select what they believe is the most popular image of a competent advertising worker.

Alvesson observes similar action in the design of the offices in marketing organizations. AD AG, he tells us, explicitly manage 'their interior decoration and physical appearance' around modern styles (Alvesson, 1994: 486). This is true of other agencies too. The result is that advertising agencies such as AD AG reference a socially legitimized aesthetic to demonstrate their 'know how' through their display of good taste. They project the image of a successful advertising agency by looking like other advertising agencies.

But, while this display work solves one problem, it creates another. Clients turn to marketing organizations, especially advertising agencies, because they are 'emancipated, sensitive and somewhat difficult to control' (Alvesson, 1994: 547). Put otherwise, they value marketing organizations because they are different from other organizations. They want them to be innovators, not followers. Yet, in proving their value through the projection of their good taste, marketing workers and marketing organizations end up appearing to be 'relatively homogeneous' (Alvesson, 1994: 540). Alvesson explains:

> The undeniable power that leads to an advertising person's habitual show of good taste, independence and casualness is representative of an ingrained conformity. The latter may be expressed in the tendency to show a lack of respect for conventionality as a particular trademark, but in a manner which follows the norms of the sub-group concerned. (Alvesson, 1994: 547)

For Alvesson, then, the lack of an explicit knowledge base or set technical competence and, in turn, the lack of an explicit way of demonstrating that they possess the knowledge or technical competence provokes a standard response in marketing organizations and among marketing workers. Without the markers of a profession, marketing organizations and marketing workers display their *professionality* by looking like each other. But, in this response, they must walk a fine line between looking like they possess good taste and looking like they lack the very independence and individuality that is the basis of their claims to *knowledge-intensiveness*. They can win the beauty contest but, in so doing, undermine the value of their winnings.

Distinctions

The relationship between marketing organizations and their clients is, in this sense, as much as threat to marketing organizations as it is an opportunity. Indeed, for Alvesson (1994), we can explain much of the action in marketing work as an attempt to both legitimize and differentiate marketing organizations from their clients. It is worth quoting Alvesson at length on this point:

> [T]he advertising agencies who deal with companies who have their own advertising department are often under the impression that the client believes that the adverts can be made just as well by using 'one's own desktop facilities'. Such understandings threaten not only the self-esteem but also the material existence of advertising agencies. Apart from putting forward one's own qualifications, it is also important to counteract the client's beliefs that he or she can also produce adverts. The claim that the judgement of advertising people is superior to the clients is of primary importance. To say that space for various ideas, opinions and proposals is great and that the client has a good professional basis, including a knowledge of their own organization, production and market, in order to be able to express themselves with regard to a good advertising suggestion would hardly be advisable. ... The success of projecting the special capability of creating a good advertisement and of being able to decide what is right is, of course, completely connected with the other parties' acceptance of this – it is the recognition that one must fight for. (Alvesson, 1994: 545)

For Alvesson, one way marketing organizations can win this recognition from their clients also supports their displays of good taste. They can claim legitimacy based on the idea that they are a different type of organization to their clients. To achieve this, they project an image of themselves as challenging the kinds of bureaucratic relations that dominate their clients. For Alvesson, the 'anti-bureaucratic metaphor' expressed in the style, mannerism, and working practices of marketing action are meant to symbolize that marketing organizations 'stand for something radically and genuinely different from that of other companies' (1994: 556). This is 'not just a matter of them having a specific competence which makes the difference, but rather that the fundamental direction, organization and "culture"' differs between marketing organizations and their clients (Alvesson, 1994: 556).

As with the display work of good taste, this response to the ambiguity of marketing work also carries a significant risk for marketing organizations. If marketing organizations present themselves as being too different from their clients, they may arouse 'suspicion and conflict' (Alvesson, 1994: 556). Alvesson tells us that it is 'important that the fun does not take over' in the work of marketing organizations such that it 'becomes foolery, which is seen to be "unserious"' (Alvesson, 1994: 550). This rule is strictly enforced and, again, puts limits on the rebelliousness and unruly nature of marketing organizations. It means that marketing workers must demonstrate both their good taste, that is their openness and emancipation, and their willingness to follow the demands and realities of business. They must be corporate rebels who do what they are told.

Here, Alvesson returns to his observations about the ingrained conformity represented in marketing workers' displays of good taste. For Alvesson, it symbolizes that they possess creative competences and are 'realistic and market orientated at the same time' (Alvesson, 1994: 547). It allows them to 'express complementarity' with their clients (Alvesson, 1994: 556). The display of good taste implies that marketing workers and organizations can do something their clients cannot do themselves but also shows they understand the client's concerns and interests.

Image

For Alvesson, the lack of an explicit knowledge base not only means that marketing organizations need to find ways to differentiate their activities from their clients, it also means that there is no clear way for clients to establish the success of marketing work nor for marketing organization to prove their value. This is what Alvesson means when he writes that the products of marketing work do not speak for themselves. Alvesson tells us that 'the criteria for evaluating work are unreliable or entirely absent' in marketing (2001: 867). It 'is characterized by work that is hard to specify and a product that is difficult to evaluate' (Alvesson, 1994: 542).

This means that the client has 'ample opportunity to take command of the evaluation processes' (Alvesson, 1994: 543). They can impose economic logics onto the symbolic work of marketing action. But marketing workers can never win at the client's game. They cannot offer symbolic resources that will directly translate into economic success.

In response, marketing organizations engage in further display work. They try to manage their client's perceptions and expectations and elevate symbolic over economic values. Alvesson writes:

> In view of the notoriously ambiguous character of (a significant part of) knowledge-intensive workers and organizations, the demands on

the agents involved in terms of providing convincing accounts of what they do, and what sort of people they are, become central. This means that rhetorical skills and rhetorical acts become highly significant for the constitution of the company, its workers, activities and external relations. ... An aspect that differentiates many knowledge-intensive companies from other kinds of companies is thus the degree of elaboration of the language through which one describes oneself and one's organization, regulates client orientations and engages in identity work. (Alvesson, 2001: 871)

Alvesson's ethnography, then, encourages us to consider the ways that the nature of marketing work, itself, conditions the ability of marketing organizations to regulate their relationships with clients and workers. He emphasizes that marketing action rarely draws on formalized knowledge nor commands socially accepted markers of a profession. As such, it lacks legitimacy. Added to this, marketing action is easy to devalue. It is hard to tell what marketing workers actually do differently from their clients and it is almost impossible to prove the economic results of marketing. As such, much marketing action can be understood as an attempt to convince clients of its value. This extends our ethnographic theory by suggesting that marketing organizations engage in display work not simply to win accounts, or justify economic inequality, but also to overcome the ambiguity of marketing action. In this sense, Alvesson's work adds a final element to our ethnographic theory of marketing.

The ethnographic theory of marketing

Having reviewed three classic ethnographic studies of marketing, we can return to the question posed at the start of the chapter: is there a specific ethnographic interpretation of marketing? Here, we can highlight some similarities in the classic accounts offered by Rosen, Moeran, and Alvesson. They each highlight distinguishing features of marketing action – things that marketing organizations and marketing workers might take for granted. They each emphasize that marketing workers and marketing organizations use the kinds of symbolic resources and creative practices typically associated with their interactions with consumers when dealing with each other and their clients. They each highlight the translation between such symbolic elements and material or economic concerns as key to marketing action.

To explain these features of marketing action, the classic studies encourage us to look to the nature of marketing work and the material relations that animate it. Specifically, they point to the relationships between marketing organizations, marketing workers, and their clients. In each of these relations, the parties can claim different symbolic and economic resources and use them in ways that complement each other's successes but also threaten them.

So, we can now outline an ethnographic theory of marketing as follows. Its essence is fairly simple: It starts from observations about the talk and behaviour of marketing workers acting together in marketing organizations. However, it seeks to explain these actions in terms of the functions they serve for marketing organizations, given the nature of marketing work and the structural relations between marketing organizations, marketing workers, and their clients.

In this regard, the ethnographic theory of marketing sits in the structural functionalist paradigm of organization theory (Burrell and Morgan, 1979). For context, structural functionalism has developed as something of a portmanteau for a range of social theory united on the simple idea that social action is oriented towards some form of collective goal – whether that is the goal of a small community, organization, or society. Talcott Parsons, one of the founders of this perspective, labelled the goals of a social group its *functional imperative* (1951: 16). In structural functionalist thought, functional imperatives drive and shape social action.

They might be conscious goals of action – sometimes these are described as *manifest functions*. They might also be less obvious to the people involved in the action but emerge when we try to make sense of what the people are doing – sometimes these are described as *latent functions*. The classic illustration of the links between these two kinds of function and social action is a rain dance (see Merton, 1957). A community might engage in a rain dance to achieve the manifest function of producing rain. However, an observer might also say that the rain dance has the latent functions of reinforcing group identity, socializing the group's problems, or establishing a social hierarchy.

Structural functionalism developed under the influence of systems theory, biology, and positivism. As such, it is often associated with quantitative research methods and mathematical modelling. It is more akin to the marketing science tradition discussed in Chapter 1. According to Burrell and Morgan, structural functionalism tends to treat 'the external social world as a concrete reality, governed by observable functional relations amenable to scientific investigation through nomothetic methods' (1979: 50). So, some readers might find it odd to see an ethnographic theory linked to the structural functionalist perspective.

However, Burrell and Morgan point out that structural functionalism 'received its first coherent expression as a theory and method of analysis ... within the realm of social anthropology' (1979: 50). Malinowski, one of the first academic researchers who left his armchair to live in the communities he was interested in, initiated a functionalist explanation of social action. For Malinowski, we should explain anthropological observations 'by their function, by the part which they play within the integral system of culture, by the manner in which they are related to each other within the system, and by the manner in which this system is related to the physical surroundings' (1936: 132; cited in Burrell and Morgan, 1979). In contrast to the then-dominant views that all societies were developing into Western-style capitalist democracies, Malinowski argued that 'the unusual or special characteristics of primitive social systems' should not be dismissed as aberrations that will be left behind as the society progresses but 'in terms of the functions which they performed' for the group (Burrell and Morgan, 1979: 50). It is not so strange, even if it is unusual, therefore, for ethnographic theory to be oriented towards a structural functionalist view.

3

Marketing in the Wild

In the last chapter we explored three classic ethnographic studies that provide a starting point for developing a unique ethnographic theory of marketing. This theory starts with accounts of events from the frontline of marketing. It explains the action inside marketing organizations as consequences of the ambiguous nature of marketing, the translation between symbolic and economic resources, and structural tensions within marketing organizations and between marketing organizations and their clients. Based on this, I suggested that the ethnographic theory of marketing is a structural-functional theory. It explains the structure of marketing actions in terms of the functions they serve.

Having set out this theoretical foundation, in this chapter I want to review more of the ethnographic observations of marketing action. My aim is to expand the discussion beyond advertising, as the three classic studies we have looked at so far focus on advertising agencies. On this point, I will argue that we need to study marketing research ethnographically. Here, reviewing the existing literature in more depth also helps to put some meat on the bones of the ethnographic theory of marketing. Finally, I will use this review to set up the questions that I want to explore as the book progresses. To this end, this chapter highlights two key themes in the existing literature: the discourses of Marketing Science and Marketing Art. These interpretative repertoires have been developed to explain marketing action and the ways marketing workers think about their activities.

Before beginning, though, let me offer some disclaimers. I acknowledge there are many other incredibly interesting accounts of marketing that do not rely on ethnographic methods but show us, in their own ways, marketing in its natural environment. These include historical (Schwarzkopf, 2015a; 2015b; Tadajewski, 2016), interview-based (Cluley et al, 2020), even experimental studies (Piercy et al, 1997). But, I will limit the discussion to ethnographic work and will leave these other traditions to one side.

I also acknowledge that many ethnographic studies include other methods, such as formal interviews with key contacts, and that many studies based on other methods often include some form of broadly ethnographic observation. When conducting interviews, for example, a researcher might spend a prolonged period of time in a marketing organization and observe the action around them (for example, Cronin, 2004a). To deal with this, and to stop this chapter's word count from ballooning, I have limited this discussion to studies which are framed by their authors as being 'ethnographies'. If their reports include other types of data, I have given myself license to include it. But, where authors frame their work through different methods, I have not included their ethnographic observations in my thinking here. This means that I will discuss some work which many diehard ethnographers might dismiss as not being 'real ethnographies' and vice versa.

I appreciate that these decisions are somewhat arbitrary. We must the draw line somewhere and, out of necessity, this is where I am drawing it. To paraphrase American sociologist Howard Becker (2008), it is impossible to digest the literature if we are forced to swallow it whole.

Let me also emphasize that, as my aim is to justify the research questions answered in the book, I have not systematically reviewed the literature. I am sure to have missed some ethnographic observations – especially those not published in English (for example, Callon et al, 2013) – and could not source others (for example, Prus, 1989). To any ethnographers whose work is not discussed, please accept my apologies. By the end of the chapter, though, I hope to show that, as marketing is adapting to a data-driven world, we need to refresh our understanding. We need to explore how the long-standing ideas that marketing workers, marketing organizations, and scholars use to make sense of marketing action are being reframed.

Two discourses

A key theme in the ethnographic literature, which I hinted at in the last chapter, is that marketing action is defined by two competing discourses – that is, two competing sets of ideas, languages, and positionings that manifest in the things marketers do, in the ways that marketers talk to each other, and in the ways they approach their clients. The first frames marketing as a cultural activity that involves creativity, intuition, and sensitivity to the interests of specific groups of consumers and clients. The second frames marketing as the application of specialist knowledge based on underlying, universal facts about how markets work. In short, they relate back to the long-standing stereotypes about marketing being either an art or a science – as discussed in Chapter 1.

There are several ways of describing these two sets of ideas. Scholars influenced by practice theory might prefer the term logics (for example, Skålén and Hackley, 2011). As we saw earlier, Burrell (2013) uses the concept of styles to suggest a patterning of organizational action and organizational design around a limited set of genres. Here, I use the term discourse as I want to emphasize the different ways of thinking about, talking about, organizing, and physically staging marketing action (see Potter and Wetherell, 1987). That is, although speaking about discourses, I am not limiting my understanding to words. I also include the ways that different ways of thinking are built into the physical environment (Deleuze, 1988).

There are also several different names offered in the literature for these two discourses. In the ethnographic classics discussed in the last chapter we saw Rosen (1985) call them the bifurcation of creative and business functions; Alvesson (1994) divide them into anti-bureaucratic and bureaucratic metaphors; and Moeran (2009: 967) describe them as 'the competing logics of "art" and "science"'. Elsewhere in the literature, scholars have developed their own terminology. Gurrieri, for example, calls them discourses of 'renegadism and professionalism' (2012: 785). Here, I will use the labels Marketing Art and Marketing Science. This is intended to simplify the fundamental distinction between the two logics and link the action within marketing organization to wider discussions in the marketing profession, marketing education, and marketing thinking.

In what follows, I will illustrate how Marketing Art and Marketing Science appear in the marketing action observed by ethnographers and link them back to the structural tensions and ambiguities of marketing discussed in the last chapter. By way of overview, I will show that, where marketers think of themselves as artists, they do so to differentiate themselves from their clients. When this happens, marketing action tends to align clients with the ideas of Marketing Science. For this reason, Marketing Science is often connected to business interests and economic values, while Marketing Art is disconnected from them. Given the structural relationship between marketing organizations and their clients, these connections create tensions and frustrations and encourage uneasy alliances within marketing action.

Marketing Art

From the 1990s, ethnographically oriented thinkers influenced by the idea of cultural mediation began to pay attention to marketing in action. Cultural mediation is a term for the production, filtering, and editing of popular culture by often overlooked or unseen actors and institutions. This idea can be traced back to Frankfurt School critical theory of the culture industries (Adorno and Horkheimer, 1944), Marxist thinking on hegemony (Barthes, 1977; Williamson, 1978; Leiss et al, 1990) as well as left media criticism and its focus on the influence of the advertising license to do business (Herman and Chomsky, 1988) – for a review of this work, see Cluley (2017). In each case, the idea is that the popular culture we consume, whether that is news, sports, or entertainment, is not value-neutral. It is popularized because it supports dominant power structures in a society.

Applied to marketing, cultural mediation suggests that marketers are, whether they realize it or not, engaged in ideological work (for example, Wernick, 1991). They are, as Ewen (1976) famously puts it, 'captains of consciousness' who shape not only what we want but the images of the good life we think with (Belk and Pollay, 1985). This idea encouraged researchers to conduct ethnographic studies of advertising so they could understand how and why advertisers use certain cultural resources and, through this, shape culture in the interests of the powerful. From this work, we inherit an ethnographic representation of marketing action as a form of cultural production. It emphasizes *productive consumption, fashion, fun,* and *emotional investments.* These are the central elements of the discourse of Marketing Art.

Productive consumption

The concept of cultural mediation forms the basis of Kelly et al's (2005) ethnographic report. In their words, they explore the 'central role' of cultural knowledge 'in many marketing organizations, especially in the most creative elements of the industry such as advertising' (Kelly et al, 2005: 508). Unlike other professions, where cultural consumption such as listening to music, watching TV, wearing fashionable attire, using social media, and so on may be seen as a distraction, the marketers Kelly et al (2005) study present it as an integral part of their work. It is not a waste of time but is a source of value. They tell us that marketing workers present themselves as 'commercial urban ethnographers' who ' "soak up" research information and nutrients from other areas of cultural and social life' as part of their work (Kelly et al, 2005: 509).

This description of marketing work frames cultural consumption by marketing workers as what Marx (1978) calls productive consumption. It is a way of producing new value by consuming other products. Indeed, Kelly et al quote an advertising worker who describes how consuming music, books, and films helps them to develop novel ideas for their clients. This advertising worker tells them that they 'flick around TV channels all the time … I watch anything … and stuff that shouldn't necessarily interest me … it just helps' (Kelly et al, 2005: 514). Here, marketing action is represented as a form of productive cultural consumption.

This frames marketing as an uncertain productive activity. It is not a linear process like a production line in a factory. It involves false starts, serendipity, and imagination. Indeed, the advertising workers, Kelly et al (2005) study appear to be constantly consuming cultural resources in the hope that they may feed into their work at some point in the future. They do not know what will be useful in advance but want to stay on top of new and emerging trends. There is always a chance that things can 'help'. Even the consumption of cultural texts that, on the surface, have little connection to marketing work can be a source of value at some point.

Here, then, the discourse of Marketing Art not only explains certain aspects of marketing action, it also helps to structure marketing action. It suggests that marketing work must involve cultural consumption and that marketing organizations must allow marketing workers freedom to consume culture. This helps us to explain why many marketing organizations include spaces which encourage cultural consumption, such as games rooms and cinemas. It also helps us to understand why many marketing organizations allow their employees flexibility and freedom over the cultural elements of work such as their dress, their workstations, and how they spend their time at work. According to the discourse of Marketing Art, this is how they produce value.

Fashion

The second element of the discourse of Marketing Art is linked to the idea that marketing involves productive cultural consumption. It is related to, but different from, Alvesson's (1994) notion of good taste. Kenny and Euchler call it the 'norm of newness' (2012: 318). Put simply, it privileges cutting-edge fashions in the productive cultural consumption that takes place in marketing organizations.

To illustrate the norm of newness, Kenny and Euchler describe ethnographic observations at Keys, 'a young, trendy organization located in a run-down but increasingly fashionable part of a large European city' that is 'in the business of cutting-edge creative work' (2012: 306). This work requires Keys to combine 'cutting-edge of cultural consumption and production' (Kenny and Euchler, 2012: 311). Kenny and Euchler (2012) tell us that action at Keys is dominated by the idea that marketing workers should be at the forefront of fashion. One way in which this is expressed is in the appearance of workers at Keys. Employees are not limited, like those Alvesson studies, to modish clothes but display a preference for 'funky clothes' and 'the latest music' (Kenny and Euchler, 2012: 311).

Behind the norm of newness, then, is an image of marketers not just soaking up culture but standing at the vanguard of culture. It imagines them as experts in culture and cultural consumption. They are meant to be aware of the latest trends. They should be rebellious, innovative trend-setters. It also suggests that marketing organizations such as Keys will encourage their employees to take risks by following fads and fashions in their daily work. The productive cultural consumption of fashions is the source of value that benefits marketing organization and their owners.

Fun

A third element of the discourse of Marketing Art is fun. Ethnographic studies show us that marketing action involves humour and sociality rather than formal professional relations. From his observations at AD AG, for example, Alvesson tells us: 'When listening to how advertising professionals describe themselves, one gets the impression that they are guided by feeling, or – and better – are inclined to present themselves in this way. ... According to themselves, it is very important that advertising persons should have "fun" and be able to laugh' (Alvesson, 1994: 550). The emphasis on fun in marketing action supports, and is supported by, the idea that marketing work should involve cultural consumption. Fun activities such as watching a movie, playing a game, or listening to music are an integral part of marketing work. They are a source of value but, as productive cultural consumption, should still be enjoyable.

As a result, marketing organizations not only allow but encourage their workers to have fun at work. The importance of fun as a criterion for evaluating marketing action affects the ways that workers, including senior leaders, interact with each other. It encourages the use of humour and emotions above formal communications. This has the additional benefit of supporting the anti-bureaucratic image that marketing organizations project to overcome the ambiguities of marketing work, as described in the previous chapter.

For illustration, we can return to Kenny and Euchler's (2012) study of Keys. In Kenny and Euchler's words, the work 'was quite informal, and socializing was encouraged through trips to the pub at lunch-time and after work' (2012: 311). In their description of the typical working day, marketing action involves hanging out, chatting, and making each other laugh. Bosses do not directly instruct their workforce but make fun of themselves. Kenny and Euchler write:

> The working day involves much hanging out on bean-bags, chatting to colleagues, or trying to beat the high score on the office pinball machine. Most of the team are comfortable with digital technology, graphic design and the Internet. At Keys, a lot of time is spent sending group e-mails to one's colleagues, e-mails that contain jokes, weird images and links to online videos: always new, always fresh, always funny. ... The nine board members, who made up a fifth of the staff, sent out almost a fifth of the total number of humorous e-mails collected. Interestingly, this ethos of being funny was by no means counterproductive in terms of the goals of the organization and management's prerogative in generating profit. ... Senior managers themselves regularly participated in using the e-mail lists for sending around humorous e-mails. ... As an example, in preparation for a weekly staff meeting one senior manager wrote: 'Please

try to furnish me with things to say at the weekly staff meeting or stare in horror as I blunder on in front of you for yet another week … 10.45 round the downstairs meeting area, cheers, MD'. (Kenny and Euchler, 2012: 306–314)

In this description, we see how marketing organizations are physically arranged and operate in ways that encourage marketing workers to socialize and have fun with each other. There are bean bags and pinball machines for them to use. These artefacts are not just for show. They are an integral part of the working day at Keys. This comes from the top down. Kenny and Euchler's key point (excuse the pun) is worth repeating: *the ethos of being funny was by no means counterproductive in terms of the goals of the organization and management's prerogative in generating profit.*

Emotional investment

The discourse of Marketing Art frames marketing work as an inherently personal activity. Traditional bureaucracies are based on a division of the role and the role holder and a privileging of the former above the latter (Weber, 1905). In contrast, and supporting the projection of an anti-bureaucratic metaphor, marketing workers 'must show more personalized qualities (i.e. creative capabilities, a feeling for what appeals, how to influence people's decisions)' than other professions (Alvesson, 1994: 545). In short, the role holder is key in marketing organizations.

Encouraging marketing workers to form personal connections helps them have fun in the workplace. But, investing emotions in their work also allows marketing workers to feel personally invested in their activities and in the products they create for their clients. An advertising concept, for example, may be considered *their idea* (Moeran, 2005). They can tell stories about where it came from that draw on personal narratives about their engagements with specific cultural texts. Put simply, marketing workers have 'high levels of personal investment and involvement in their work' (Kelly et al, 2005: 516).

As with productive cultural consumption and fun, this supports the anti-bureaucratic image projected by marketing organizations. It means that friendship, sexuality, and romance replace professional relations among marketing workers (Alvesson, 1998). Here, Alvesson writes:

When the advertising workers … are asked to describe themselves, their workplace and advertising work the following themes are salient. … Friendship and 'personal chemistry' are vital. It is important that people are having fun and can laugh; that advertising workers are emotionally involved in their tasks; that they are free, independent, and even a bit lawless. (Alvesson, 1994: 549)

As illustrated in Alvesson's words, the four elements of Marketing Art are complementary. The idea that marketing work involves productive cultural consumption facilitates organizational practices which encourage fun and personal relationships in marketing organizations. These, in turn, encourage marketing workers to form personal connections with their work and to other marketing workers. These emotional investments mean that marketing work can be sold to clients based on the personal skills, track records, and identities of marketing workers. It grounds marketing action in symbolic values. Indeed, we have seen evidence of this already. As we saw in the discussion of Moeran's studies in the last chapter, when Frontier explained their decision to hand their International Division's advertising account to Asatsu, they emphasized the commitment demonstrated by Asatsu's presenter as the reason behind their choice.

Using Marketing Art

These four elements of the discourse of Marketing Art help us to make sense of much of the action ethnographers observe in marketing organizations. As a discourse, though, they not only act as a sensemaking device for marketers and ethnographers. They also structure the way that marketers work together. They manifest in the organization of marketing action and, literally, appear on the wall of marketing organizations.

Through this, the discourse of Marketing Art helps to establish a value claim for marketing action as an art that does not go too far and become unserious (Alvesson, 1994). It remains focused on the translation of symbolic resources into economic rewards. It is a way for marketing workers to demonstrate their good taste and for marketing organizations, in turn, to promote the creative competence of their workers. At the same time, by emphasizing the anti-bureaucratic nature of marketing work, the discourse of Marketing Art helps marketing organizations to differentiate themselves from their clients. As Alvesson might put it, it lets them project an 'anti-bureaucratic metaphor'. It suggests that marketing organizations 'stand for something radically and genuinely different' from other companies (Alvesson, 1994: 556).

It is notable here that the discourse of Marketing Art draws on a specific image of creativity. In place of the archetypal artist, struggling to express their authentic voice or vision and unwilling to sacrifice themselves on the altar of commerce (Bradshaw et al, 2005), Marketing Art imagines creativity as the appropriation of existing cultural resources. This image has an affinity with pop art. Interestingly, this is a style of art that developed in the same milieu as consumer culture. It is a mode of creative production in which artists take images from popular culture and recombines, reframes, or satirizes them. As a result, the discourse of Marketing Art draws, intertextually, on some wider cultural resources about the value of creativity.

Marketing Science

The second discourse that structures marketing action is a companion to Marketing Art. If Marketing Art helps to distinguishing marketing organizations from their clients, it relies on a second discourse that it is distinguished from. As an anti-bureaucratic metaphor, it assumes a bureaucratic metaphor for its comparison. This is represented in the discourse of Marketing Science. It appears most often in the ethnographic literature as a negative frame that helps to articulate Marketing Art positively. The ethnographic literature defines this discourse through three elements: *information*, *self-evidence*, and *stupidity*.

Technique

The first element in the discourse of Marketing Science is the idea that marketing action involves gathering and transmitting information and facts. This is informed by a positivist image of science and manifests in the tendency towards quantification. Numbers are assumed to communicate information free from outside influence – as the saying goes, two plus two equals four. According to the discourse of Marketing Science, marketing workers use quantitative research methods and statistical analysis to document consumer behaviours and report their findings to others. The idea is that accurate information and proper analysis should lead to proven, almost guaranteed, results. It should identify the one 'best' decision.

We have seen an example of this framing in Moeran's (2005) account of Asatsu's pitch at Frontier. The presentation team introduced their creative ideas with statistical reports and market analysis. These were presented as an objective picture of Frontier's markets. The implication, and the image that was projected, was that the team based their creative ideas on this information.

The discourse of Marketing Science is often used to make sense of marketers' engagements with quantitative research practices. However, it is not quantification in and of itself that is the driving force. Quantification is the manifestation of a belief it is possible to objectively document consumer behaviours, link them to product and brand details, and, thereby, achieve marketing objectives (Ariztia, 2015). Put simply, Marketing Science assumes that there is something outside of marketing action and that the task of marketing is to represent it.

Underpinning the emphasis on quantification is, then, a belief that marketing work involves the execution of technical skills that are independent of the marketing worker. It presents marketing as an activity that will produce the same results no matter who the individual marketing worker is. This, of course, is the opposite of the underlying logic in the discourse of Marketing Art. In Marketing Art, there is a belief that marketing action creates something new, something that could not be seen, let alone counted, in advance. According to the discourse of Marketing Art, this relies on the individual marketing worker's grasp of culture and fashion, their rebelliousness, and their willingness to invest themselves in their work. In the discourse of Marketing Science, in contrast, the value of marketing comes from following a predefined method.

Self-evidence

The second element of the discourse of Marketing Science is a claim that markets and consumers operate according to universal and fundamental laws that exist outside of marketing action. These can be documented through validated marketing techniques and can be communicated objectively through the universal language of numbers. In the discourse of Marketing Science, marketing organizations offer their clients access to these laws thanks to their technical expertise. In so doing, marketing organizations confirm something the client might be dimly aware of but cannot articulate because they lack the right skills. The facts of Marketing Science are, in this sense, not based on their correspondence to external reality but, rather, on their self-evidence.

This is powerfully illustrated by Ariztia's (2015) analysis of 'insight' in advertising agencies in Chile. The notion of insight is 'one of the cornerstones of the creative process' Ariztia witnesses (2015: 152). Unpacking the way this term appears in the action inside advertising agencies, Ariztia tells us that it is based on 'an imaginary collectivity of consumers' who have 'inner truths' (2015: 151). Although they are originally 'buried deep in the consumer', such inner truths become 'self-evident after a process of professional work and intuition ... as one expert explains: "Insight is something that is in the unconsciousness of all people, people realise that when you tell them"' (Ariztia, 2015: 150). The imaginary collective of consumers also includes marketing workers and their clients. So, when describing an inner truth, marketing workers allow their clients to connect with 'some common experience regarding themselves' (Ariztia, 2015: 151).

Here, raw numbers and statistical analysis are insufficient to deliver the promise of Marketing Science. Marketers do not simply provide their clients with numbers but, rather, a way to relate them to the inner truths of consumers. They integrate real people into their analysis. Ariztia, again, provides a description of this action:

[It] involves moving from the space of defining general properties of the consumer in general terms to being able to purify a very specific experience or value that might guide the campaign. Creative professionals in agencies used several words to refer to this further translation. They often talked about being able to 'turn the key' of the consumer or 'to open the door' to the consumer's soul. All in all, these further steps mean changing the logic of description, moving from raw data or description to specific qualities that might be the touching point for a given campaign. This work is often understood by professionals as moving from abstractions to 'real people', and being able to connect with them. They are often contrasted with the 'colder' consumer qualifications provided by quantitative market research. As one interviewee explained when describing how creative insight is produced: 'You talk to a person, a name, you get it? You don't talk to C2, C3, you talk to Arturo Gonzalez who lives in a particular neighbourhood, you don't talk to a number, or a segment. You talk to a person and to make sense to him, what you say, your content has to be related to him, otherwise it will bounce back'. (Ariztia, 2015: 156)

We can see, then, how the idea of self-evidence structures marketing action. Marketers relate quantified representations of consumers to their clients' pre-existing ideas, assumptions, and experiences. They start with cold information but then draw on an imaginary of collective consumers, which includes the client themselves, to animate these quantifications towards real people. If they do this successfully, the client will realize the truth of these translations when they are presented with them.

The stupid client

The final element of the discourse of Marketing Science positions it negatively. It frames this discourse as something that is imposed on marketing action by people who do not fully appreciate it – primarily, clients. The client is pictured as someone who does not know what they want, is not able to understand their own consumers, and wants to be told what to do. It is clients who believe that marketing, if done scientifically, can guarantee results.

For an example of this, we can return to Kelly et al's (2005) study of cultural mediation in advertising. They report a 'common pattern' in their interviews with advertising agents. Advertising agents tell them that advertising is 'not a science' but emphasize that their 'clients would like to turn it into a science' (Kelly et al, 2005: 517). According to the advertising agents Kelly et al speak to, this desire is self-defeating. The 'research tools used by clients within the advertising process "killed" advertising ideas' (Kelly et al, 2005: 518). Here, Kelly et al quote an interviewee as saying that, when considering a new creative idea, their clients 'analyse it and analyse it and analyse it … like a poem that is overanalysed … eventually it's not a poem anymore' (2005: 518).

In this way, the talk in marketing action recruits the discourse of Marketing Science to distinguish marketing organizations from their clients. Alvesson notes that it 'is striking that advertising people often make rather negative comments about their clients. ... The client is seen as someone who is always wrong' (1994: 548). They are assumed to be uncomfortable with novelty and individuality and only willing to accept the products of marketing work when accompanied by scientific proof – even though this undermines its artistic value. Alvesson explains:

> The relationship between the client and advertising people is often brought to a head when a solution is presented for evaluation. The employees of the agency are often in agreement that something 'feels right' but sometimes the client is 'completely lost'. It will then appear as if the advertising people are inclined to attribute every possible negative quality and motive in order to explain the lack of understanding ... the client is stupid because he (or she) pays the advertising agency a great deal of money for 'a hell of a lot of work and analysis', and then does not accept the proposal but presents his own idea instead. (Alvesson, 1994: 548)

More sympathetically, Ariztia (2015) reframes *the stupid client* as *the myopic client*. Ariztia (2015) details how advertising workers reframe their clients' original, but limited, understanding of their own problem. This starts when the client submits a document called a creative brief to an advertising agency setting out its marketing objectives. From the advertising agent's perspective, the typical creative brief is too focused on economic outcomes. Ariztia tells us that 'the consumer is often embedded in a commercial "problem" ... usually framed in terms of a set of "targets" defined by socio-demographic variables and contextual data' (2015: 152). Ariztia explains: 'The versions of the consumer, as they appear in the client's first brief, are often regarded by advertisers as too poor; as one advertiser explained, "it has to be fattened"' (2015: 153). Ariztia continues:

> During my fieldwork, I was able to examine several briefs. In some cases they were presented in meetings as emails with marked words and phrases. In other cases, they were presented as a PowerPoint presentation with a fairly standard structure, often a template produced in the agency. For example, during my fieldwork I participated in a meeting that had as its purpose to interpret and adapt the client's briefs for an advertising campaign. (The client was a non-governmental organisation [NGO] that wanted to create a new donation campaign.) To interpret the brief, we used a board on which we wrote a list of the 'qualities of the good' as suggested in the brief (in this case the good

was the donation campaign). With this list, we focused on discussing possible connections between the listed elements and the consumers (target) at who the campaign was aimed. (Ariztia, 2015: 153)

This suggests that marketing workers assume that the client does not understand their own problem. Marketing action is, accordingly, understood as a process that translates the client's limited thinking into universal laws, self-evident facts, and inner truths. It takes information and links it to an imaginary of consumers. Through this, it shows clients what they do not know, but should know.

Using Marketing Science

Most existing ethnographies tell us that marketing workers have traditionally thought of themselves as artists. They believe, or would like to believe, that marketing organizations bedazzle their clients with their creative skills, productive cultural consumption, fun working practices and personal commitments. In response, they emphasize their good taste, their authentic understanding of consumers and markets, and their ability to work in different ways to their clients.

In establishing this view of marketing action, marketing workers align the discourse of Marketing Science with their clients. They claim that clients, who are imagined to be fearful, uninformed, and in need of constant support, require them to present their work as if it was objective information based on fundamental laws of markets. It is on this basis that they will accept the symbolic value of marketing work. This is why, for example, clients demand that marketing workers rationalize their creative ideas in objective analysis – as we saw in Moeran's account in the previous chapter.

As such, the Marketing Science discourse often appears in the ethnographic literature as something imposed on marketing action from the outside. It marks elements of marketing action that are external to it but, typically, cannot be ignored due to economic imperatives. Here, the elements of Marketing Science are often associated with business and accounts functions in marketing organizations. These are, as we saw in the sartorial divisions evidenced in Chapter 2, most closely related to clients. They are not real marketing.

So, while Marketing Art is an enabling frame, Market Science often appears in the ethnographic literature when marketing workers are frustrated with marketing action. It refers to bureaucratic, formal, impersonal working practices, and economic imperatives. But, given the relationship between marketing organizations and their clients, Marketing Science cannot be eradicated. Marketing organizations are economically dependent on clients and, by association, must always frame their work in the discourse of Marketing Science. The best marketing organizations and marketing workers can do is minimize or ignore the features of Marketing Science. Summarizing this sense of frustration, Kelly et al write:

> Creative practitioners in advertising agencies occupy a cultural industry which is driven by the economic capital and strategy imperatives of their corporate clients, and have to try to negotiate their symbolic capital within the advertising process. However, they find they are often constrained in their work by the scientific ideologies of large clients and by the power relations of economic dependency that exist between the advertising agency and the corporate client, which often results in a frustrating creative dilemma for these occupational groups. (Kelly et al, 2005: 521)

One way to manage this frustration is to divide creative and business functions – allowing one group of specialists to engage in Marketing Art and another in Marketing Science. This prevents a permanent resolution between the 'competing logics of "art" and "science" held by different sub-teams (creative and marketing, respectively)' (Moeran, 2009: 967). Unfortunately, though, the need to win and keep accounts forces ongoing collaborations between them.

Moeran's (2009) description of a photo shoot for an advertising campaign demonstrates how this is managed in action. He emphasizes how the physical layout of a photo shoot is designed to offer a single point of contact for clients and, as such, to limit their ability to bring the discourse of Marketing Science into the creative action. It is worth quoting Moeran at length on this point:

> Although the art director moves about the studio, giving instructions or consulting staff as appropriate, his 'home base' – or fixed point of return – is a table set up in one unused part of the studio (but almost invariably near the studio entrance). It is here that client personnel, and random visitors (of whom there tend to be many, including the occasional anthropologist) are invited to sit, and to which other personnel will gravitate during a slack moment during the day's work. This is the client base, which serves as a general liaison point between client, agency art director and subcontracted freelance personnel. ...
> The location of these points of reference reflects the importance of each of the tasks being carried out, as well as of their personnel and the relationships among them. Thus the 'outsider', the client, is located at the point nearest to the studio entrance and thus the 'outside' ... while the camera and set are located in the 'interior' ... of the studio. It is in this highly charged symbolic space that the two pivotal actors, the art director and photographer, take up their positions, although the art

director is obliged, as an 'employee' of the client, to move back and forth between interior and exterior locations. (Moeran, 2009: 970)

What we can see, then, is that Marketing Art and Marketing Science each emphasize different aspects of marketing action. They help to valorize and differentiate marketing work and support the attempts by marketing organizations and marketing workers to overcome the ambiguities of marketing work. Here, we must recognize that, while the existing ethnographic literature is relatively consistent in its depiction of Marketing Art and Marketing Science, most ethnographic accounts focus on the more creative element of marketing – notably advertising. They see Marketing Art as the source of value. Indeed, in Moeran's words, 'creativity is the magic' by which clients are, ultimately, 'dazzled' (2009: 967). But what of the less creative aspects of marketing work?

Art and science outside advertising

Since the ethnographic classics, there is a growing concern for thinking about marketing in action more broadly. As we have seen, ethnographic studies developed with a focus on advertising as the most obvious form of cultural mediation. More recently, reflecting a growing interest in understanding the representation of marketing in work that has applied science studies to markets (reviewed in Chapter 1), the ethnographic lens has turned towards other marketing functions, primarily marketing research, strategy, and digital marketing (Cluley, 2022; 2023). This thinking suggests that, while the discourses of Marketing Art and Marketing Science remain, they are used within marketing action in different ways. To illustrate these changes, and open up the questions I want to address in the next sections of the book, I will review J. Nilsson's (2019; 2020; 2021) ethnographic account of Norna, a market research branch of an international marketing group based in Denmark.

The individualized client

Reporting the ways that clients are discussed at Norna, Nilsson highlights that they 'are not discussed as monolithic entities benefiting from a better position in the market but as people who have needs that can be met by research' (J. Nilsson, 2019: 157). The marketing workers Nilsson observes talk about clients as 'individual actors, located within commissioning organizations' (J. Nilsson, 2019: 156). In short, market researchers at Norna work on the basis that their clients are other marketing professionals who do not need to be convinced of the value of marketing work nor the difference between them and marketing workers. Instead, they need a marketing organization to support their own work within the client's organization.

Nilsson tells us that a 'recurring phrase' at Norna regarding these individual client contacts is the need to 'make them the hero' (J. Nilsson, 2019: 156). The goal of the marketing action at Norna is to support the in-house marketer who works at a client organization to establish the value of *their* work or the robustness of *their* decisions within *their* organization. To do so, marketing workers at Norna engage in action to understand the individual client in the context of their organizational setting. In Nilsson's words: 'The implied client is someone who has to be known and whose position matters. It is their needs and ways of receiving market research reports that researchers try to anticipate and manage' (J. Nilsson, 2019: 156).

To illustrate how this plays out in practice, Nilsson reports how the research team at Norna discuss their clients in weekly catch-up meetings. In these meetings, 'many explicit expressions are made about the work market researchers do, the benefits provided to clients and how to work with them' (J. Nilsson, 2019: 156). However, the discussions tend to be centred on specific individuals. Nilsson reports:

> During the Monday meeting, the client is typically referred to by organization name. Beyond casual mention, however, most speculation is about the individual client representative. ... Speculation about the position and needs of clients is part of discussing research projects at Norna. In one Monday meeting, account manager Alex described one of his client representatives as: 'the type of manager who's just been appointed to a top position and is now overwhelmed with all the figures and studies. I think she tries to establish some stable ground'. Other formulations included the following statement during a Monday meeting: Alice outlined a sales meeting for a focus group project with a local tourist destination. She noted that the client representative seemed excited about this and 'will be trying to sell it' to the client organization. 'We', Alice added, 'will try to aid her in that work'. (J. Nilsson, 2019: 157)

The action described here allows marketing workers to develop shared accounts of clients as individuals. They identify 'their needs within organizations and how to unite with them in sales efforts' so that a marketing organization wins more business (J. Nilsson, 2019: 157). This understanding is necessary for marketing workers to deliver their promise and make the individual client into a hero in the commissioning organization.

We might assume that all marketing organizations pay such close attention to their clients, but if we contrast Nilsson's observations with Moeran's (2005) account of Asatsu, we see that this is not always the case. As we saw in Chapter 2, while there was a concern to understand the preferences of the 'target man' at Frontier, this concern developed late in the presentation team's work. In fact, the need to consider the target man only emerged in the post-mortem after the presentation team had rehearsed their offering for the client in the pre-presentation. The target man might have been powerful but, in terms of the marketing action, he was a peripheral figure much of the time. Instead, the account team worked with a general idea of their client.

The embedded client

Nilsson shows us how individual clients can come to occupy 'centre stage' in marketing action (J. Nilsson, 2019: 150). At Norna, he witnesses researchers shaping 'materials to suit the interests of the client representative in relation to the client as a whole' (J. Nilsson, 2019: 161). They also directly integrate their clients 'throughout the research process' (J. Nilsson, 2019: 155).

For example, Nilsson witnesses marketing workers providing ongoing updates to their key contacts while collecting data. Here, Nilsson observes that the researchers at Norna are 'pleased when collected responses suited the clients' agenda' (J. Nilsson, 2019: 161). Nilsson provides a detailed illustration of this from Norna's work for an activewear brand. It is worthy ethnographically quoting this case:

[W]hen respondents in an online focus group on active-wear provided interpretations of the brand's positioning that were in line with the client representatives' own vision, there were expressions of contentment within the Norna team. … [At the end of the] online qualitative project about the positioning of a brand of active wear, there were several discussions within the Norna team about the extent to which client representatives were on the researchers' side. Alice, the account manager in charge, noted that for the next meeting with the clients there would be 'higher-ups' from the client present. These people did not need details for the study and were to be presented with 'actionable insights from the get-go'. She had already been in contact with part of the client team and knew that they were happy with the results. Alice noted that the important thing at that point was that 'it becomes both a workshop and presentation' to keep the client buying. She also mentioned about the client representative commissioning the project that 'he is on our side' and that he would work with Norna to continue the study with more commissions. I asked Pia, one of the project managers who took part in the active-wear project, to explain more about this during an interview. She explained that there was an understanding between the team within the client and the project group at Norna and that the results appeared to work well for the client at large. When I wondered what this understanding pertained to, Pia answered: 'The alliance between our and the client's project teams is to work towards more research projects, to find out more. That means that we need to – and I say this as speaking for the project – unite with the client to talk to their CEO to open the wallet, so to speak.' (J. Nilsson, 2019: 161)

So, while marketing research firms such as Norna are often formally organized around a distinction between accounts teams (Cluley et al, 2020), who liaise with clients and sell research products, and field teams who conduct the actual research, in reality the client's voice echoes throughout the entire research process. The client is not someone who must be fought or kept at a distance – as Kelly et al (2005) argue. They are welcomed into the marketing action. Here, Nilsson suggests that the more combative relationship between marketing organizations and their clients described in earlier studies may have been replaced by an 'alliance mode of dealing with clients' (J. Nilsson, 2019: 161). This is facilitated by new relationships between marketing organizations and their clients. Clients are individualized and brought into marketing action.

This suggests that the bifurcation of creative and business functions in marketing organizations, each associated with their own opposing discourse, may no longer hold. It hints at a new structural relationship between marketers and their clients. But what does this mean for the ways that marketing organizations use the discourses of Marketing Art and Marketing Science to manage the structural uncertainties that form the basis of an ethnographic theory of marketing? Are they no longer relevant? Or are they now used in new ways?

These questions are particularly prescient given broader changes in the landscape of organizational decision-making that have moved towards data-driven decisions. As I suggested in Chapter 1, in this context, it is easy to assume that Marketing Science has pushed Marketing Art off the stage. Certainly, this is a claim many in marketing theory and marketing education have made (for example, Wymbs, 2011; Nunan and Di Domenico, 2019; Paas, 2019). There are too many calls for prospective marketers to be taught data science, computer programming, even neuroscience for me to list. Yet, given the previous suggestion that Marketing Art is what really distinguishes marketing from other types of organizational action, if these claims are true, we might assume that the triumph of Marketing Science is actually the end of marketing (Ahlberg et al, 2022). As such, I want to better understand how the discourses of Marketing Art and Marketing Science now structure marketing action.

4

Studying Marketing Ethnographically

Having outlined the underlying theoretical perspective and set up the research focus of the book, in this chapter, I will discuss what it means to conduct an ethnography of a marketing organization. To do so, I first explore the methods used in existing ethnographic research and review some of the general methodological issues involved in studying contemporary marketing action ethnographically. I will then detail the ethnographic methods that I used and describe the site of my research.

Studying marketing

As discussed in the last two chapters, there are different ways of studying marketing. Ethnography has some unique advantages. Ethnography is primarily about observing what happens – not relying on people's accounts of what they do. It involves a researcher spectating and, possibly, participating in marketing action. As such, it has the potential to open up more realistic accounts than methods that rely on predefined ideas about what marketing is or rely on marketers' own reflections of their activities. Ethnographic research can allow the researcher to see things that everyday participants take for granted.

Ethnography also allows researchers to document specific incidents and events. Ethnographic studies offer us moment-to-moment commentaries that go into 'incredible detail' and, from this, to provide 'the backdrop for a developing understanding of what is going on' (Neyland, 2008: 17). Ethnographers call such accounts 'thick description'. This is a key element of the ethnographic method. It is typically traced to Geertz's (1973) account of betting in Bali. Geertz's idea, as I understand it, is that by providing as much detail as possible about a specific incident one may uncover something inherent not only to that specific incident but to the action in general. In other words, an ethnography of a night of betting, a health organization, a theatrical performance, or an advertising agency should not only tell us about the action in that setting but, through the detail they offer, also tell us something more profound about the ways that societies, organizations, industries, and individuals work together (Becker, 2007).

According to Braverman (1974), a foundational theorist in work sociology, ethnographic methods are particularly powerful for understanding work relations. He argues that we simply cannot get to grips with productive activities unless we go to work ourselves. Braverman explains that 'active and interested parties' offer interpretations that 'are enriched by their efforts at practise' (1974: 21). They can 'convey a solidarity, a depth and a subtlety of observation, and anticipation of changing moods, and an ability to disentangle the durable from the ephemeral' (Braverman, 1974: 21). Braverman continues:

> [W]here some sociologists have themselves gone to work in factories either as part of their professional training or out of necessity, or whereas sometimes happens they have put aside their questionnaires and listened to workers with both ears, they have often established relationships of trust, learned to comprehend the milieu, and written credible accounts. (Braverman, 1974: 21)

This ethos lies at the heart of ethnographic accounts of marketing. Here, advocates point out that ethnographic fieldwork has the potential to shed new light on marketing action precisely because it allows the researcher to leave behind the baggage of their pre-existing theoretical assumptions and learn from the field. Nilsson, for example, explains that being there 'where marketing happens' is a way to develop a 'rich description of various marketing phenomenon' (T. Nilsson, 2019: 235). Reflecting on ethnographic observations at a multinational advertising company, Wang, too, concludes that 'an industry-bound approach' encourages the academic to 'stop theorizing about the consumer from their perch in the ivory tower'. This 'not only yields rich empirical details but also opens up new conceptual windows' (Wang, 2010: 305–306). Wang continues: 'access to industry vantage points helps researchers quicken the pace of conceptual discoveries' (2010: 101).

What has been done?

Table 4.1 summarizes ethnographic research of marketing action. It is not an exhaustive list. I have not included autoethnographic studies (for example, de Waal Malefyt and Morais, 2010; Muniesa, 2014) as these are hard to distinguish from biographical accounts written by marketers which, themselves, have their own biases and limitations (for example, Ogilvy,

1963; Wells Lawrence, 2003; Fletcher, 2008). The list also misses some ethnographic accounts which I was unable to source and non-English language work. But, despite this, it does provide a fair account of the state of knowledge.

Table 4.1 suggests that, despite the espoused benefits of ethnographic methods, and despite ethnographic methods being widely used to study consumers in both academic and commercial settings (Zaltman, 1997; Goulding, 2005; Arnould and Cayla, 2015), there are relatively few ethnographic studies of marketing action. Indeed, two decades ago, Cronin (2004b: 352) observed that 'detailed ethnographic accounts of practices' are 'lacking in the field and their input is urgently needed in order to fully appreciate this complex arena'. At best, Cronin's (2004b) call has been only partially answered.

Not only are there relatively few ethnographic studies in total, several reports appear to be based on the same observations. Moeran (2005), Moeran (2006), and Moeran (2007) analyse the same events. As do J. Nilsson (2019), Nilsson (2020), and Nilsson (2021), and Cluley (2022) and Cluley (2023). There is, of course, absolutely nothing wrong with authors reporting different aspects of their observations across multiple reports (indeed, in the world of contemporary academia where one must 'publish or perish' this is a necessity) but it means that the breadth of marketing functions and contexts have yet to be studied. Most accounts focus on advertising and there is a skew towards Scandinavian settings. Two of the historically most influential marketing industries – the United States and the United Kingdom – do not dominate the ethnographic literature in the same way they do other areas of marketing and consumer research.

Existing ethnographic observations also tend to be limited in scope. Some are based on short-term observations. For example, Kelly et al (2005) conduct a seven-week ethnography. Alvesson (1998) conducts a three-month observation.

Neyland (2008), an advocate for organizational ethnography, equates such studies to visits to drive-thru fast-food restaurants. The researcher does not 'intend to stay around too long' and, instead of allowing the field to direct their interests, moves through the setting collecting what they 'assumed were the important ingredients' they required to produce their research reports before they arrived (Neyland, 2008: 18). In other words, rather than going into marketing action with open eyes, in the drive-thru model of ethnography, researchers arrive at the research site knowing what they want to see and only stay for long enough to see it.

Other studies listed in Table 4.1 appear to be what Bate (1997) calls jetplane ethnographies. Here, 'fieldwork is a matter more of a series of flying visits to the research site' than a prolonged single stay (Watson, 2011). Svensson (2007), for instance, reports that he attended 14 meetings and 14 events but

Table 4.1: Ethnographic studies of marketing action

Paper	Method	Function (topic)
Cluley (2023)	1 Unspecified onsite full participant observation at Super Tech, a European-based business strategy company 2. 12 months digital ethnography 3. 23 unstructured interviews	Market research and strategy (performance space)
Cluley (2022)	1. Onsite participant observation lasting six months at Super, a European-based research, media and AdTech company 2. 23 in-depth ethnographic interviews	Market research and AdTech (insight)
Nilsson (2021)	1. Six months full participant observation in the Swedish-based consumption and technology department of an international marketing group (Norna) 2. 28 interviews with employees	Market research (knowledge)
Nilsson (2020)	1. Unspecified full participant observation in the Swedish-based consumption and technology department of an international marketing group (Norna) 2. Interviews with 23 co-workers resulting in 28 transcribed (27 recorded) interviews and about 120 pages of single-spaced research notes	Market research (focus groups)
T. Nilsson (2019)	1. Three years fieldwork in Sweden including unspecified observations, semi-formal interviews and everyday conversations with ten professionals 'with responsibility to "do business" by means of marketing and sales activities' (2009–2012)	Sales (rhetoric)
J. Nilsson (2019)	1. Nine months full participant observation in the Swedish-based consumption and technology department of an international marketing group (Norna) 2. 28 interviews with employees	Market research (market shaping)
Ariztia (2015)	1. Forty interviews from eight agencies and observation of four meetings in advertising agencies in Chile	Advertising (insight)
Kenny and Euchler (2012)	1. Unspecified participant observation as a 'creative consultant' at an Irish creative advertising agency (Keys) 2. 655 emails collected over four months	Advertising (humour)
Moeran (2009)	1. One-year participant observation at an unnamed Japanese advertising agency (1990) 2. Occasional follow-up visits to the Japanese agency	Advertising (creativity)

Table 4.1: Ethnographic studies of marketing action (continued)

Paper	Method	Function (topic)
	3. Several days 'concentrated participant observation' in a studio setting observing the production of an advertising campaign (2002) 4. Follow-up interviews with an unspecified number of freelance fashion personnel in Denmark	
Wang (2010)	1. Participant observation ('a double life as an academic critic immersed in the cris-ridden daily routine of an agency' at Ogilvy & Maher in Beijing for 'two summers' (2002 and 2004)	Advertising (globalization and cultural mediation)
Moeran (2007)	1. One-year participant observation at an unnamed Japanese advertising agency 2. 15 years of 'frequent follow-up visits'	Advertising (creative production)
Svensson (2007)	1. Unspecified 'observer-as-participant' in 14 meetings, 14 events, 20+ interviews and informal discussions	Advertising (ideology and discourse)
Moeran (2005)	1. One-year participant observation (1990) at a Japanese advertising agency (Asatu)	Advertising (authenticity)
Kelly et al (2005)	1. Seven weeks non-participant observation at an Irish advertising agency 2. Five 'ethnographic interviews' with eight employees	Advertising (cultural intermediation)
Alvesson (1998)	1. Unspecified participant observation ('about three months') at a Swedish creative advertising agency employing 21 people 2. An unspecified number of interviews with representatives from other agencies and one interview with an ex-employee	Advertising (gender)
Brownlie (1997)	1. Six months shadowing six marketing directors	Strategy (representation)
Alvesson (1994)	1. 'Field observations of a few months' at a small Swedish advertising agency 2. An unspecified number of formal interviews and informal conversations with agency staff 3. An unspecified number of formal interviews and informal conversations with 'a few senior members of other agencies'	Advertising (identity)
Rosen (1985)	1. Unspecified ethnographic observations	Advertising (symbolism)

does not tell us what action he observed in between. The problem with such approaches is that they tend to produce 'quick descriptions' rather than 'thick descriptions' (Bate, 1997).

In my opinion, this is a critical weakness of the existing literature. There are few concrete accounts of specific marketing actions of the sort provided by Rosen (1985) and Moeran (2005). For example, we have seen tht Kenny and Euchler (2012) tell us that senior leaders at Keys would socialize with their employees in the pub. Yet, they do not provide a description of these visits. We are left to imagine what kinds of pub they visit, how they socialize, what they talk about, and how they interact. Alvesson (1994) offers a detailed theory of a marketing organization but few descriptions of concrete actions. He reflects a tendency in the literature to preference *telling* above *showing*.

There are also significant issues in the methodological reporting practices displayed in the existing literature. Key details are often not reported or left ambiguous. For example, Alvesson (1994) reports that his observations lasted 'a few months'. Kenny and Euchler (2012) do not specify the length of their ethnographic observations. Wang (2010) only reports details of their fieldwork in the preface of their book. It amounts to telling us that they were 'given the opportunity to work at the transnational advertising agency Ogilvy and Mather in Beijing for two summers, in 2002 and 2004' (Wang, 2010: xi). We are offered no detailed on the nature of Wang's fieldwork, how they entered the field, how they recorded their observations, their ethnographic approach, method of analysis, and so on. The result is that aspiring ethnographers of marketing action will find little methodological guidance from existing research.

But where academic researchers gain access to marketing action, it is not necessarily easy for them to apply ethnographic methods given the nature of marketing work. As we have seen in Chapters 2 and 3, impression management is a core element of marketing action. This necessitates backstage areas where people prepare, cool off, and rehearse. These are, by definition, hard to access. It is easy to miss them if we are only driving-thru or jetting in and out.

Brownlie (1997) provides a telling illustration of this danger from his study shadowing marketing directors. He offers a thick description of an incident in which he learned that a marketing worker he was shadowing was carefully editing what he saw. It is worth ethnographically quoting Brownlie on this:

> One Friday night in the pub, after a particularly grueling ten hours shadowing, the marketing director shot off home, the weekly ritual duty of socializing with his troops duly discharged. I was left with his marketing manager, advertising manager, marketing research manager, new products manager, a secretary and a new member of the brand management team. After a few drinks they started speaking

to me and with me. It suddenly dawned on me that they were feeling sorry for me, even if they were feigning this to influence me in some way. They told me tales of the director and how he had carefully orchestrated his diary for my visit. He was doing things while I was there that he never did, except perhaps when the board or his wife were visiting. … They also told me that he was having important meetings with senior staff that he was not telling me about; that my visit was putting him under incredible stress because he was trying to operate in two modes simultaneously – one was apparent and meant for my consumption; the other was covert and more akin to his normal mode of operating and was not meant for my eyes. They told lurid tales of wrongdoing, of pelvic political intrigue, of hypocrisy and betrayal, of harassment, of incompetence; of the coming of major changes in the market environment and a likely reorganization of the sales and marketing functions. They insisted that what they said never got back to him. They put the knife in deeply and twisted it. I was dealing with appearances. My ethnography was his public relations exercise, his impression management test. And he had to pass. In the other mirror, that supplied by the marketing staff, I was dealing with other appearances. My ethnography was their PR exercise too; and they had to pass. Just like their boss, they were struggling to project appearances, to re-present before my eyes and ears, their interpretation of what they would like me to say about them in my journal. Isn't it funny how the outsider forces a social group to confront its own understanding of itself; for the normally invisible and uncontested conventions and rituals, the taken-for-granteds, to suddenly become transparent and open to question? (Brownlie, 1997: 270)

These weaknesses undermine the empirical insights and theoretical innovations of ethnographic studies of marketing action. Moreover, they might be self-replicating. Aspiring marketing ethnographers may follow the existing literature and omit thick descriptions, methodological details, and lengthy observations. To counteract this, and hopefully help others get into marketing action, in what follows, I offer a thick description of my methods. My aim is to give the reader a sense of the difficulties, frustrations, and challenges involved in the ethnographic study of marketing action.

Getting into marketing action

Most ethnographic studies of marketing do not tell us how the researcher negotiated their way into marketing action. Where this is discussed, existing research suggests that ethnographic studies of marketing tend to occur by chance. For instance, Wang tell us that their ethnographic research proceeded by 'mere fluke' (2010: xi). Wang explains: 'I have little doubt that the MIT [Massachusetts Institute of Technology] brand name helped me a great deal in securing an opportunity to work at Ogilvy and to conduct my research there' (2010: 328).

Sadly, I lack the credibility of MIT's brand (although any readers who sit on hiring committees at MIT are welcome to change this situation – please contact me with any job offers via the publisher). So, I was forced to pursue other ways into marketing. Around 2015, I began attending marketing and advertising workshops looking for materials to support my teaching and a textbook I was writing (Cluley, 2017). I also hoped to identify potential research partners. I found them curious events. Industry speakers normally repeated Marketing Science buzzwords (Cluley, 2013a). They spoke about data-driven marketing, big data, and analytics, neuromarketing, dopamine hits, and feedback loops without ever really showing they fully understood what these terms meant.

On other occasions, the presenters would revel in challenging these trendy buzzwords. Championing more craft-based and artistic views of marketing, they garnered loud applause from the audience but, again, seemed to be talking about stereotypes and strawmen. For instance, at one event, a creative director for a large advertising agency described the design process for an award-winning ad campaign. She made a point of emphasizing that her team ignored all scientific approaches and based their ideas on the inner truths that drive consumers: 'sex and death'. The comment almost instantly appeared on the event's social media feed. I wondered if it was true or just good impression management.

Typically, the presentations were followed by drinks. I struggled to get into conversations with other attendees and, having a young family at home, tended to leave these gatherings at the first chance I could. An event before Christmas 2017 was different. It was a panel on data-driven marketing. One speaker caught my attention. While the other speakers from major brands wore suits, this speaker wore jeans and a fleece. He looked more like he was on his way to an indoor climbing wall than an industry workshop. He was younger and much more relaxed than the others. He was introduced as Dan – director of research at a marketing agency I had not heard of. I anonymize it here as Super.

The other speakers explained the difficulties they had encountered getting data-driven marketing to work with a resigned tone. They appeared frustrated that the industry hype might be just that. In contrast, Dan was funny, honest, and sanguine. 'If we don't have the data, or can't do the analysis', he explained, 'we just buy it. Data isn't a problem'. When he said he was reading Byron Sharp's *How Brands Grow: What Marketers Don't Know* (2010), the audience laughed. It was not a joke, he explained. He found Sharps' explanations of consumer behaviour essential to make sense of data. The audience laughed again. Was this really a room full of marketing industry workers laughing at a key pillar in 'Marketing Science'? This was not what I expected having read the pages of academic journals in my ivory tower.

As the talks at this workshop finished, and a queue formed to speak to the presenters, I found myself looking at my watch, trying to figure out if it was worth missing my connection home for the chance to say 'Hello' to Dan. For some reason, I ignored the queue and went directly to Dan to introduce myself. 'Your talk was great', I said. 'It's exactly what I think. I need to catch a train, but can we talk sometime?'

'You're going now', Dan replied. 'I'll walk with you to the subway. I have to get home for my dog. You've given me the perfect excuse to leave.' Dan asked me to wait for him while he fetched his coat.

Following a five-minute conversation on the way to the subway, we exchanged business cards. The next week we spoke about potential research collaborations over the phone. We arranged for me to visit Dan at Super's European head office to discuss the idea in more detail.

A month later, I made my first visit to Super's head office. Following my journey to Super's city and 30 minutes on the subway, I arrived at the head office an hour early. It was strange to walk around the local area as, nearly a decade before when researching for my PhD (Cluley, 2011), I had arranged to interview a store assistant at a new record shop in the same neighbourhood. Back then, the area was run-down and largely populated by immigrant communities. Indeed, I had struggled to find the record store and no one I asked for directions could believe someone would open one in their neighbourhood. After I found it, I spent a morning in the store and was the only person present who did not work there until a famous national radio DJ came in.

In the decade since that visit, the area had been transformed. It was now a thriving creative industry hub with independent clothing stores, restaurants, hotels, and a large, open-air street market. While I waited in Super's reception for Dan, I saw several 'Street Art Walking Tours' taking tourists down the street to look at suspected Banksy pieces. I noted the exposed wooden floors and the Ikea display cabinet that contained awards recently won by Super in the reception. Eventually, Dan and his dog came to meet me. He gave me a tour of the building. I was impressed by the sprawling kitchen that dominated the open-plan office space on the second floor of the building. I noticed the numerous artworks on the walls and toys and figures that seemed to be scattered throughout the building.

After this, we went to a nearby restaurant for lunch. We talked about data science and marketing. At one point, Dan's dog sat on my lap while Dan spoke on the phone. When he returned to the conversation, Dan told me that his dog was normally shy and that I should consider myself lucky to win her favour. I decided to see if I was lucky. As we drank coffee, I asked Dan if I could conduct an ethnographic study at Super.

Dan, who had an MSc in Management and Marketing, thought the idea of studying marketers at work made sense. 'Research the researchers', he said, 'I like it!'. He asked what I had in mind. I did not have a clear plan but suggested I could work in his team and observe how they did things. I explained that we could explore potential research collaborations. Dan said that he would be happy to host me in his team and had an idea for a task I could execute for him. He asked if I would be willing to conduct an extended literature review for his team. But, he told me with a note of caution, I would need to pitch the idea to Super's senior leadership team. 'We love working with academics. So, it won't be a problem,' Dan explained. 'But you need to tell them what they'll get out of it.'

I went back to my university office and wrote up a proposal over the next few weeks. The day after my visit, I sent Dan a pack of organic dog treats (for his dog, I clarified on a note). My initial proposal said I wanted to understand data-driven marketing as a process involving researchers, software, data, space, and physical objects. I wanted to write about this and bring the findings into my classroom. I also emphasized that the University of Nottingham, where I taught marketing at the time, had recently invested in a business analytics lab (see Smith, 2019). As a result, I might be able to engage in knowledge exchange with Super.

A few days later, Dan emailed to say that Super's senior leadership team had approved my proposal. I could work as an unpaid junior executive in Super's research team for as long as I wanted. This role would have responsibility for reviewing survey results, preparing slideshow presentations and research reports, coding media content, and attending meetings and presentations.

As I will detail later, Super's senior leadership team may have been willing to support the research because of a broad commitment to knowledge exchange with academic institutions. Members of Super's senior leadership team hold teaching affiliations at local universities and Super have established collaborations with a number of business schools. They regularly host academic researchers onsite in their offices. In fact, by the end of my ethnographic observations, I had to hot-desk with a cultural anthropologist who was also visiting the company as part of a knowledge exchange programme at a large European university that one of Super's senior leadership team taught on. I later saw that these relations with academic institutions were promoted in Super's marketing materials and learned that they had led to new product innovations.

For the time being, though, having gained access to a potential research site I encountered some practical problems typical for a modern ethnographer. How could I travel to Super's offices? It was too far to commute everyday but I could not afford to rent a room nearby. How could I balance working at Super with my academic job? Could I work as a full-time intern and continue to fulfil my teaching, administration, and research requirements?

The answer to these problems, like many others in life, was money. Fortunately, I had a sympathetic research director at the University of Nottingham who allowed me to repurpose a small budget normally used for travelling to academic conferences. This would allow me to travel to Super and covered accommodation for the first few weeks of my fieldwork.

A few months later, before I had started my fieldwork, I was awarded support from the British Academy's Small Grant Scheme (SG161403). This provided me with enough funding for travel costs and meant I could to rent a room near Super's head office. It also covered costs for transcribing recordings and professionally illustrating my observations. I was, and remain, incredibly grateful to Nottingham University Business School, the British Academy, and the reviewers who supported my bid. That just left the small matter of explaining to my partner, who had recently given birth to our first child, that I was going to spend time away from home. Even worse, I had to convince the timetabling department to reschedule my classes.

An introduction to Super

After I received formal confirmation that I had access to Super from Dan, I began to research the company in more detail. It is a global marketing company that was started in the late 1990s by a small team of 'founders' – as they are called at Super. Inspired by the growth of the internet, and as part of one of the founder's computer science degree coursework, they created an aggregator website that listed the 'hottest' online videos using publicly available viewing information. Soon, this chart attracted attention from the marketing trade press and rumours emerged suggesting that advertising agents were increasingly desperate to get their videos listed in the site. Eventually, an established European marketing industry magazine approached the founders to ask if they could publish the chart. The founders agreed and soon found themselves being courted by advertising agencies who wanted to know how to get their adverts listed. This prompted the founders to turn their hobby into a business. Super was born.

Two of the founders quit their full-time jobs working as cultural studies academics. They began to analyse popular adverts that appeared in their chart using semiotic and literary ideas they had taught in their academic careers. They formally coded the adverts in their charts following a content analysis approach. They came to realize that the adverts that did best tended to replicate other viral content: they were catchy, short, and funny. To support their conclusions, they started to conduct occasional market research studies using standard advertising and branding effectiveness measures they had researched online. This led them to conclude that online videos created by brands which produced an intense emotional reaction tended to perform best on social media metrics. This might seem obvious now, but in the early days of online advertising, any insight was valuable. The founders had a ready-made market for their research. They sold it to advertisers and brands on a consultancy basis.

At this point, the founders had a database of coded online videos created by brands and records of their online performance taken from publicly available sources – specifically the number of views and shares. They approached a local business school to see if an academic would analyse this data for them. One lucky academic accepted and found themselves in possession of a large database. They ran various econometric analysis that all pointed towards the idea that branded online videos which generated a strong emotional response did, indeed, perform the best. This study was published in a series of papers and the academic soon left their institution and opened their own marketing consultancy.

In the meantime, the founders from a computer science background tried using Super's database to develop a predictive model. Their idea was simple: could they accurately predict the viewing and sharing figures for an online video if they knew the emotions it provoked through Super's marketing research studies and content analyses? Following a standard data science method, they trained a model using a portion of the database and then compared the model's predictions against the actual viewing figures for adverts in the other portion of the database. The model performed remarkably well and Super began to sell access to this model to brands and advertising agencies. It allowed them to test their how well their online marketing content would perform by running Super's emotional test and analysing the results through Super's predictive algorithm. Here, while the use of machine learning was new, their work echoes with Hopkins' (1923) logic of testing adverts. At this point, Super began to bill clients not only for creative advice but also for access to its databases and research. The founders recruited staff to support them – including Dan, who was tasked to lead a dedicated research team.

As the research side of the business was taking off, the founders had another idea to develop the company. Why rely on publicly available data? In fact, this was becoming increasingly difficult as social media platforms and websites began to realize the value of their data and lock it behind paywalls, walled gardens, and ring fences (Cluley and Brown, 2015). The founders developed a media player which online content providers could use to serve online adverts, collect data, and conduct targeted digital marketing. This ad network, as these systems became known, was not only an early entrant into the then emerging AdTech and MarTech markets (Cluley, 2020), it also increased the data Super could access and, through this, strengthened their research offerings.

For context, an ad network is a marketplace that matches publishers and online content providers who have online advertising space to sell with brands and advertisers who have adverts they want to display. In marketing and advertising circles, this area of business is sometimes known as programmatic advertising because it is automated. In the most straightforward systems, advertisers can bid for advertising space depending on the context in which an advert is displayed (Turow, 2012). This can involve placing an ad based on keywords used on a webpage or even features assigned to the web user who is browsing it (Zuboff, 2019). Despite some notable controversies (Cluley, 2013b), programmatic advertising has been a significant growth area and has supported the development of many social media platforms and technologies we currently have access to.

Super's ad network came to be distinguished by the idea of 'emotional targeting'. They used their studies of the emotional reactions generated by an online video produced by a brand to programmatically display it with relevant content and to potentially interested consumers. For example, if they were placing an advert targeted at generating happiness and their research indicated the video produced this emotional reaction most strongly among 20-year-olds, their network would place the advert on webpages viewed by users they inferred were aged around 20 years old.

From the mid-2000s, thanks to its success leveraging its emotional research and emotional targeting through the ad network, Super grew rapidly. It leased a large building in an up-and-coming creative area of a large European city and began to hire more staff. Initially, all staff joined the company as shareholders. Super attracted investment from venture capital funds and government support and continued to grow. The headcount increased – reaching 500 staff by the mid-2010s. Alongside this, Super expanded into new geographical territories and opened small branch offices in roughly 20 countries. Shortly before ethnographic observations commenced, Super had been acquired by a Fortune 500 media conglomerate, with the founding members, now multi-millionaires, tied to the company by 'golden-handcuffs'.

Getting into Super

At the time of study, Super is split into five functional teams (creative, coding, sales, research, and admin). Each team is organized hierarchically with junior and mid-level executives reporting to a team director who, in turn, reports to one of the founders. Each team is led from Super's European-based head office.

As discussed, Super's head office is located in a large European capital city. The surrounding area is focused on a main high street that is occupied by a mix of food stalls, coffee shops, bars, clothing stores, offices for creative and cultural organizations, and apartments. The streets in the area are clean but most buildings are adorned with street art, stickers, and posters. Several international advertising agencies have offices in the area. There is also an art and design college nearby. As a result, throughout any given day, the area is busy with local people, students, commuters, shoppers, and tourists enjoying the local landmarks. There is also an assortment of homeless people, street performers, and street sellers.

Super's office building is set back from the main high street on a side road. Its immediate neighbours are converted and new-build apartment blocks. If you walk further along this street, away from the high street, you come to local university's business school. This academic institution has had a long-running relationship with Super. They helped them design their original emotional measurement instrument. Ever since, Super has hosted an annual 'Superversity' event for the business school's academics and students to share ideas with Super's staff.

The head office itself comprises a basement, street-level reception area, and three storeys of offices and meeting rooms. The basement is made up of four main rooms: a small glass-walled meeting room used by the company's senior leadership team for one-to-one meetings with Super's staff; a chill-out room with incense, mood-lighting, and ambient music; a gaming area with sofas and bean bags also offers storage for bikes and staff lockers; and the Lab. The ground floor houses Super's reception desk and waiting area. The first and second floors are open-plan offices. The top floor comprises a small meeting room for internal meetings called the Study, an outside roof terrace, and a large meeting room known as the Townhall.

Day-to-day production activities take place in the open-plan offices on the first and second floors. These activities cover typical office work: writing emails, participating in conference calls, producing electronic documents and computer code. Teams are organized physically in 'neighbourhoods' – that is, they are clustered together on shared open-plan desks (see Figure 4.1). Most workers listen to music through headphones and engage in online meetings with colleagues and clients over headsets. No staff wear uniforms or identifying documents.

There are daily online meetings with international team members and regular in-person visits to the head office by all staff. The head office is also a central meeting place for Super's clients and executives from its holding company. It is a key part of its brand. The creative team has formal responsibility for all aspects of the built environment.

Introducing the research team

The research team is responsible for four research products (Heartbeats, Virality, Compare, and Emotionality). These are described in more detail

Figure 4.1: A view of the open-plan office from the research team's neighbourhood

in Chapter 7. They also complete bespoke one-off pieces of research known as Big Picture Projects. The head office-based research team members sit together at a large open-plan desk. The area is known as the research team's neighbourhood. They work on laptop-computers supplied by the company. Each team member has multiple computer screens on their desks.

The research team is led by Dan, the team director. He joined Super five years ago after completing a Master's degree in Management and Marketing from a large European business school. He is in his late thirties, confident, and outgoing. He lives with his partner, a psychiatrist, and pet dog, who he brings to work with him most days.

Dan is supported by Becky, a mid-level executive. Becky is in her late twenties. She joined Super shortly after Dan, having graduated with a Bachelor's degree in Medieval History from a world-leading European university. Becky is quick-witted and sarcastic. She wears casual but fashionable clothes to work such as colourful dungarees. Becky is primarily responsible for Emotionality studies. This is Super's facial coding product – discussed in detail in Chapter 8.

There are also three junior executives in the head office team. Joanne joined Super three years ago. As an émigré, she speaks occasionally broken English with a slight accent. She is primarily responsible for Virality EQ studies. Andy and Greg joined Super in the last 12 months. They started on the same day and are treated as something of a double-act. Andy holds a Bachelor's degree in Psychology. He joined Super having worked in consumer research for a large airline. He says he did not fit into the corporate environment there. He has dreadlocks and a punk style. He spends his weekends attending raves across Europe. Greg joined Super after finishing a Bachelor's degree in Marketing from a European business school. He has a style most similar to that described by Alvesson (1994). He wears smart, modish clothes and has a neat haircut. He is quiet and has a withdrawn nature. Andy and Greg are primarily responsible for completing Compare and Heartbeat studies.

In addition to completing research activities, the research team spends much of its time and effort liaising with other teams. They work particularly closely with the admin and coding teams to ensure that the technical system is in place to run their studies. They are also responsible for supporting the sales team to sell the research products to Super's clients. Indeed, shortly before my visit, Super had just launched Emotionality. This was a significant investment for the company as Super had to partner with expert facial coding specialists. Much of the research team's work around this launch involved pitching to members of the sales team in international branch offices to convince them to pitch it to their clients.

The research team spends time reminding the sales team to charge clients for research products. Since the development of the ad network, which can involve much more significant sums of money than contracts for research, the sales team use research products as add-ons to win accounts for the ad network.

Not so fast

I started my first day onsite at Super like any other new starter. I reported at the reception desk around 9:30am, as I had been instructed by Dan. The receptionist told me that Dan was working at home but that Becky would welcome me. She made a call to Becky to tell her I was waiting in reception.

After brief introductions, Becky showed me to a desk. It was next to her in the research team's neighbourhood. Becky called a man over from the IT neighbourhood and told him I was a new starter in the research team. He asked me what computer equipment I needed. I said I had my own laptop but needed access to the company wifi. He took my laptop away. While my laptop was with IT, Becky showed me how to use the coffee machine in the kitchen, walked me round the fire-escape routes, and said I could shadow her for the day.

After a few minutes, as I sipped a Nescafé espresso from the company machine, the IT assistant returned my laptop. It was now connected to Super's network. The IT assistant said he had signed me up to the all-company email list and the research team's email list, board, and shared drives (these are described in Chapter 5). Becky told me that Super runs most of its work through free apps such Gmail, Drive, and Hangouts. IT had logged into my Google profile and added me to their systems and online groups.

A few moments after getting my laptop back, someone from admin emailed to ask me to fill out a new starter questionnaire. It included questions such as 'What is your favourite film?', 'If you weren't working at Super what would you be doing?', and 'What is the most surprising thing about yourself?'. As Becky returned to her work, I spent some time thinking of answers that would present me in the best light. I sent it back to the admin email address and went out of the office in search of lunch and to collect the keys to my rented apartment.

While I was out of the building, my answers were sent to the all-company email list. Within seconds, people had emailed me with memes related to my favourite film and other answers. I returned to the office and began working through these emails. Then Becky leaned over and asked, 'Have you called Dan yet? You need to call him now.' I saw I had an email from him. It read: 'We've got a problem, call me.'

I immediately called Dan on my mobile phone. He explained that one of the recipients of the all-company emails was the human resources team at the Fortune 500 holding company who now owned Super. On reading my introductory email, in which I said that if I was not at Super I would be teaching my class at the University of Nottingham, they had immediately contacted Super's admin team to ask what I was doing and, upon learning I was an ethnographer, asked if we had a Non-Disclosure Agreement (NDA) in place.

We did not and the holding company demanded that the research stop immediately. Dan apologized but told me I had to pack my things up and leave the office straight away. I asked if I needed to take my laptop to IT to sign me out of their systems. He said it was already done.

Dutifully, I left the building and headed to my rented apartment. It was located around the corner from Super's head office. After a flurry of phone calls back to the University of Nottingham's legal team, I was advised to return home while they completed the necessary paperwork for an NDA. As it turned out, this was more complicated than expected. Getting an agreement delayed my observations for several weeks. The university's legal team would not sign an NDA if it impinged on my academic freedom, but Super's holding company wanted the right to stop me publishing what it deemed to be commercially sensitive material.

Eventually, after much negotiation, both parties agreed to an NDA. It granted me the ability to report my ethnography and formalized a schedule of anonymizations that I needed to adhere to. This dictated, among other stipulations, that I change all names – including those associated with specific people, clients, partners, techniques, and products. The anonymization was implemented to textual data after recordings and notes were transcribed by a university-approved professional transcriber. A university-approved graphic designer anonymized images through line drawings. As this was planned from the start, and set out in my funding bid, I was unconcerned by the effect of the commitments in the NDA on my research. Indeed, this is an example where an early engagement with research ethics facilitated empirical research.

Even before the NDA issue, I had committed to myself that I would change any details needed to protect the people I worked with at Super. Unlike research techniques such as interviews, where participants can edit what they reveal to researchers, ethnography, particularly more the long-term and immersive form of ethnographic study, grants people involved in the action less discretion in the way their actions are presented and represented – in fact that is the point. This means that the ethnographer must be sensitive to the possible implications of their reports for the people they observe. For example, if I report that someone is critical of their manager, or a client, or behaves unethically, or reveals trade secrets, this could have serious consequences for their career, reputation, or company. As such, some of the details of action I observed have been changed in this report to protect people from potential harm.

Getting back in

With funding and the NDA in place, onsite data-gathering started in earnest. This led to a 'You're back' moment when I returned to the research team's neighbourhood which suggested my absence had, somehow, facilitated acceptance into the team. I went back to Super, having arranged to meet Dan in the reception again. As he escorted me back to my desk, I noted in my diary that the 'office seemed more relaxed' to me for some reason.

Indeed, no one acknowledged my return until, after 20 minutes, Becky sat at her desk following a meeting. She turned to me and, in a warm, if slightly sarcastic, tone, stated: 'You're back! I hope it's for good this time!' She asked if I was staying in the same apartment and then turned to her laptop and began to work. Strangely, this acknowledgement encouraged others in the research team to start to talk to me. Throughout the rest of the day, I recounted the story of the NDA several times and people told me they were happy I was back. I wondered why. Maybe they assumed that the senior leadership team had insisted on my return? Maybe my absence was framed as a battle between them and the new owners of the company?

Super's IT team reinstated my access to their digital systems and my laptop became an indispensable data-collection tool. Not only did it give me access to the electronic files and systems the research team used, it also provided a convenient way for me to keep notes on the action I was observing. The first morning I was onsite, prior to being asked to leave, I noted that people worked predominantly on laptops. At Super, people seemed to always have a laptop in hand. They sat in meetings tapping on their laptop's keyboards. They sat in the kitchen, eating lunch or drinking coffee while watching videos on their laptops. This meant I could make notes on my laptop throughout the day, and use my laptop to take photographs, save screengrabs, and make audio recordings of meetings and interviews without drawing attention to myself. Finally, at the end of each day, either in Super's offices or back at my rented apartment, I would type up detailed reflective fieldnotes on my laptop. Here, I recorded what I observed, what I felt about it, and what I was learning about marketing action.

I participated in onsite observations for six months. This was followed by eight months of virtual participation which I conducted around my teaching duties. In this time, I took 250 photos and saved over 200 screengrabs – I selected 30 to be anonymized by a graphic designer. I recorded the audio from ten company meetings and presentations and 30 research team meetings. All recording were transcribed by a professional transcriber. I archived over 3,000 emails and over 150 digital documents. I also collected physical documents, such as print-outs and brochures, which I digitized after my onsite observations.

I augmented these ethnographic materials with 23 unstructured ethnographic interviews. These were also audio-recorded and transcribed by a professional transcriber. They helped to formalize the research focus and probe for relevant details. Three interviews took place prior to the ethnographic observations, nine during and 11 after. The interviewees came from the coding, research, and admin teams and Super's external partners including Analytico – a company described in Chapter 8.

Writing an ethnography

According to Neyland (2008), there are three fundamental approaches to reporting ethnographic research. One may aim to produce a *realist ethnography* by assuming that what one witnessed really happened and that one's account captures the reality of the action. Alternatively, a researcher may write a *narrative ethnography* in which they accept that their position as a researcher means they will experience a partial account of what is happening around them. The narrative ethnographer accepts that there are things that they will not see. They believe that they will bring their own assumptions and interests to the research site and that these will influence what they pay attention to and how they interpret the action. Finally, for Neyland (2008), we may engage in a *reflexive ethnography*. Here, the object of interest shifts from the research site to the researcher's experiences within the site. Such ethnographies privilege how the action affects the ethnographer as much as detailing the action itself. More recently, we have seen additional approaches put forward, including affective ethnographies, virtual ethnographies, multisite ethnographies, post-human ethnographies, and netnographies. As with Neyland's categorization, each brings with it a particular way of engaging with the research site during fieldwork and engaging with one's observations when reporting them.

It is rare for ethnographers of marketing action to detail which approach they have adopted. Most engage in organizational ethnography as they limit their studies to a single organization and many implicitly adopt a realist approach. Perhaps the most detailed description of the relationship between data and theory in the existing marketing literature comes from Alvesson's (1994) classic study. He suggests that ethnographic studies of marketing action should not offer 'procedural accounts for the generation and processing of empirical material' because 'the material is too multifaceted and "rich" to be easily categorized or compared' (Alvesson, 1994: 541). Rather, Alvesson argues that ethnographic reports should focus on 'elements that spontaneously surprised' the researcher in the field (1994: 541). He continues: 'An important element in research of this type concerns "surprises" which occur when the researcher's framework "breaks down" in the face of actions, circumstances and talk pertaining to the framework of the "natives"' (Alvesson, 1994: 541). Rosen (1985) and Moeran (2005) are representative of this surprise-led approach. They each focus on a single event that neither author expected to interest them at the start of their studies. In Moeran's (2005) case, it was serendipity that meant he was invited into an otherwise closed-off space as the account team at Asatsu needed to recruit a foreigner.

Alvesson's (1994) advice might explain the lack of methodological reporting in the ethnographic literature. However, I disagree with Alvesson that a focus on surprising aspects of the field necessitates that we do not document procedural accounts of our observations nor follow protocol or procedures when in the field. We can still explain what we did and why. I accept, though, that it means that we cannot follow a vulgar understanding of 'transparent' analysis. The surprise-led approach means that 'research themes' may be 'decided relatively late in the research process, based on a combination of the researcher's interpretive repertoire ... and interesting themes emerging from (the interpretations) of the field' (Alvesson, 1998: 974). As a result, the criteria for presenting and assessing research must differ from those typical of other methods. Alvesson writes:

> The central element in research then becomes the researcher's ability to interpret the material in an interesting way. This is better indicated by reproducing the text in its entirety. Success must be evaluated by seeing whether the text convincingly provides grounded insights and points, and not on whether the research effort has been guided by methodological conventions. (Alvesson, 1994: 541)

To this end, I began my study at Super with a broad interest in understanding how Super worked as a marketing research organization. I adopted an organizational ethnographic approach informed by Watson's (2011) vision of a 'how things work' study. Such studies sit between Neyland's (2008) definitions of narrative and reflective accounts. They involve the researcher learning how an organization, profession, or industry works. They focus on both what kinds of actions are appropriate for the given setting and how these conventional actions impress themselves on participants. This is achieved by the researcher reflecting on their experiences learning to fit in. As such, Watson, who is himself a trailblazer of organizational ethnography, asks ethnographers 'to write about the understandings' they learned during ethnographic observations so that 'any reader would be able to cope and survive on board such organizational vessels – whether they board those vessels as sailors, passengers, or officers' (2011: 209).

Where my approach differs from Watson's is that, following the innovations of science studies discussed in Chapter 1, I was interested in understanding the action at Super beyond human participants. I entered the field with an interest in understanding marketing research practice, particular research practices that used data science approaches, as an assemblage of humans, knowledge, symbols and physical, representational and technical objects (for more on assemblage theory, see Diaz Ruiz, 2013; Hill et al, 2014; Franco et al, 2022).

By the end of my observations, I recognized that the non-human elements of marketing actions are organized around discourses of Marketing Art and Marketing Science – just as human talk and interactions are. They structured my participation at Super. They were not only part of the talk at Super but were so embedded in the action that they had become literally materialized in the spaces, tools, and objects at Super. The impressed themselves on the action, then, in ways not represented in the existing ethnographic literature.

As I reflected on my experiences, which are summarized in Chapter 5, I saw that the research activities at Super are better understood as science fiction than science or an art. This is an understanding which I detail in the following sections of the book. It starts from a belief that clients turn to marketing organizations to reduce the complexity and uncertainties that would, otherwise, stop them from making decisions. Organizational theorists call this kind of sensemaking activity 'uncertainty absorption'. I describe how this belief structures action in Chapter 6. To absorb uncertainty, the action at Super uses ideas, discourses, and methods associated with a range of scientific practices – which I detail in Chapters 7 and 8. These are intended, consciously or otherwise, to present Super's activities with a sense of certainty. No one believes that Super is engaged in genuine scientific activity. Rather, the final stage of marketing science fiction involves creativity. Here, marketing action is about giving meaning to data and telling stories that interest clients. I call this artistic qualification and describe it in Chapters 9 and 10.

To present the ethnographic observations and theorize the process of marketing science fiction, in what follows, I enter into a theory–data dialogue. In some chapters, I start with an existing academic theory that provides a way into the ethnographic observations. In other chapters, I describe marketing action and then engage with related theory or develop new concepts. In each, I provide concrete examples of specific actions that illustrate my experiences and present detailed accounts through line drawings, fieldnotes, and commentaries. My aim is, following Alvesson (1994), to allow theory to develop from the field as I explain how things work with people who claim to be doing marketing science.

5

Marketing Work

To begin the ethnographic account, let us take our first step into Super by exploring how the research team works together in a coordinated way. This not only illustrates how Super operates but, also, provides a general sense of the organization of marketing research. From talking to the research team, from ethnographic interviews and from subsequent conversations with marketing researchers about my experiences, it is clear that the action at Super is fairly representative of the ways that marketing research – indeed, marketing action – happens generally.

There is good reason for this level of standardized action. It means that marketing researchers can move between marketing organizations without having to learn new ways of working and, thus, supports seniority and a power structure in marketing organizations. It also reflects the account model discussed by Moeran (2005). Advertising agencies say that the conformity that Alvesson (1994) finds so curious is functional. It reduces the transactions costs for clients looking to move from one agency to another.

The same is true for marketing research organizations. In fact, it is common for key contacts in their clients to work towards bonuses tied to key brand performance indicators that are measured by their marketing research organization. These include standard measures such as brand awareness or brand recall. If a market research agency does not measure these indicators or measures them in a unique way, it creates a significant challenge when it is trying to win new business.

For now, though, we will consider what these standardized practices look like. I will describe the working day and the atmosphere in Super's head office. I will review the ways that the research team coordinates their work and highlight the importance of automation in their activity. I will also describe the human relations with the team.

Getting to work

As discussed in Chapter 4, Super's head office is located in an up-and-coming neighbourhood in a large European city. Like many similar areas, nearby accommodation is both in short supply and prohibitively expensive given the kinds of salaries paid to the research team. At the time of writing, new hires to the research team are offered a salary roughly equivalent to US$50–60,000. This is around 30 per cent higher than the national median wage but in a similar range to the median wage for the city where Super's head office is located. The result is that many of the younger, and typically more junior, staff at Super have no choice but to commute to Super's head office from less fashionable areas of the city and beyond.

As typical accommodation in the area is poor quality and small, the area is also unattractive to older, and more senior staff, with young families – even though they are more able to afford to live there based on their salary. They can live in larger residencies and in more family-oriented areas of the city or use the premium salary to acquire much more palatial properties in the commuter belt outside of the city. The result of this is that many of the older staff also commute to work. I am relatively unusual in this regard as I have a junior position at Super, a young family, and I rent an apartment in Super's neighbourhood.

The fact that so few employees live nearby has two effects that I noticed soon after beginning my work at Super.

First, it means that there is very little socializing outside of the workplace. Given the nature of the host city, commuting means relying on notoriously unreliable public transport. This encourages staff to 'head home' as soon as they can and to work irregular hours so they can minimize the time they have to spend on their commutes. The lack of social activities outside of work contrasted with my expectations based on previous ethnographic accounts (Kenny and Euchler, 2012) and my own studies of other marketing companies (Green and Cluley, 2014; Cluley and Green, 2019). Here, we are given the impression that it is common for marketing workers to turn off their computers and head to the pub both during and after work, as we saw in Chapter 3.

Second, given the geographic dispersal of its workers, Super has to make special accommodation for its staff. There is, for example, a dedicated bike park in the building to support staff who commute by bicycle. The kitchen in the open-plan office is equipped with the necessary implements to allow staff who arrive early or stay late to prepare meals. It is not simply a place to make coffee but includes toasters, ovens, and cooking equipment. Similarly, Super uses hybrid working. It is common for meetings to take place virtually and all staff, especially senior staff, are free to manage their physical attendance in the office as they see fit.

The working day

There are few formal policies structuring the working day at Super. On my first day, before I am asked to leave while a Non-Disclosure Agreement is put in place, Becky tells me that I am free to come and go as I please, although she asks me to record my plans on a shared online calendar. When I log into this calendar for the first time, I am surprised to see that not only am I able to view the calendars of everyone in the company but that I can book time with anyone as well. For example, when arranging times to conduct ethnographic interviews, most respondents ask me to book a time directly in their online calendars. Occasionally, they might come back to ask if we could reschedule a meeting to accommodate their other plans but, more often than not, if I booked an interview in, say, the Townhall at 3pm on a Friday with the creative director, the creative director would be in the Townhall waiting for me at 3pm.

This was very unusual for me given my experiences working in UK universities. While we have similar flexibility to manage our time, booking meetings with other staff members is a tortuous process typically involving Doodle polls, Microsoft Teams, Outlook calendars, emails, and room booking systems. The idea that I could, for example, go into the vice chancellor's online calendar and book a meeting with them is laughable. Here, it is more likely that I would only be able to apply to their personal or executive assistant for a ten-minute consultation slot that would be scheduled three months into the future and in which I could only discuss pre-approved topics. Yet, at Super, I could simply drop a meeting into the chief executive officer (CEO)'s diary.

There is no official start of the working day when members of the research team are expected to be present in the office. Yet, the working day follows a regular rhythm. The offices are unlocked from 7am. Members of the research team, indeed most other workers, arrive over the next few hours.

Those who arrive in the office before 9am include staff with caring responsibilities who want to leave as early as possible, staff who want to miss peak-time travel and rush hour traffic, and staff who have specific work tasks to complete such as calls with clients in different time zones. The only members of the research team who regularly arrive early are Dan, who often does so to work around a family illness, and Becky, who occasionally arrives before 9am for meetings with international clients or to meet a specific deadline.

Perhaps because the group who arrive early is self-selected and because the majority have not arrived early because they have too much work to do, there is a relaxed atmosphere in the offices between 7am and 9am. As evidenced in fieldnotes, before 9am most staff spend time socializing in the kitchen. They prepare breakfast and discuss non-work topics. Only staff who are there out of a sense of obligation, needing to complete a task, seem focused on work. They tend to ignore their socializing colleagues:

Today I arrive at Super's offices at 7:30am. As I walk in, the shops and cafes on the local streets are opening and the pavement was a rush of commuters, students and school kids. I enter the building, walking past rubbish bags in the un-manned reception area. I don't see anyone in the coding neighbourhood. In the main office, the first thing I see is Graham's [mid-level executive, business development] computer screen. He sits opposite the entrance to the office. He is talking to Becky on a video call. There are a few other people in the office. Most are chatting in the kitchen. I walk to the research neighbourhood and am surprised to see Becky at her desk. I presumed she was on a video call with Graham because she was working from home. I set up my laptop and listen in to their conversation. They are talking about a gig they both went to last night. Becky notices me. She leans over to me and says, in her typical sarcastic tone, 'We're waiting for an international client who hasn't turned up. I can't believe I got out of bed for this!'. I ask Becky if she wants a coffee and walk to the kitchen. In the kitchen, as I load pods into the single-shot coffee machine, I chat to two girls from the coding team. They are talking about suffering back pain from sitting down at a computer all day. I suggest they try doing Jefferson Curls – a technique I had picked up from a YouTube video recently. When I get back to the research neighbourhood, Ross [sales team director] comes over with a sense of purpose. He abruptly asks when Dan will be in the office. He is very frustrated when Becky says she doesn't know and that his calendar says he should be in already. 'Do you know?', Ross asks me aggressively. I say I don't. Becky rolls her eyes at me as Ross walks away and tells me that Ross is pulling together a presentation for a major client.

The relaxed atmosphere before 9am is supported, even encouraged, by Super's management. Not only does the company provides a well-stocked kitchen, but fresh bagels and cereals are delivered each morning at 7am. There is a gym in the building equipped with kettlebells, yoga mats, a punchbag, and a weights bench. There are also showers and washroom facilities. The CEO and founder, Bella, explains that Super incurs these 'expenses' for two reasons. First, it is 'the kind of thing companies like us do, people we want to work here expect it'. Second, it is intended to maintain 'a start-up culture'. Bella says:

> The company grew because we [the founders] worked every hour we could, not because we had to, or because someone told us to, but because it was our life. We want everyone to feel like that. We want people to be here working to push the company forwards. If a box of bagels is enough to twist their arm, it's worth it.

As the clock ticks towards 9am, more people begin to arrive in the office. As they do, the atmosphere in the offices gives way to a gentle hum of office work. At 9am, the reception formally opens. Now there are around 100 workers in the open-plan office. Despite this, it is remarkably quiet. I took audio recordings of the ambient noise in the office but they did not even register on my recording equipment. Most workers listen to music through headphones and engage in online chats with colleagues and clients over headsets. When people need to have discussions, they tend to move to the kitchen or one of the meeting rooms in the building.

There is no scheduled lunch break but, around midday, members of the research team tend to stop working. They sometimes stay at their desks and log onto social media or watch TV online. They may relocate to the social spaces in Super's offices such as the kitchen or games room in the basement. Sometimes they leave the office altogether.

Interestingly, these freedoms produce a number of routine working practices at Super. In Week 3, the fieldnotes describe the familiar rhythms of the office:

> Things are becoming a bit clear to me now. The days aren't always the same, but they do seem to vary around a common theme. Becky and Andy tend to sit at their desks listening to music through headphones. Greg and Joanne don't listen to music. After we meet for an update meeting in the morning, the time before lunch tends to involve concentrated work. The Research Team does not often book meetings for this time – although people might be needed in meetings organized by other teams. They usually involve Dan though. Dan's activities are represented by a bag of satsumas. In the morning, he brings a bag of around 6–8 satsumas with him. He puts the bag on his desk and, throughout the day, as he returns for short periods, maybe 10–30 minutes at a time, and eats a satsuma. As he does, he will lean back on his chair and asks how we all are. Often someone has a query and Dan will either speak to them about it, tell them he is already 'on top of it' or take them to the Kitchen to discuss the matter in private – or as private as the Kitchen gets. It always seems to have someone in it. Occasionally, lots of people. There is a constant flow of traffic round the office and a very distinct sound. It is quiet. It almost sounds like an office with one person in it. As the day passes, some of the Research Team migrate from their desks to other spaces in the building. Andy, in particular, will move from the Research Neighborhood to one of the many little liminal workspaces dotted throughout the building. These tend to be in corners, corridors or other out the way places. They each have a personality. For example, one behind the Research Team's Neighbourhood has a modern theme with a high-sided armchair, shag rug and large arc lamp. These are arranged around a mock fireplace filled with a pixelated image of a fire.

There is no formal end to the working day. The office stays open until 9pm – with a security guard, who begins working at 4pm, standing on duty at the entrance to the building until the main door is locked. Some employees stay late to complete their work tasks, some use the staff gym, others make food in the kitchen before they leave. Like the early morning, the atmosphere in the offices becomes more relaxed from about 5pm. There is a sense that this is not typical working time. This is a time when, for example, the senior leadership team hold many of their meetings. It is a time for strategy and blue sky thinking.

For instance, the ethnographic interview with Bella, the CEO, takes place at 7:30pm. As we sit down together at an empty desk in the open-plan office, which is now darkened as most lights and computers have been switched off, Bella apologizes for keeping me in the head office late. She explains that 'this is the only free time I get'. As this interview takes place, only Bella, myself, and Bella's personal assistant are present in the office. We had booked 30 minutes and Bella makes it clear at the start of the interview that she will not give me any more of her time. She explains that she 'has to get home to put her kids to bed'. I assume that her personal assistant has stayed in the head office to ensure that this happens.

As with the early starts, only Dan and Becky from the research team regularly work after 5pm. As more senior staff, they engage in some management activities and video calls with international colleagues. For Bella, the CEO and founder, this is a worrying sign. As the ethnographic interview with her turns to the organizational culture, she points to the empty office and comments: 'People should want to be here. It hurts me to think people treat this as a job.'

So, despite the appearance of flexible working, beneath the surface there are tensions around the organization of the working day at Super. The working day appears to be unstructured and unmanaged, but this is intended to maximize the amount of time people work. Despite this intention, the flexibility afforded to them is embraced by most of the staff to manage their work and commuting time. Rather than increasing their efforts, they treat their marketing work as a job and resist the invitation to stay for longer than necessary. They impose a more conventional working day on themselves and choose to reject this aspect of the start-up culture promoted by Super's senior leadership team.

Huddle time

The typical working day for the research team begins with a 'huddle'. This is a short meeting led by Dan. It usually takes place in the kitchen or, if Dan is away from the office, online in a video call. Everyone in the head office-based research team is expected to attend. International colleagues occasionally sign in too. In fact, every team at Super holds a huddle meeting once a day – normally shortly after 9am. This creates a buzz in the kitchen as the teams vie for space on the benches for their huddles (see Figure 5.1).

Figure 5.1: Teams gathering in the kitchen for their huddles

The research team's huddles focus on an electronic project management system known as the 'board'. It is essentially a collection of online kanban boards. There is a board for each member of the research team. They are split up into different tasks organized around the products the team offers. Each product is listed in a column. An electronic 'card' is placed in the relevant column with the client or project name when a new job comes in.

The individual boards for each research team member are linked to a collective research team board which is split up into columns for each team member. These list the cards that have been assigned to each team member. So, for example, if a new Emotionality study comes in, a card is created and added to Becky's column on the team board and the Emotionality column on Becky's personal board.

Dan is responsible for managing the research team's board and has oversight of each team members' individual boards. As work comes into the team, Dan first creates electronic cards on the research team board and assigns the task to a member of the research team by dragging and dropping the card into their column in a huddle. This populates a card on their individual board which they, or Dan, place in the appropriate product column. Once a task is complete, a team member can mark it complete on their board. This then flags it as completed on the research team's board and Dan can archive the card. This is typically discussed in the huddles.

The fieldnotes in Week 10 illustrate a typical huddle:

> We Huddle around 10:30am in the Kitchen. On the way from the Research
> Neighbourhood, Becky says she 'can't be bothered to Huddle today'. But she
> dutifully walks with us to the Kitchen. We make coffees, grab fruit and bagels
> and sit down together at a bench. As the meeting starts, Dan asks how everyone

is. No one has much to say. Dan turns his laptop round so everyone can see the Research Team's Board. Dan asks each team member for an update on their completed cards and to identify which outstanding cards and tasks they did not complete yesterday. He starts with Andy, who is working a one-off study. Andy says he hasn't completed any cards as there was a problem getting OTC [over the counter] data. Dan says he will take this up with the Project Manager at the OTC data provider. Joanne reports that she is 'pretty snowed under' as she has client visits planned for the next few days. Dan asks if anyone else could 'jump in' and work on any of her cards. Greg responds that he can help. I also offer to help. Greg and Joanne pointed at cards on Dan's laptop and decided which cards can be reallocated. Dan finishes the huddle by asking everyone to attend an internal training session later that day He says it is important that the Research Team has a good presence at the sessions. He adds this as a card to everyone's Board. Everyone goes back to their desks.

The board coordinates tasks and allows work to be moved around within the research team so they can maximize the productivity of their resources. This is possible because, while each research team member has primary responsibility for a specific research product, many tasks in the research team are standardized. As described in Chapter 4, the team's work is primarily focused on four products. Each has a clear remit but each speaks to Super's underlying brand position of emotional targeting. Indeed, they each use a set of standard measures which Super describe as the 'Elements of Emotionality' (discussed in more detail in Chapter 7). These measures include common brand metrics such as brand awareness, top of mind recall, and purchase intent as well as measures from Super's earliest research. They test audience's emotional and affective response to test adverts.

For the research team, the focus of these measures provides a heuristic for interpreting their research results across all the products. No matter which method a product is based on, they focus their analyses on the links between emotional and affective responses and brand outcomes. For example, when reviewing audience responses to an advert in Compare studies, members of the research team tend to look for differences in brand metrics first and then for differences in emotional responses. If they find a notable difference, their conclusion will, inevitably, be that the advert's success is due to the emotional responses it evokes.

This standardization has not occurred by chance. It is embedded in the tools the research team use. The research team report their four standard products to clients through a PowerPoint slideshow called 'The Deck'. Each product has its own Deck design that has been created by the creative team. However, each Deck design includes a number of shared methodology slides which emphasize the importance of generating an emotional response – as detailed in Chapter 6. The Deck for each product also demands that the research team include visualizations which compare emotional measures and brand metrics. This, of course, encourages them to focus on these relationships in their interpretations.

Illustrating this interpretive heuristic in action and the ways that it is linked to the research product's methods, fieldnotes from Week 2 of the onsite observations document a presentation in which Dan and Becky review an updated methodology for Virality studies to internal stakeholders – primarily, the sales team. In this meeting, they make it clear that the product focuses on the link between emotional responses and brand outcomes. The meeting takes place in a hybrid form. Dan, Becky, and I are in a small meeting room in Super's head office, known as the Study. This room is described in more detail in Chapter 10. The audience for the meeting has signed into the meeting from Super's international offices using a video-conferencing platform:

> Dan begins by working through a new Deck design for Virality. He presents as if he is talking to clients. He says that the key point is that 'emotionality is linked to memory' and says this is what Ehrenberg Bass 'prove'. He tells us that academic research shows that, to be successful, 'you must link that emotional reactions to your brand'. He then tells the meeting that Daniel Kahneman's work 'supports need to study unconscious and rational responses'. He says that to measure Kahneman's concept of System One or automatic responses, Super use through facial coding. These studies don't rely on audiences thinking about their responses. Super measure System Two thinking, or rational choices, through their survey-based methods like Virality. It includes '18 psychological responses'. He explains that these have been selected 'because they help to inform brand decision making. They are things marketers care about'. He says: 'We are actually trying to sell something. We aren't in the business of making videos that get shared and viewed all over the world cause we like making videos!'. To measure 'rational messaging', Virality uses unprompted brand recall and brand statements. Virality also allows a client to include up to five unique brand statements that specific to the brand such as 'Brand X care about the environment'. Dan explains: 'it sounds quite basic but advertisers care about this sort of thing'. He then explains that they have added a new 'compound metric' based on a large competitor research firm about the information conveyed in the video and a new measure of enjoyment as it is 'something other people are reporting on'. After about 30 minutes. Dan asks if everyone can hear him okay. Up to this point no one has asked any questions. Dan waits for a moment and is met by further silence. He shrugs his shoulders to Becky and I and introduces Becky as the 'go to' if people have any further questions. Becky takes over as presents a 'use case' for a confectionary brand.

As this fieldnote suggests, not only is the design of Super's research products based on the link between emotional responses and brand outcomes, a link which supports the emotional targeting approach offered by their ad network, but the measures are designed around brands' expectations and industry norms – that is to say, like a Keynesian beauty contest, because other research firms include them in their products. They have added new metrics because they are things other people are reporting on. In short, this extract shows us how standardization, as much as their brand position, legitimizes Super's research approach.

The ability of the research team to shift work around is supported by this standardization. Standardization, in turn, facilitates the automation of the research process at Super. Data gathering begins with an electronic Request for Data (RfD). This specifies which of Super's four research designs the study involves. The RfD also specifies the desired sample characteristics and timeframe for a study. Samples can be defined by demographic features such as age and gender or predefined psychographic features offered by Super's OTC data provider – anonymized here as Aloha. These are external companies who run panels of research participants. They offer access to groups such as such as 'active consumers', 'ethical consumers', and 'new parents'. The default data request is for a 'Nat Rep' or nationally representative sample for the client's home market.

Completing a RfD request is a skilled task and requires a developed understanding of the client's needs and Super's product offering. I was not permitted to do this during my time at Super. The process is typically started by Dan, or Becky when Dan is unavailable, and moves to research team members for further elaboration if needed. After it is completed, the RfD is 'signed off' by Dan and is entered into Super's OTC data provider's system. This is the point at which Super formally commissions the data collection and commits to cover the costs of collecting the data. It ignites an automated data-gathering process.

Data gathering itself is a black box at Super. After submitting the RfD, the research team wait for notification from Aloha that the task has been completed. Typically, this is done with remarkable efficiency. Nat Rep samples cost a few dollars per respondent and are returned to Super within 24 hours – even for studies involving thousands of respondents. More specific demographic or psychographic features incur higher costs and take longer to get back. Yet, even in these cases, data collection rarely takes more than a few days.

The completed data is delivered as an electronic file that is automatically uploaded to Super's analysis system by Aloha. This system revolves around an electronic database that stores all study results. It includes an online dashboard that allows the research team to perform standard analyses for each research product. Once Aloha has uploaded data to the database, the dashboard automatically sends an email notification to the relevant research team member, as indicated on the original RfD.

Charting and scripting

The main work of the research team that is allocated during the huddles is 'charting' and 'scripting'. Charting refers to the production of visual artefacts for the research products. The most common artefacts are bar charts, line graphs, and spider diagrams. Scripting refers to writing titles and notes to go alongside these visual artefacts.

Most charting is automated. Once the data had been uploaded into Super's database, a member of the research team downloads a copy as an Excel file and creates a new Deck. They use a bespoke computer program to automatically populate the charts in the Deck using the data from the Excel file. The most common charting task, then, is actually checking that these automatically generated visual artefacts are error-free.

Errors occur if, for example, the data in the Excel sheet is corrupted. Blank cells or incorrectly formatted data might mean that a chart is not generated correctly. In these cases, the researcher must manually edit the data and rerun the bespoke charting programme. Other problems occur when the automatically generated charts interfere with the position of other elements of the Deck. A bar on a bar chart might cover a textbox. When this happens, it must be manually corrected.

The exception to this automated charting occurs in Big Picture Projects such as the Luxury Car Social Media Playbook discussed in the next chapter. Often, as in the Luxury Car Social Media Playbook, Big Picture Projects use some data from Super's database and include a mixture of existing research products combined with one-off analysis. In these cases, the researcher completing a Big Picture Project can use Super's online platform to generate standard-format charts but has more freedom about which data to report compared to other products. As demonstrated in the Luxury Car Social Media Playbook, Big Picture Projects can involve a one-off research design to meet a specific objective. This means the research team member conducting the Big Picture Project must decide the study design, analytic approach, and format of the final report. This can include manually designing one-off charts using a variety of non-standard tools.

If charting is about creating visual outputs, scripting is about creating text. Once the charts are complete, the research team add titles and notes to them on a Deck. This is called 'scripting'. It is important because all Decks are sent directly to clients once complete and are not always presented in-person by one of Super's team. In these circumstances, scripting is the research team's main chance to influence how the research is received by clients. According to Greg, the scripts for most products follows a 'say what you see' approach. For example, when scripting many of the brand metrics such as purchase intention, a script may read 'Purchase intention increased by 4% among viewers of the ad.'

But certain measures and certain products provide more space for the researcher's input. In particular, Super's facial coding product, Emotionality, and its predictive ad-tests, Virality, require more detailed interpretations and explanations. As a new product, Emotionality is scripted by Becky because she is the most senior and experienced member of the research team, other than Dan. Not only must Emotionality studies be introduced to clients with more explanation about the method but, as they produce time-series plots that visualize viewers' responses over the duration of an advert, they require more active interpretation.

As described in depth in Chapter 8, Becky must identify a particular moment or movement in the time-series plot as the basis for her interpretation. She typically focuses on 'smile tracks' – these are time-series plots showing how happy audiences were while watching the advert. If the smile track moves upwards, suggesting that viewers found what was happening at that moment amusing, Becky analyses the advert to see what might explain this response at that particular moment. Sometimes it is obvious. But sometimes she struggles to see a clear explanation and needs to conduct further research. When analysing an advert targeted at the Indian market, for instance, she has to translate the advert and conduct a web search to identify a celebrity Indian actor.

Once they have completed charting and scripting, members of the research team email a copy of the Deck to Dan for approval. After this, it is uploaded to Super's database through a drag-and-drop function in their online dashboard. It is then either emailed directly to a client or to an internal contact in the sales team who presents it to their client. This is dictated at the start of the research process and is recorded on the RfD. The speed of this process is revealed in a fieldnote recorded in Week 1:

> At the end of the day, I just had to call Prof Russell Group [a senior colleague at a UK university] to tell him about how they work here. I can't believe how fast it is. Dan approved my RfD yesterday, this morning I had the data from Aloha [an OTC provider], analysis and results! The study was based on over 1,000 people!

Meeting and presenting

The other set of tasks that are discussed in a huddle are 'meetings' and 'presentations'. Although not always used consistently as distinct activities in the same way that charting and scripting are, meetings generally refer to gatherings where the research team is part of the audience. In contrast, presentations generally refer to events where the research team are performing for others. Put simply, the research team's presentations are someone else's meetings and vice versa (see Figure 5.2).

Both meetings and presentations can take place in-person, online, or in hybrid form. To support these interactions, Super have designated meeting

Figure 5.2: A research team meeting with the sales team

Note: From left to right: sales executive, Becky, Andy, sales executive.

rooms in their head office with full video-conferencing facilities. We will look at two of these spaces later (the Lab and the Townhall). They also have a preferred online video platform for internal meetings and a different, more stable but also more expensive one for presentations to clients.

In a huddle, Dan asks each member of the research team which meetings they have been invited to that day and if they are planning on attending them. He creates cards for meetings they plan to attend. If someone is too busy, he might ask if anyone else wants to go in their place in the huddle. If so, their card for the meeting will be moved to their colleague's board.

There are regular internal meetings organized around specific clients and products. Each research product has a dedicated support team in the admin team and coding team. They meet regularly with the research team to identify issues and problems. The research team also regularly meet with other internal stakeholders, particularly the sales team, to keep them up-to-date with the products, present 'use cases', and encourage them to sell their products to their clients.

Dan makes requests in the huddle for people to represent the research team in meetings he has been invited to but does not want to attend. He uses this as an opportunity for professional development in the team. Delegates can learn about discussions in the company beyond their everyday activities. I took advantage of many of these opportunities during my onsite observations.

There are many meetings going on in Super throughout any given day. One reason for this is Super's 'open door' strategy. Essentially, they accept all pitches for new technologies, methods, and innovations. These are seen as being both strategically and culturally important. Much like the *productive cultural consumption* and *norm of newness* evidenced in other ethnographic studies described in Chapter 3, Super hope that they might gain competitive advantages over other research firms by learning about cutting-edge new techniques and technologies. They also want to project an image as being an innovative company and have a strong presence in the local start-up ecosystem. This not only supports their brand position as a technology company but also helps them win accounts among fast-growing businesses. Indeed, the founders have recently begun to use this knowledge to make investments in local start-ups. In short, the open culture symbolized by their willingness to receive pitches helps them to present themselves as an anti-bureaucracy (Alvesson, 1994) and suggests the norm of newness in terms of technology rather than cultural consumption and clothing (Kenny and Euchler, 2012).

However, these pitches from external suppliers are often seen as a drain on the research team's time. While they have developed their facial coding product following a pitch from a start-up anonymized in Chapter 8 as Analytico, most pitches come to nothing. As a result, in the morning huddles, Dan has to cajole, encourage, and sometimes demand that someone attend. I served a useful function here and was often sent to represent the research team in pitches.

In contrast to meetings, presentations primarily refer to events where the research team report their research to their clients, either in-person or online. Sometimes these are small-scale affairs and are barely discussed in the huddle. For example, it is common for Greg and Andy to talk a client through the Decks they chart and script on short phone calls or online meetings. In these presentations, they talk through the script written on the Deck almost verbatim unless the clients ask for elaboration or explanations. This tends to happen when the client is going to re-present the research to an internal audience. Here, Greg's and Andy's presentations serve as pre-presentations, as discussed by Moeran (2005), but also mark a chance to help make their clients look like heroes, as Nilsson suggests (J. Nilsson, 2019).

There are also significant presentations, although these are less common. They occur when Super pitches to win new accounts or presents Big Picture Projects to blue chip clients. These presentations are considered one-off events. They are not only a chance to win accounts but also a chance for Super to display their expertise, good taste, and openness to their clients. They are also an opportunity for key contacts from different client organizations, who work together in their marketing activities, to come together on neutral ground. Presentations are social gatherings as much as anything else. We will look at one such event in Chapter 10, when I describe the final presentation of the Luxury Car Social Media Playbook.

As with Moeran's (2005) account of a pitch at Asatsu, the significant presentations involve a series of relatively routine preparatory activities. Big

Picture Projects build up, much like a theatrical performance. They start with meetings I call 'table reads'. Here, a small group sit in the kitchen or in a meeting room and discuss the key themes that should be developed in the presentation. We will look at one of these events in the next chapter. Big Picture Project presentations then progress to what I call 'rehearsals'. The audience for these presentations includes Super's teams and representatives from clients. They provide feedback on the staging of the presentation. Eventually, there is a final 'performance'. These are designed to be one-off events – never to be repeated to the same audience – where the entire head office building is put on display for the audience.

In huddles, presentations are generally sacrosanct and other activities are organized around them. Other than illness, if someone is requested to present, they present. In some cases, Dan asks if members of the research team want him to accompany them and, for important meetings, he invites himself.

No one's bothered

Despite the standardization and automation of activities, two organizational techniques associated with deskilling and increased drudgery (Braverman, 1974), relations in the research team are generally positive. People are friendly and polite. But relations do not involve the kinds of highly personal and emotional ties discussed elsewhere in the ethnographic literature (Alvesson, 1994; Kelly et al, 2005; Kenny and Euchler, 2012). They are professional.

As discussed, most members of the research team choose to work a fairly conventional working day. They come into the office around 9am and work until around 5pm. Then they go home and, presumably, enter into different social relations. Other than occasional social activities in the working day, there is very little socializing among the team.

Indeed, in Week 6, in preparation for a social event in work time – the annual Super Chilli Cook-off, a cooking competition judged by Super's founders – Dan is asked to provide an interesting fact about the research team for an all-company quiz. He emails the research team's shared email list to ask if any member of the research team has any interesting secrets they are willing to share. When no one responds, he brings up the request in a huddle. After a prolonged silence, with members of the team trying not to make eye contact with Dan, Greg offers one. He tells us that, outside of work, he is a competitive lacrosse player and has represented his national team in international competitions. Everyone is shocked. Even though he has been working in the research team for nearly a year, no one knew this. In the days following the quiz, Greg is treated as a minor celebrity.

Despite these professional relations, members of the research team are not cold or uncaring towards each other. Dan, in particular, demonstrates a duty of care to the team. He always seems in a rush but he is incredibly responsive to the research team. He deals with any problems raised with him on the spot and he makes quick decisions. He also empowers the research team and encourages junior executives to make decisions themselves. When they do, he supports them even if he does not agree with their decision. He also takes a genuine interest in the team's professional development – as we will see in Chapter 10.

It is also clear that Dan takes seriously the idea of protecting the research team. If he gets a sense that a senior member of another team, often the sales team, is making unreasonable requests of a member of the research team, he is quick to intervene. In huddles, he often tells people not to do tasks given to them by other teams and says he will 'sort it out'. He says that all work should come into the team through him. He talks about the team's time as a finite resource that must be invested in the most productive and profitable activities. Much of his work, therefore, involves negotiating which work the research team will take on with the directors of other teams or the senior leadership team. Dan is willing to push work away when it affects the performance of the research team. In Chapter 9, we will see that Dan stops Andy from collecting data for a Big Picture Project because he feels that is a job which the sales team should do. This results in the project not recruiting its target number of participants and causes significant issues that jeopardize the project being released.

When a member of the research team says they have been tasked with an activity from another team, Dan asks why they want to do it. One reason is that Super operates a transparent reward process called 'Pow Points'. Essentially, any member from any team can post a message to the 'Pow Points' email address that highlights the work done by someone else in the company. These messages are aggregated by an admin team app, programmed by the coding team, and distributed to all staff by email on a Friday afternoon. The people named in the 'Pow Points' email are rewarded with 'Pow Points' and, at the end of the business quarter, those with the most 'Pow Points' are considered for bonuses by the senior leadership team.

The messages on the 'Pow Point' email can be made anonymously, such as 'Pow Points to Greg'. They can also be authored by a team such as 'Pow Points to Greg from Sales' or by an individual such as 'Pow Point to Greg from Ross'. They can also detail the reason for the Pow Points such as 'Pow Points to Greg for his work on the Luxury Car Social Media Playbook'. The result of this system is that members of the research team are often willing to do extra work so they can earn 'Pow Points'. In some instances, they tell Dan in a huddle that they feel obliged to do extra work to justify 'Pow Points' they have already been awarded.

Overall, though, Dan's attitude to the research team is based on the idea that team members approach their work as 'just a job'. As we have seen, the

CEO, Bella, says that the senior leadership team want Super's employees to work as if they have a stake in the company. In contrast, when asked about commitment in the research team, Dan says he makes no such demands on his team. He explains that he was appointed in the early days at Super. At this point, the company ran as a cooperative with each employee taking a stake in the firm and a seat on the 'Council'. This was a strategic decision-making body for the company that met each month and voted on a majority basis on major issues. Dan says that, as the company grew, the Council decided to end this arrangement for new staff. It voted to replace itself with an executive body comprising the founders. Thinking back to these earlier arrangements, Dan recollects: 'You can't expect people to work as if they own the company, when they don't.'

First impressions

Overall, the organization of market research at Super has all the hallmarks of a scientifically managed production process (Braverman, 1974). While there are symbols of a start-up culture, the processes are highly designed, and the autonomy of individual team members is relatively low. Members of the research team tend to engage in repetitive tasks in which they use shared heuristics to categorize their charts and scripts into various standard practices. As a result, the research studies often blur into each other. For all the freedom and flexibility offered to staff, the games room and stylish design of the building, working life at Super still has a bureaucratic tone – at times even an industrial one. It can sometimes feel like an assembly line for the mind.

6

Clients Get Hung Up
on a Number

Having described the general organizational culture at Super and the working practices in the research team, in this chapter we will look at the relationship between the research team and their clients. Specifically, I want to explore the ways that the research team talk about their clients in the course of their work and consider what this tells us about the service that the research team thinks it provides for their clients. In keeping with our earlier discussions of discourses of Marketing Art and Marketing Science in marketing action, we might expect that they either emphasize their creativity and imagination or their ability to produce truthful, objective, and robust information.

My argument is that the research team at Super act on a more sophisticated understanding of their clients as organizational decision-makers. Their action is based on the idea that their clients need help making decisions. This is not a matter of telling them what to do – whether that is justified through scientific methods or artistic innovation. Rather, the research team seek to increase their clients' ability to make decisions. They do so by providing them with simple accounts of their markets and consumers that facilitate clients' decisions by aligning their clients' pre-existing assumptions and enrolling a wider network of symbolic and economic resources to support them.

I began to recognize this as I witnessed the research team describing their products to internal stakeholders. In a presentation to the sales team, for example, Dan explains why the research team have modified an element of their Virality product – the predictive algorithm for what is called the Virality EQ score – away from offering concrete predictions. Previously, Virality EQ predicted the 'share rate' for an online advert based on its performance in a test market. A Virality EQ of 2 per cent meant that the client could expect 2 per cent of viewers to share their advert among their social networks. The problem, Dan explains in the presentation, is that this number is taken too literally by clients. 'We have been burned by predicting a share rate that did not occur. Clients can get hung up on achieving a number and we can get our fingers burnt', Dan tells the audience. The new method 'mitigates against this', he continues. It does so by offering a number that is far less exact. Instead of predicting the actual share rate, the new Virality EQ score is a probability that an online advert will achieve a share rate of 2 per cent. Dan says that the benefit of this is that it 'allows us to have a cool-looking graph and not hang our hat on a particular number!'.

I experienced this intervention as the kind of ethnographic surprise that Alvesson (1994) writes about. Why would a marketing researcher not want to offer their clients an exact number that could inform their decision-making? Why not 'hang their hat' on a number? Why is it important that they can offer a cool-looking graph? Is it more important, I wondered, to not be wrong than it is to be right?

To answer these questions, we need to understand the relationship between marketing organizations and their clients differently. As we saw in Chapter 3, much of the ethnographic tradition starts from observations about the anti-bureaucratic nature of marketing action and works backwards to hypothesize the structural conditions between marketing organizations and their clients that necessitates them. My aim in this chapter is to do something similar but look through different marketing action. Here, the chapter takes a detour into organization theory. I argue that marketing researchers think about clients as a general category through the lens of bounded rationality. They appreciate the difficulties organizational decision-makers face in an information-rich world and seek to help them make decisions by absorbing uncertainty.

What are marketing researchers selling?

Why do organizations employ marketing researchers to study their markets for them? Or advertising agencies to create their advertising campaigns? Or any other type marketing organization for that matter?

As we have seen, the existing ethnographic tradition emphasizes differentiation. Marketing organizations are specialists (Alvesson, 2001). Their clients, being primarily organized around other tasks, lack marketing expertise. Even dedicated marketing departments in client organizations are, primarily, focused on marketing their brands, products, and services to their customers (J. Nilsson, 2019). The twist developed in the existing ethnographic literature here is that, in marketing action, the appearance of specialization may be more powerful than its actual presence (Moeran, 2005). That is to say, whether or not marketing organizations actually possess authentic creative skills or scientific prowess is less important than convincing their clients that they do.

This perspective assumes that marketing organizations interact with clients on the basis that they make rational decisions. Clients are imagined as choosing marketing organizations because they efficiently and effectively do marketing work. But are client organizations really this rational?

The ethnographic tradition suggests that marketing workers adopt a more cynical attitude towards their clients than this rational interpretation. Clients, as we have seen, are considered to be stupid, cowardly, and myopic. They are perceived as acting irrationally. For example, clients employ specialist creatives but then question their creative ideas – to the point where they 'kill' them (Kelly et al, 2005). To explain this sort of marketing action, Moeran (2005) quotes Goffman's observation that service providers 'are sometimes forced to delude their customers because their customers show a heartfelt demand for it' (1959: 29).

Here, it is worth thinking about marketing as a response to uncertainty. Explaining the development of marketing and markets in the early 20th century, Braverman (1974) argues that marketing developed, fundamentally, as a response to market uncertainties faced by firms. He suggests that the historical emergence of marketing follows the path charted by scientific management, which developed in response to the uncertainty of production. That is, if you pay people to work for you, how do you know they will work hard enough? Scientific management met this challenge by allowing an organization to design and automate work processes in ways that removed workers' freedom. As such, it guaranteed that workers would be productive.

According to Braverman, marketing is a response to the second uncertainty facing capitalist organizations. It relates to markets and consumers. If you have produced goods and services, how do you know people will buy them? The answer offered by marketing is to use persuasive techniques to influence what people spend their money on and to engage in research to understand what people want so you can make that to begin with.

In my work at Super, I found, too, that many of the activities of the research team are best understood as a response to the uncertainties faced by their clients. In this regard, my sense was that the research team's work is designed to facilitate decision-making. But this is not achieved by presenting clients with facts and information nor telling them what to do. This is clear in the ways that they speak about their clients. As the earlier example from Virality EQ illustrates, the research team do not want their clients to 'get hung up' on a number.

Instead, the research team design projects, script Decks, and present their research in a style that follows Callon's (1984) notion of translation. They problematize, align, enrol, and mobilize their clients to act. Through building networks, they create certainty. To do so, the research team focuses on what they think their clients want to be told. This is not always straightforward and is not always what their clients tell them they want to hear. Figuring out the points of alignment can be a drawn-out process and translating them into their research can be challenging.

The Luxury Car Social Media Playbook

Early on in my onsite ethnographic work, I was invited to a meeting to discuss a Big Picture Project. This is a type of research activity that the research team conducts alongside the four standard products outlined earlier in Chapter 4. Big Picture Projects are sometimes designed by the research team to promote their services. Such projects are treated as PR material and are disseminated through industry press. They may also be designed in collaboration with other teams, notably the sales team. They use Big Picture Projects to leverage meetings with potential clients – as we will see in Chapter 9. Finally, Big Picture Projects maybe designed with an existing client who is interested in looking at a particular business issue. Precisely because Big Picture Projects are not standard, much of the activity that goes into them involves thinking about their scope and content. As such, they offer us a good perspective on the ways the research team negotiate what they can and should provide for their clients.

The meeting concerns a Big Picture Project for a large car brand – anonymized here as Stormer. It takes place in the kitchen. Dan, Greg, and I sit at a bench while other staff are working and conversing around us. The meeting represents the kind of 'table read' session introduced in Chapter 4. Here, we have two basic outline scripts. First, Greg brings his thinking about the data he has collected to the meeting. Second, Dan brings his understanding of the client's needs to the meeting. Our discussions are not focused on analysing the data but thinking about the final messages, key themes, and general approach of the Big Picture Project. We are discussing how to integrate Greg and Dan's two scripts.

Dan starts the meeting establishing the background to the project. Even before we look at the data, he provides a lengthy history of the project and introduces some guidelines around our discussion. Dan explains that Stormer approached Super's sales team director, Ross, saying it wanted a better understanding of social media tactics in the luxury car market. In discussion with Ross, Dan offered to produce a 'Social Media Playbook' for Stormer that follows a model of other Big Picture Projects. 'Playbooks' are a generic term used at Super to refer to research projects which review good practice and analyse case studies. Stormer liked the idea and instructed its creative advertising agency – anonymized here as Splash – to partner with Super in the design of the study. Dan says that Stormer left the discussion at this point and will not engage with the project again until the final presentation of the Playbook in a few weeks' time. As far as Stormer is concerned, Splash should have a strong enough grasp of the problems to direct Super.

However, Splash has proven to be unhappy with this situation. According to Dan, Splash is concerned about introducing a new marketing organization into its relationship with Stormer and is suspicious of Super's motivations.

Is Super a rival? Is Super using the opportunity to get closer to Stormer? Is Super going to undermine Splash's work?

To smooth the relations, Dan tells us that he and Ross hosted a brainstorming event with Splash a few weeks ago. From this, they believe that Splash is hostile to the project because it thinks it is being set up to fail. Like Moeran's (2005) account of a competitive pitch, Spalsh appears concerned that the research will start the process of Stormer taking the account elsewhere. Dan says, 'They think it's a chance for Stormer to beat them up.'

Dan talks through this background. He goes on to explain that he handed the Big Picture Project design to Greg as part of his professional development. Greg says that the project background provided by Dan explains why Splash has been unresponsive in interactions with him. Greg tells us that he has 'pretty much had to make this up on my own. They've not helped at all'. Dan responds: 'The good news is they don't actually hate you! They hate us!'

Dan tells us that he and Ross have decided that the Playbook needs to 'smooth this relationship' between Stormer and Splash. He explains that, while there is a possibility of Stormer moving some of its budget to Super, there is also a risk that this will upset Splash. This could be a bigger problem as Splash works with many of Super's ad network and research clients. If Super upset Splash, it might put these accounts at risk. The Playbook, then, needs to serve three masters: it must tell Stormer something useful to justify its expense, it must support Splash's relations with Stormer, and it must meet Super's business interests. To this end, Dan tells us that the Social Media Playbook is not intended to reveal any striking insights for Stormer. 'They aren't paying us enough to give away all our secrets', he says.

He now asks Greg to speak through the data he has collected. Greg opens a PowerPoint on his laptop and begins to speak through the methodology. He says that Splash's team provided him with a list of Stormer's 'competitor set'. This is a list of 11 brands Stormer likes to consider itself competing against. He says that he used this list to source social media content via two over-the-counter social media data providers. One provided him with a database of 5,000 videos, the other 1,000 videos. Each entry in the databases links to an online video and records the number of views on different social media, the number of shares, and the share of voice for a 12-month period. He has compiled these datasets into a spreadsheet for analysis and manually calculated the share rates.

At this point, Greg begins to refer to the slides. The first slide explains that share rate is the key metric he has focused on. It is calculated by comparing the number of views to the number shares and, essentially, represents the number of views needed to gain an additional share by a viewer on their social media accounts. Greg tells us that views are largely driven by paid-for distribution such as so-called 'pre-roll ads' which appear before or during another video. Here, the viewer has little choice but to watch an ad, at least until a 'skip ad' button appears. In contrast, shares are voluntary actions taken by a viewer. In Greg's words, 'the viewer has seen the ad and decided to share it in their social network. It is an indication of quality content as we know that good adverts are not just shared more but have higher share rates'.

After reviewing this methodology, and indicating the average views, shares and share rate for all the ads in the database, Greg highlights the 'Superstar' adverts that will form the basis of his analysis and the key lessons or 'plays' he wants to emphasize in the Social Media Playbook. He tells us that the first lesson he wants to focus on is the importance of environmentally related content.

He flicks to a slide with an embedded video from one of Stormer's competitors and presses play. The video is very famous. It begins with a close-up of a Hollywood celebrity and the camera pans backwards to reveal them sat on top of an electric truck. Greg gives a short explanation of the 'key learning' for Stormer from this ad. He emphasizes that videos which are most shared tend to relate to social and environmental causes.

Indeed, in the next slide he highlights another video to prove his point. He says that one of the most viewed and most shared videos of the year is a 'behind the scenes' video about the making of an advert. It explores environmental issues involved in the advert's production and the brand's attempts at responsible marketing. The brand posted this video to its social media feed. It has, subsequently, 'organically' outperformed the advert on which it is was based. In other words, more viewers had chosen to watch the behind-the-scenes video than watched the original ad through paid-for distribution. Greg then flicks to a slide which uses the Emotionality product to assess this advert. It shows that viewers most felt 'social warmth' after watching the behind-the-scenes video.

At this point, Dan interrupts. He says that his is concerned about focusing on the creative content of the ads too much. This would be difficult for Splash to support as it would direct Stormer to question their creative work. He advises Greg that it would be better 'for key insights and learnings to focus on distribution. There's got to be a lesson there about distribution. Let's direct them to stronger distribution'. He asks if Greg can 'tell a story' from the videos that 'focuses on things like the reason for sharing such as kudos, cool hunters, opinion seeking'. Greg and Dan then discuss how Greg could reframe his analysis around distribution. They discuss Super's measure of 'social warmth' from the Elements of Emotionality and discuss ideas such as virtue signalling. The meeting ends with Greg saying he will look into reasons for sharing and will study notable adverts through Super's Emotionality product. We return to the research team's neighbourhood.

Later on, I ask Greg how he feels about this new focus given he had spent time analysing the videos and Dan had not even watched them all.

He explains that, in Big Picture Projects, you need 'to focus on a story'. He reflects that this is not natural for him. I ask why. He continues: 'I'm learning that I tended to be too critical. Dan simplifies things down to the key story. I need to work on that.' Greg says that he finds it easier to script standard products where he can describe the results. Big Picture Project require that he tell a 'good story'.

The idea that the research team is telling a story for their clients about the data they have gathered reveals something about what marketing researchers at Super think they are doing. It will appear several times in this book. A naïve interpretation of this – one that takes the notion of storytelling at face value – would suggest that marketing researchers see themselves as little more than used car salesmen, making up bullshit, selling the dream to gullible clients. As we have seen, there is an element of this in existing interpretations (Moeran, 2005). It suggests that, in its own way, marketing is an art.

My sense on the ground was quite different though. Telling a story is a way of supporting their clients. In the Luxury Car Social Media Playbook meeting, we see the research team working with data to support a relationship between a brand and its advertising agency. They certainly hoped to tell the client, Stormer, something useful and certainly were not simply making things up based on the kinds of flimsy research Moeran (2005; 2006) describes. But they engage with data by making explicit their assumptions about what their clients want and need from the research (J. Nilsson, 2019). In the table read, for instance, Dan directs the interpretation towards distribution. This has the potential to tell Stormer something they might find interesting without undermining their faith in their creative agency. In other words, there are many stories that can be told about any dataset. All of which are true to some extent or other. The skill displayed by the research team is selecting the right story.

Bounded rationality

What do we learn about the ways that marketing researchers at Super think about their clients from the Luxury Car Brand Social Media Playbook table read meeting? It is apparent that Dan brings a great deal of background knowledge to the meeting. It is not knowledge about research techniques nor the data that Greg has gathered. It is knowledge about the clients, their relationships, and their relationships with Super. So, while Greg designed the study, the meeting is a way of aligning his research to Super's perspective on the clients. It is a way of selecting the right story. Here, Dan provides a filter. In the meeting, we implicitly ask: does the data let us say something that the clients want to hear?

To answer this, we do not look at the raw numbers nor do we translate them into inner truths about some general idea of consumers as Ariztia

(2015) describes. Rather, we explicitly establish what the clients want to get out of the analysis and try to balance any competing demands. At the same time, of course, we edit this through Super's business needs. Cluley (2022) calls this process the production of *interesting numbers*. By this, he refers to the ways that the concerns of different stakeholders influence how data is interpreted through the process of translation. Interesting numbers enrol people by piquing their aesthetic interest and matching their material and economic interests.

In the background to the production of interesting numbers is a general understanding of clients as individual actors – that is, individual people or teams – who have their own interests and their own problems that can be solved through marketing research (J. Nilsson, 2019). But what are those problems? Here, the members of the research team talk about clients in line with the notion of bounded rationality – although they do not use the term explicitly.

Bounded rationality is a concept that is associated with Nobel Prize winner Herbert Simon and his collaboration with James March. Interestingly, given the ethnographic focus of this book, this idea developed from a quasi-ethnographic study of the administration of public recreation facilities in Milwaukee that Simon conducted in the mid-1930s (Simon, 1945). These observations provoked a fascination for Simon in understanding why organizations fail to agree on the most rational course of action. He saw that the two agencies responsible for local recreation facilities in Milwaukee continually disagreed on the best way to work. 'Why did they not', Simon later commented in his Nobel Prize acceptance speech, 'as my economics books suggested, simply balance off the marginal return of the one activity against that of the other?' (1979: 500). He continues:

> Further exploration made it apparent that they didn't equate expenditures at the margin because, intellectually, they couldn't. There was no measurable production function from which quantitative inferences about marginal productivities could be drawn; and such qualitative notions of a production function as the two managers possessed were mutually incompatible. ... How can human beings make rational decisions in circumstances like these? How are they to apply the marginal calculus? Or, it if does not apply, what do they substitute for it? (Simon, 1979: 500)

To answer these questions, Simon suggests that we think of an organization as 'a complex network of decisional processes, all pointed toward their influence upon the behaviours of the operatives. ... The anatomy of the organization is to be found in the distribution and allocation of decision-making functions' (1945: 305). Most obviously, organizations make direct decisions for their members. Forms, manuals, instructions, plans, and schedules tell an individual in an organization how and when something must be done.

But it is usually impossible, or at least inefficient, for superiors to make every decision for their subordinates. The general cannot tell every soldier when to pull the trigger. At a certain point, the subordinate must make decisions themselves. Here, organizations can indirectly influence the choices of their members by specifying 'the particular values, facts, and alternatives upon which [decisions] in the organization are to be based' (Simon, 1945: 278).

Going back to his experiences in Milwaukee, Simon suggests that the reason the two organizations he observed could not agree how best to organize public recreation facilities was that they each influenced their members by orienting them around different values. For one organization, 'a playground was a physical facility, servicing as a green oasis in the crowded grey city' (Simon, 1979: 500). For the other, a playground was taken to be 'a social facility, where children could play together with adult help and guidance' (Simon, 1979: 500).

Based on this, Simon argues that rationality in organizations is not absolute. It is, instead, 'perfectly flexible and adaptable to abilities, goals, and knowledge' (1945: 323). To act rationally, in this view, is not to maximize some abstract notion of utility that is the same in every situation. It is to work effectively and efficiently towards an organization's goals. Simon (1945) calls this 'bounded rationality'. It has affinities with structural functionalism as it, too, focuses on the goal of action. As Simon puts it, the 'basic task' facing an administrator or manager is 'to provide each "operative" employee with an environment of decision of such a kind that behavior which is rational from the standpoint of the organization is also rational from the standpoint of the group values and the group situation' of individual employees (1945: 325).

Simon develops an elaborate justification for his view. For our purposes, his key point is that bounded rationality not only allows an organization to influence its members' decisions but is necessary for them to make decisions at all. This is because it 'permits conservation of mental effort by withdrawing from the area of conscious thought' those aspects of organizational life that are repetitive or unconnected with the organization's aims (Simon, 1945: 99).

Uncertainty absorption

This line of thinking is developed by Simon in his collaboration with James March. For March and Simon (1958), it is a practical necessity that organizational decision-makers make decisions based on limited information and heuristics that help them to interpret that information quickly. The world is, simply, too complex and information-rich otherwise. Trying to gain a full grasp of all the facts will overwhelm decision-makers with uncertainty about the best course of action. March and Simon explain:

> An individual can attend to only a limited number of things a time. The basic reason why the actor's definition of the situation differs greatly from the objective situation is that the latter is far too complex to be handled in all its detail. Rational behaviour involves substituting for the complex reality a model of reality that is sufficiently simple to be handled by problem-solving processes. (March and Simon, 1958: 173)

March and Simon (1958) argue that this rule is not only true for individual decision-makers but is also true for organizations. It is rational for them to substitute the complexity of reality with simple models because their environment provides them with too much information. Organizations, Simon tells us in his Nobel Prize acceptance speech, 'either have to simplify the world (abstract it – e.g. do this cause it makes more profit) or deal with concrete but confusing reality (but doing this also costs more!)' (1979: 498). Faced with this choice, working with limited models is actually a more rational way of operating.

Here, Simon tells us that the kinds of models which support organizational decision-making must be 'fashioned with an eye to practical computationability, no matter how severe the approximations and simplifications that are thereby imposed on them' (1979: 498). What he means by this is that models must be bounded by the organization's aims and values. They should, he tells us, represent the 'simplified world of our assumptions' (Simon, 1979: 499).

Is this not what we see happening in Moeran's (2005) story about sampling half a dozen 40-year-old American actors to gauge their opinions about potential ads? Was the agency not developing a sufficiently simple model of reality to help the client make the decision it wanted to make? Was their 'back up reasoning' not helping Frontier make a decision that was already made? And was the client not happy to be presented with a model that not only made the world understandable but stood in harmony with its pre-existing assumptions?

Is this also not the basis for the discussion in the table read meeting for the Luxury Car Social Media Playbook? Were we not establishing the bounded rationalities of Stormer and Splash – not to mention Super? Were we not seeking out their goals, values, and assumptions?

The obvious question that arises from this is: How can organizational decision-makers work on the basis of simplified models that confirm their existing assumptions? Is this not irrational? The answer, March and Simon (1958) argue, is another consequence of bounded rationality.

If the aim of modelling is to replace a complex world for a simple one, interrogating every model would be counterproductive. All people would find is their assumptions, flawed evidence, and occasional leaps of faith. In short, we would be back at the disabling complexity that modelling is meant to avoid.

The answer is to focus on the modeller not the model. Put simply, as long as the source of information is believable, the model of reality they offer can serve as a basis for organizational decisions. Evaluating models in terms of the modeller is, in this sense, a way of modelling models. It simplifies how organizational decision-makers can interpret models.

March and Simon (1958) call this side of modelling *uncertainty absorption*. They write: 'Uncertainty absorption takes place when inferences are drawn from a body of evidence and the inferences, instead of the evidence itself, are then communicated' (March and Simon, 1958: 186). This process has two effects. First, uncertainty absorption is a way of producing simplified models. Second, by shifting emphasis from the evidence to the source of a model, it makes it easier for organizational decision-makers to trust the models. Both the modeller and the model absorb their uncertainty. In March and Simon's words:

> [T]he person who summarizes and assesses his own direct perspectives and transmits them to the rest of the organization becomes an important source of informational premises for organizational action. The 'facts' he communicates can be disbelieved, but they can only rarely be checked. Hence, by the very nature and limits of the communication system, a great deal of discretion and influence is exercised by those persons who are in direct contact with some part of the 'reality' that is of concern to the organization. (March and Simon, 1958: 187)

Interestingly, for our discussion of the research team at Super, March and Simon offer the 'successive editing steps that transform data obtained from a set of questionnaires into printed statistical tables' as an example of uncertainty absorption (1958: 186). In other words, they identify marketing research as an example of uncertainty absorption. Working on the basis of such transformed data, they write, involves a shift from a 'direct examination of the evidence' to a concern with the organizational decision-makers' 'confidence in the source and his knowledge of the biases to which the source is subject, rather than on a direct examination of the evidence' (March and Simon, 1958: 187).

As this quote indicates, the ability to edit, filter, and translate models for organizational decision-makers gives the actors who perform uncertainty absorption great power and influence. This helps us to explain why organizations may turn to outsiders to absorb uncertainty for them. They are neutral – in theory at least – even if they owe a debt to those who hand them the account. At the worst, their models will reflect the assumptions of these key decision-makers.

Magic realism

The idea that marketing researchers' work is oriented around producing something their clients can 'buy into and believe in' has led analysts of marketing to suggest that marketing research has magical elements (Arnould and Cayla, 2015: 15). On this view, clients take a leap of faith when they employ marketing research organizations, in the same way they do when they appoint an advertising agency. They allow themselves to be bedazzled by what they already know by fetishizing the research skills of marketing organizations.

But this misses something important: the reason why. Through administrative theory, we can suggest that, as organizational decision-makers, bounded rationality pushes clients to search for actors who can absorb their uncertainty by providing them simple models and, as a result, facilitate decision-making. This, in turn, pushes clients to focus on the people absorbing uncertainty rather than the models they produce.

Whether or not the marketing researchers at Super were consciously aware of this or not, this understanding emerges from their actions and interactions. They are working from a shared understanding of their clients, considered as a general category, as needing marketing organizations to help them make decisions. Reflecting Braverman (1974), they approach marketing action as a way of reducing uncertainty that is inherent in consumption and market relations. This is not done by providing clients with facts or direct instructions for action. It is not a question of making decision for clients. Rather, it involves offering believable accounts which help clients to make decisions. It involves absorbing their clients' uncertainty by picking the right story to tell them.

As such, the actors involved in the Luxury Car Social Media Playbook table read (Dan, Greg, myself and, although not physically present, Ross) are not dealing with either Stormer nor Splash as perfectly rational decision-making entities. We approach them as two distinct decision-making systems with their own interests, aims, and values. In this sense, the action in the meeting is reminiscent of the action Simon observes in his study of the administration office for public recreation facilities in Milwaukee during the mid-1930s. Where it differs is that Super's enrols its clients through a single model. We discuss how to align their interests, needs, and expectations.

On the surface, Stormer has approached Super to better understand social media marketing and, through this, improve its organizational performance. Splash, as Stormer's creative advertising agency, wants to support Stormer here. But, if this was all that was involved in the action, we would expect the analysis to focus on the data that Greg had collected from Super's data providers. The table read would have involved looking at the data and exploring different analytical techniques and testing different interpretations.

This did not happen. Stormer might have been motivated to develop its understanding of social media marketing. Splash might have wanted to develop this understanding too. But, in the action at Super, it was established that Stormer and Splash had very specific motivations for the study – albeit latent functions in the language of structural functionalism. They each wanted to be told a particular story. Dan and Ross thought that Stormer wanted an outside research agency to provide it with ammunition to 'give Splash a kicking'. Stormer already thought that Splash's work was not up to standard and wanted Super to prove this. Stormer wanted to be provided with a model of social media marketing in harmony with these assumptions. Splash, in turn, wanted to keep Stormer happy so it would not lose the account. Splash did not want Stormer's story to be true as it might call their relationship into question. Once this was established in the table read, the discussion focuses on how to use the data as a post-rationalization for the interpretation.

The work establishing these understandings of Stormer and Splash happened outside of the meeting. It was done as Dan, Greg, and Ross interacted with Splash and Stormer. But it was brought into the table read. The meeting was a space to experiment, role play, and workshop stories that might align Stormer's and Splash's interests into a story, or simple model.

7

Scientism in Action

In the last chapter, I showed how the research team's initial engagements with the data they collect is influenced by their understandings and assumptions about a client. I argued that they work on the basis that their clients are bounded rational decision-makers who turn to marketing organizations to absorb uncertainty for them so they can make decisions. As we saw in our discussion of administrative theory, uncertainty absorption occurs when organizational decision-makers allow others to create simple models of their external environment for them. For this to be effective, organizational decision-makers must have confidence in the people absorbing uncertainty for them. Uncertainty absorption works through the modeller more than their models.

In this chapter, I want to explore how marketing research is organized to absorb uncertainty. Here, we will see that the discourse of Marketing Science plays an important role. Market researchers at Super integrate scientific discourses, images, and artefacts, not to mention the very idea of 'marketing science' as it appears in academic and industry discussions, to encourage their clients to believe them. Science, in particular computational science, is materialized in the objects and built environment in Super's offices. The products and services Super sells to its clients are packaged through references to scientific ideas and Super uses computational scientific discourses to communicate with its clients. My claim is that, thanks to the social legitimacy of the ethos of science discussed in Chapter 1, this is a powerful mechanism of uncertainty absorption.

It is important to note at the start that this is not necessarily a false impression. As we will see in Chapter 8, where I document Super's research processes and practices in more detail, Super's research involves a great deal of data, computational analysis, and is supported by many academic ideas and Marketing Science conventions. The key point here, though, is that the way Super display its work to its clients is largely unrelated to these activities and is better explained through the lens of uncertainty absorption.

Scientism

To begin with, let us think about the ways that images of science have traditionally been used outside of the lab. As discussed in Chapter 1, scientific knowledge has a special value in many societies (Merton, 1973). Scientific facts can trump folk, spiritual, and other knowledge claims (Adorno and Horkheimer, 1944). Even though scholars of science tell us that scientific endeavours rarely live up to the image of science at the heart of this social legitimacy (Latour, 1987), the scientific privilege means that framing a statement as a scientific fact is a way to grant that statement legitimacy (Callon, 1984).

Indeed, seeking to establish their own legitimacy, many non-scientific practices claim that they are scientific. In academia, for example, we have seen many fields of study repackaged as 'sciences' (Burrell and Morgan, 1979). This not only involves changing their names but also what Nobel Prize winning economist Friedrich Hayek describes as the 'slavish imitation of the method and language of Science' (1942: 269). Hayek (1942) calls this scientism. It can be a misguided or unintentional aping of hard sciences. But it can also be an intentional and possibly cynical rhetorical manoeuvre that uses the social legitimacy of science instrumentally.

Here, Hayek rallies against the 'trespasses of scientism' into social theory (1942: 270). The problem, as Hayek sees it, is that the social legitimacy granted to genuinely scientific endeavours is based on their disinterested inquiries. Science is meant to look neutrally and objectively at the world and draw inferences from the evidence. Scientism, Hayek argues, is based on the opposite approach. It occurs when someone wants to hide their existing prejudices and wants to convince others of their position. Where one finds scientism, one finds 'a very prejudiced approach which, before it has considered its subject, claims to know what is the most appropriate way of investigating it' (Hayek, 1942: 269). Hayek tells us: 'This way lies charlatanism and worse. To act on the belief that we possess the knowledge and the power which enable us to shape the processes of society entirely to our liking, knowledge which in fact we do not possess, is likely to make us do much harm' (1975: 441).

The same argument appears the section on 'Scientism' in *Organization Man* by William Whyte (1956). He argues that social theorists, and those they influence in business and policy, have been led astray by their faith in hard science. He puts this in stark terms: 'only the arrogant – or the stupid' can aspire to scientific knowledge of society, markets, or organizations (1956: 30). Social phenomena, Whyte (1956) argues, are not governed by natural forces and fundamental laws in the same way the physical world is. Social knowledge cannot let us engineer fully functioning societies free from alienation, deviance, discontent, and disorder because social knowledge is productive of the very social relations it claims to study (Pickering, 2010).

Our understanding influences the kinds of political choices we make, the social interactions we prompt, and the products we sell. It affects how people, organizations, and institutions interact and shapes what people think, feel, and know.

But, despite these limitations, the appeal of scientism rarely diminishes. In particular, Whyte notes that the supposedly 'new-found ability to measure more precisely' through innovations in technology leads us, again and again, to believe that 'there is nothing that can't be measured' and that 'somehow by the sheer accumulation' of bias-free findings 'we will have the basis of a theoretical formula that describes all. Just like physics' (1956: 30–31). The problem is that this promise has 'a long and dismal record of achievement; even its proponents readily admit its bugs are appalling' (Whyte, 1956: 27).

There is, then, something unscientific motivating scientism. It is a contradiction. It does not live up to the normal tests of scientific knowledge. Like Hayek suggests, it is based on a pre-established claim. Reflecting this, Whyte argues that scientism is not scientific. It is a faith – even a blind faith. Whyte writes: 'Dip into personnel journals, advertising trade journals, and you will find the same refrain. A lot of it is sheer malarkey, of course, but I think most of it is evidence of a genuine longing to be related to a faith' (1956: 29).

For Whyte, this faith is most clearly displayed by organizational decision-makers – the people who, as we saw in the last chapter, are faced with uncertainties in their production lines, offices, and markets. They move from one technological revolution to the next and from one branch of the natural sciences to another in the hope that they might discover 'an exact science of man' (Whyte, 1956: 27). Indeed, for Whyte, it is 'the sense of being on the frontier that gives scientism so tremendous an appeal' (1956: 28). Yet, 'in reality' each new science of markets, societies, or organizations 'is a cliché that has been kicked around for centuries' (Whyte, 1956: 28).

In this respect, I was unsurprised to find numerous examples of scientism on the ground at Super. Much of the action has echoes of Hopkins' (1923) writing on scientific advertising as it approaches markets through an experimental logic. In what follows, I will evidence this in terms of the design of Super's head office, the ways in which it packages its products, and, finally, the ways its communicates its research findings to its clients in a standard Deck. In each of these areas, it is hard not to understand the activities at Super as scientism in action (Latour, 1987). The fact that these displays tend to be directed to clients suggests that Super uses scientism to increase its appeal to its clients.

Spaces of scientism

The most obvious imitation of the method and language of science one encounters when entering Super is the physical space in its head office. As with other marketing organizations, this building plays a key role in Super's interactions with its clients. It is not just a productive space designed to allow workers to perform their functions as efficiently as possible. It is also designed as something to show clients. It is a key part of Super's brand offering. In the words of the creative director, it is meant to 'bring clients into Super'. However, while we have seen in the existing ethnographic literature discussed in Chapter 3 that it is common for marketing organizations to incorporate non-working spaces and objects such as games rooms in order to project an anti-bureaucratic theme (Alvesson, 1994), there are many areas of Super's head office that reference science. Interestingly, these are mainly the spaces used for recruiting new clients.

The Lab

The most obvious manifestation of these is a dedicated space for pitching to new clients in the basement of the head office. It is called the Lab. As the name suggests, this space explicitly evokes a scientific theme. It includes two areas demarcated by separate colours. The first area one enters from the single entrance to the Lab is painted white. It is organized around a large white vinyl conference table (see Figure 7.1). With three bright overhead lights, this table has the air of an operating table. It is spotless.

Next to the entrance in the first area of the Lab, white lab coats hang from the wall. There is a large monitor for conference calls on the wall opposite

Figure 7.1: Looking in the first room in the Lab from the entrance

Figure 7.2: Props on the wall in the second room of the Lab

the entrance as well as smaller LCD displays housed in ornamental picture frames hanging on this white-washed wall. When you touch these smaller displays, pre-recorded videos play about Super's business, interviews with consumers (actually Super's staff acting as consumers), and other brand-related clips. Display frames with various scientific objects such as DNA strings hang on walls in the first area of the Lab.

In the second area, which is painted grey, there are two rows of green plastic chairs facing 11 wall-mounted touchscreens. Each plays a set of interactive slides that make up Super's sales pitch. Large telescopes and other scientific artefacts are scattered around this section of the room. One wall includes 12 display cases, each housing a scientific object including DNA strings, test tubes, and petri dishes (see Figure 7.2).

The Lab is closed off from the rest of the organization and the outside world. Access is limited to a single entrance. Indeed, during the observation period, only Dan admitted me into the Lab. In other cases, for example, when Super's staff need a meeting room, the Lab is never used. When there is a sales pitch taking place in the Lab, everyone in the company is informed via an all-staff email. A sign in the main reception area is put up to both welcome the clients and inform everyone that a pitch is taking place. In these cases, the entire basement is avoided by staff who are not involved in the pitch.

I noted this controlled sense around the Lab in fieldnotes taken during the ethnographic observations. In Week 4, the fieldnotes document my first trip into the Lab following an invitation from Dan. These emphasize that staff outside did not acknowledge us as we entered the space. My view is that there was a cultural norm in the organization to act as if people going into the Lab are not there and, in turn, as if the Lab is not there either. The fieldnotes read:

> Dan returns from lunch and asks me if I want to go to the Lab. In the basement outside the Lab, three girls sit on bean bags. I recognize one from the desk in the Reception. Even though I'd spoken to her at length earlier and I try to make eye contact, she doesn't look at me nor Dan. Dan ignores them. He opens the door of the Lab and says 'Here's where the magic happens'. He offers to talk me through the pitch as if I were a client. I have to wear a lab coat. I ask if clients do this. 'Sometimes', he laughs, 'We always ask them'. Dan explains, Super's Sales Team use this as a form of cold-reading to profile clients. It reveals clients' attitudes to Super and power relations within client teams. Such information is later used in the presentations just as a hypnotist 'gets a read' on suggestible audience members before they begin their performances.

The pitch delivered in the Lab involves a script choreographed to the material space. After getting clients to put on lab coats, Super's salespeople and researchers work through their presentation, seamlessly tapping the large wall-mounted touchscreens in the grey area of the Lab to bring up pre-loaded slides, charts, graphs, and videos. The script is standard but elements within it are tailored to the specific client. For example, statistics and videos are designed for the client's sector with examples and case studies drawn from their adverts and social media. Each slide in the presentation is arranged in specific order on a specific screen in the grey area of the Lab so that presenters need to press the correct screen to access the correct image. Their movements, words, and visual artefacts are carefully choreographed and built into the physical surroundings. This is very impressive. It appears spontaneous when it works but it carries some risk. A presenter might touch the wrong screen or a slide might be loaded incorrectly. To mitigate against these risks, Super's admin team ensures that all the materials are in place days before a pitch and presenters use rehearsals to check, and double-check, that things are as they should be.

Not only is there a danger that the slides will not work, or not work in the order they are supposed to, but also it is possible for a client to voice concerns, ask questions, or press a touchscreen and, thereby, interrupt the flow of the performance. However, there is a sense that these actions are prohibited. One reason for this is that the second, grey presentation area of Lab is organized with a clear physical distinction between the audience and the presenters (see Figure 7.3). Clients sit together as an audience on the green plastic chairs and are distanced from the interactive screens. Presenters stand in front of them and create a barrier between them and the touchscreens. Perhaps because of this, clients tend to allow presenters to work through their script uninterrupted.

Things change after the presentation component of a pitch. As it ends, clients are invited back into the first area in the Lab. Here, the spatial division between

Figure 7.3: Looking into the second room in the Lab from the first room

the presenters and audience is removed as both sit around the conference table. This is intended to spark conversations between them. Indeed, at this point, the presenter might link to other representatives from client organizations using the conference call facilities in the white area of the Lab.

Does the design of the Lab represent scientism? Certainly, the space includes a number of scientific objects that have little direct connection to the activities that take place in the room nor Super's other activities. That is, Super's pitch could just as easily take place in a room without DNA strings and telescopes in it. They could deliver their pitch to clients without them and the representatives from the clients' organizations wearing lab coats.

So why has Super chosen to include these things in the room? My sense is that it is not meant to convince potential clients that Super's activities are actual science. I do not think that anyone involved thinks that Super is engaged in research on DNA or uses microscopes. Rather, these artefacts indicate to clients that Super will engage in scientism. They speak to Super's willingness to dress up its workers and present their activities in the discourse of science. As a socially legitimate knowledge regime, this shows Super has the ability to absorb uncertainty.

Materializing code

After a pitch in the Lab, the second space that prospective clients encounter when they move through Super's building is the space where the coding team work. It also includes a number of objects and artefacts that follow a scientific theme. In this case, though, these objects are not a random assortment of scientific objects from different branches of scientific enquiry. They suggest a particular type of science: computational science.

The coding team's neighbourhood is on the first floor of Super's head office. Typically, after a prospective client has watched the pitch in the Lab, they are walked up from the basement to the kitchen on the second floor. In the process, they walk past the coding team's neighbourhood. It is the first working space they see. As such, it offers another chance to shape clients' perceptions of the action at Super.

Ironically, the coding team occupy this visible space after they initiated a move from the main open-plan office in Super's head office. This was intended to create their own coding island and to impose a physical division between the coding team and the marketing work occurring in the rest of the building. Dan explains that the coding team collectively lobbied Super's senior leadership team, complaining that they could not concentrate on their work in the open-plan office. They convinced the senior leadership team that there was no benefit to their work being surrounded by marketing workers and that they would, instead, be more productive if they isolated from them. Perhaps reflecting the strategic importance of the coding team to their growth and, no doubt also accepting their argument, the senior leadership team supported the move.

But, once they were in the new location, the coding team encountered their new visibility. They realized that the space they had requested lies on the main thoroughfare through the building. Workers whose neighbourhoods are on the second floor of the office walk past the coding team's neighbourhood throughout the day. As do clients, on their way through the building.

In response, the coding team again lobbied the senior leadership team. They claimed that the passersby disturbed their work and risked revealing Super's trade secrets. With nowhere else to go, they were allowed to purchase cardboard partitions to offer them increased privacy. These are about four-foot high and block sight of the programming team's desks (see Figure 7.4). They were also invited to return to the main open-plan office. A neighbourhood was left empty for them to use on the second floor.

The partitioning cardboard walls are an interesting physical object (see Figure 7.4). If they are designed to move the coding team out of sight from passersby, they are only partially successful. They offer shelter to individual members of the coding team when they sit at their desks but they leave much on show. Walking past the coding team's neighbourhood, you can see seven large flatscreen monitors positioned on the external walls that surround the space (see Figure 7.5). These are around eight-foot high – high enough that they are still visible above the partitions. Two show computer code being executed. I was unable to establish whether this was Super's actual code or a video. The other screens show various logs and dashboards displaying the

Figure 7.4: Walking past the coding team's neighbourhood from reception

performance of Super's systems. Again, I was unable to verify if these were displaying real-time data or were pre-recorded. Certainly, I did not observe the coding team looking at them or discussing them. My sense was that these are placed on display for visitors.

Below the screens, there are four large whiteboards which are also visible to passersby. Two of these display notes for workflows and examples of computer code, while the other two have kanban-style task boards. These have coloured A4 sheets of paper stuck to them. Each sheet has a project title and a task name written on it. They are organized into columns for each team member. This is notable because, as we have seen in Chapter 5, the other teams at Super also operate through kanban-style task boards but run them on a digital platform. The coding team is the only team that uses physical cards and boards. The result is that, even though members of the coding team use the whiteboards as partitions, and position them to shield themselves from view (see Figure 7.6), the display of the team's boards on the whiteboards makes the coding team's work visible to passersby.

We can ask if the design of the coding team's neighbourhood represents scientism. If we accept that the space is consumed by Super's clients as they walk through the offices, I think it is fair to say that it does – but of a particular kind. It relates to the work of programming. It suggests that a specific kind of work is taking place in the office – one involving computers, computation, data, and numbers. In this sense, the coding team's neighbourhood materializes

Figure 7.5: Looking over the coding team's partition into the coding team's neighbourhood

Figure 7.6: A member of the coding team using whiteboards as walls

something that is normally immaterial: computation. It puts coding on display and expresses a sense of what we might call 'computationality' to Super's clients that serves a similar function to the sense of professionality described by Alvesson (1994) in his classic ethnography of advertising.

The objects on view to clients suggest that the coding team conducts highly technical work with computers and data. The whiteboards, likewise, literally show code being written. They display workflows, tasks, and technical jargon relating to computer programming. In the process, the work of the coding team is symbolized not as enigmatic, artistic, or creative work typically seen in other ethnographic accounts of marketing work. It is displayed as being structured, numerical, and formally organized. It is fair to say that the objects reflect the methods and language of computer science.

As a display to clients, it does not matter that the coding team are involved in computational practices. For the most part, members of the coding team are educated in computer science and use these skills at Super to administer the technical infrastructure for Super's research processes and Super's ad network. The point is that Super displays these practices with objects that, in actual fact, have little to do with the computational work of the coding team. They work in the same way that Goffman (1959) describes professional service workers cynically displaying their value to their clients such as beauticians wearing lab coats.

Indeed, the display of computationality is reminiscent of Goffman's (1961) thoughts about prisons which hang their inmates' artwork on the walls for visitors to see. For Goffman (1961), while artworks might be painted by prisoners, the decision to display them has little connection with the work of a prison. It is, he argues, an attempt by a prison to present itself to visitors, inmates, staff, and wider society as a space of rehabilitation not a space of incarceration. My sense walking past the coding team's neighbourhood was that the objects on display served a similar purpose. The space performs scientism through its computationality. The important thing is not the objects, but the choice to put them on display.

Signs of scientism

So far, we have looked at how Super uses physical objects to frame its work in the eyes of clients. The next set of materials I describe helps Super to package its research products for its clients. Specifically, I will explore how Super describes its standard research products – paying particular attention to their names, research designs, and justifications.

Products

The research team offer four standard research products in addition to Big Picture Projects such as the Luxury Car Brand Social Media Playbook discussed in Chapter 6. As we saw in Chapter 5, all of these standard research products are based on the idea that emotions drive brand outcomes. One way they achieve this is by drawing on the same measurement device. This is described as the 'Elements of Emotionality' in Super's sales material and is visualized through a modified periodic table. It is an inventory of questions that measure emotional responses to an advert using concepts such as happiness, fear, anger, social warmth, and brand metrics such as liking, brand associations, and brand recall. It was first designed by the founders as they began their market research activities and has since been refined in collaboration with European business schools.

The packaging of the research products through this measurement device not only distinguishes Super's research offering from its competitors but draws explicitly on scientific terminology and artefacts. The products are each built on experimental logics that can be traced back to Hopkins' thoughts on scientific advertising. For example, Super conducts within-subject ad-tests known as Heartbeat studies. These are standard pre-/post-tests in which a group of participants is asked to complete a survey based on the Elements of Emotionality, watch a test advert and then fill out a second version of the survey. The idea is that the advert will have provoked a change in the participants' responses. The name Heartbeat emphasizes the focus on emotions in the survey. But it also evokes a sense of a physical response. Just as a medic might measure someone's pulse, Heartbeat suggests Super can read the physical signs of the market. Indeed, in marketing research jargon, these kinds of studies are sometimes called 'tracking' studies. They form the basis of ongoing research for clients studying their 'brand health'.

The second research product is called Compare. Compare studies involve between-subject ad-tests. Here, Super recruits two samples of participants and asks each to complete a survey based on the Elements of Emotionality but related to the client's brand. One group will watch an advert before completing the survey, the other will not. Any differences between the two samples are assumed to have been caused by the advert. So, while the name Compare does not, in itself, evoke a scientific message, the methodology it evokes explicitly draws on experimental logics. It is designed on the basis that consumer responses can be standardized. Compare is also a 'tracking' product through which Super measures its clients' 'brand health'.

The third product is called Virality. Virality studies draw on computational notions of contagion and prediction based on big data and machine learning. In these studies, a sample is recruited to watch an advert and complete a standard Elements of Emotionality survey about it. Virality studies are primarily self-contained, one-off pieces of research. However, as they are also based on the Elements of Emotionality questions, Virality studies can be compared against each other. Here, Virality studies follow a data science method. Using viewer response data from Super's ad network for previous ads that have been tested using the Virality survey, Super makes a prediction about the likely viewer responses to test adverts based on its Virality survey scores. This is known as the Virality EQ – discussed in the introduction of the previous chapter.

Finally, Super sells one-off ad-tests using facial coding techniques. These studies are called Emotionality. Emotionality studies, which are discussed in detail in Chapter 8, utilize facial recognition algorithms to establish consumers' emotional responses to an advert. Unlike the other products, they allow Super to study how consumers' responses change over the duration of an advert. So, while a Virality study might reveal that consumers feel a certain level of happiness after watching an ad, Emotionality studies can pinpoint the exact moment when a consumer began to feel happy while watching the ad.

These products, generally, follow an experimental logic. They involve standardized tests, typically, conducted on two different groups. One is exposed to a stimulus, the other acts as a control group. Any differences in the results are used to draw conclusions about the potential effectiveness of the interventions. In this sense, each product has an affinity to a medical trial. An advert stands in place of a drug.

So, the packaging and promotion of these standard research products draws on discourses of the body, emotions, experimentation, and standardized testing. The naming of the products brings with it a sense that Super's research involves scientific measurement apparatus. Heartbeats, for example, suggest that Super can 'take the pulse of the market'. This is a phrase used when describing them to clients. Emotionality studies work in a similar way by using facial coding algorithms to read consumers' responses. Through these choices, and the experimental logic, it is fair to say that Super is imitating the methods and language of science. Following the discourse of Marketing Science, they emphasize the standardized measurements, not the imaginations of the researchers who complete the projects.

Results

Now, let us look at the ways these products are framed in action. To do so, I will speak through a typical report that is given to clients following a Virality study. As with the other products, these are presented in a standard format called 'the Deck'. This is a PowerPoint presentation that may be emailed to a client or presented to them in-person or virtually by a member of the research team. This means that the Deck must often communicate Super's message on its own. It must prove its value to clients alone.

The Decks for each research product are designed by the creative team and follow a standard template. For instance, the Deck for a Virality study begins with a series of methodology slides. These reference academic papers published in leading marketing journals and popular psychology theories to establish the power of emotions. The first slide in this methodology section compares 'rational' and 'emotional' advertising campaigns. It includes a bar chart from an academic study comparing the 'business effects' of each type of appeal. An annotation on the slide tells us that 31 per cent of emotional adverts create 'very large business effects' while only 16 per cent of rational adverts have this effect. Another note accompanying this chart on the slide says that adverts with an emotional appeal are both 'more effective' and 'more profitable' than other advertising strategies.

Working through the methodology section, we encounter direct references to scientific methods. A subsequent slide includes an infographic based on a Nielsen Consumer Neuroscience study that compares the changes in sales volume for emotional adverts compared to changes in sales volume for all other adverts released by the same brand. Here, emotional adverts were measured using an electroencephalogram test (EEG). This measures electrical activity in the brain using small metal discs (electrodes) attached to the scalp. A bold annotation next to the graphic tells us: 'Ads with above-average EEG scores increase sales by 32%.'

Subsequent slides follow a similar trend. On one, the headline is: 'Ehrenberg-Bass prove that positive adverts are most likely to be remembered.' Ehrenberg-Bass refers, here, to the Ehrenberg-Bass Institute for Marketing Science. It is based at the University of South Australia and links back to academic marketing science as discussed in Chapter 1.

Another slide displays four scatter charts using Super's own data. The charts compare viewing figures to adverts measured on Super's ad network against their Vitality EQ scores. There appear to be millions of data points on them. But the slide has a simple headline: 'Emotional ads drive viewer behaviour.'

The final slides in the methodology section of a Virality Deck provides an explanation for the focus on emotional responses. One slide, in particular, introduces a theoretical framework that is often referenced by the research team to justify their research methods. It refers to the ideas of behavioural scientist Daniel Kahneman (2011) – specifically, his distinction between System One and System Two thinking. The slide includes a picture of the cover of the book *Thinking, Fast and Slow*. The title of this slide says that brands need to measure the effect of their ads on both System One thinking (which is equated with emotional advertising) and System Two thinking (which is equated with rational advertising). In other words, despite the preceding slides establishing the importance of System One thinking, as a label for emotionally driven, almost automatic responses to adverts, this slide allows Super to hedge its bets. The implication is that it is worthwhile measuring both System One and System Two responses to advertising. Possibly, this reflects the need for industry standards discussed in Chapter 5.

The final slide in the methodology section on the standard Virality Deck shows how Super measures System One and System Two thinking through a graphic representation of the survey measures. The slide offers a periodic table modified around the Elements of Emotionality. One section is highlighted as the measures of System One thinking. It includes symbols for Ha (Happiness), Sh (Shock), Sv (Social Vibes), among others. Another section is highlighted as the measures of System Two thinking. It includes symbols for BrP (Brand Perception), BrR (Brand Recall), and BL (Brand Liking). To the side of this image is a text box that tells us that Super's 'Elements of Emotionality' has been 'developed based on over 3 trillion ad views by over 1 million viewers'. It says that this data has been analysed by 'modified predictive algorithms' and using 'logistic regression'.

As we can see from the methodology section of the Virality Deck, Super references academic studies, scientific techniques, and popular psychology theory when describing and justifying methods to its clients. Super draws on the legitimacy of academic institutions and large commercial research centres. It uses scientific jargon. Each of these is a way to persuade clients of the validity of the Virality studies. Or, put otherwise, a means of absorbing clients' uncertainty about their findings.

The presentation of the 'Elements of Emotionality' in a periodic table provides a clear example of scientism in action at Super. It is a direct translation of Super's brand position in the language and imagery of science. It presents a model of consumer interactions with advertising as if they were comparable with the structural relationships between fundamental elements of the physical world. There is, of course, all sorts of intertextual work going on that links back to the discourse of Marketing Science, academic ideas, popular theories, and the ethos of science. But, for our purposes, the key thing is that this image makes Super's measures of emotion equivalent to chemical elements. This substitution is not shocking or jarring. It does not require explanation and is frequently accepted without question. It is attractive. It is part of Super's appeal to its clients.

General and specific scientism and uncertainty absorption

In this chapter, we have seen how Super presents marketing action to clients using references to science. To paraphrase Latour (1987), I have argued that Super engages in scientism in action. For instance, to win new accounts, Super stages its pitch to clients in a space called the Lab. Here, clients are asked to don lab coats and are surrounded by DNA strings and telescopes. Rather than dazzling clients with creativity, then, Super dazzles them with scientism. Later, Super invokes experimental methods and natural imagery in the names of its research products and, when reporting to clients via a Deck, offers a methodology section packed full with marketing science models, neuroscience, and popular psychology.

In this action, Super makes general use of scientific ideas. Its displays often do not acknowledge any differences between different scientific practices or disciplines. Super engages in what we might call *general scientism*. This involves a bricolage of different scientific references. Experimental science, physics, chemistry, DNA strings, telescopes, and so on are combined without a second thought for the different methods and knowledge claims they imply. They are used as generic symbols for science. They simply represent 'science'.

Things are different in the coding team's neighbourhood. Here, Super invokes a specific scientific practice: data science. Super displays the computational nature of its work by materializing code and the practice of coding. This scientism works into the ways Super presents products such as Virality EQ. Here, Super emphasizes that its work is predictive. It is also based on big data. It is executed by computers. What we might call *specific scientism* is, in other words, an attempt to present an activity as a certain kind of scientific endeavour. It seeks to make an explicit comparison between an activity and a single field of science. This is another Keynesian beauty contest. It is not important that the references refer to the specific field of study – only that those they are seeking to convince connect them with it. In attempts at specific scientism, references to other fields of science are out of place and possibly undermine their success.

What is the purpose of these displays of scientism? Are they functional? In the last chapter, I argued that market researchers assume that their clients need them to absorb uncertainty. That is, to produce simple models of their external contexts, markets, and consumers that accord with their clients' assumptions and, thereby, facilitate decision-making. I also showed how this understanding of a client's needs is implicit in the ways they think about a Big Picture Project. As we saw, this understanding does not necessarily make the task of market research any easier. As in the Luxury Car Brand Social Media Playbook, a study must often serve multiple masters and align competing interests. Added to this, market researchers must fit their own business needs into the equation. We might think that things would be easier if all they had to do was discover a fact – or live up to the ethos of science.

Thinking in terms of uncertainty absorption offers a way to explain why marketing organizations such as Super spend so much effort on display work – particularly displays using *general scientism* and *specific scientism*. To absorb clients' uncertainty, Super needs to build clients' confidence in it, as it is only once clients give it license to absorb uncertainty that it can begin the editing steps involved in building simple models.

Scientism is a powerful tool here because it references the socially legitimate ethos of science – with its particular appeals to those in business that are highlighted by Whyte (1956). Presenting its work as a scientific practice helps clients to shift their attention towards the people modelling their environment for them. Ironically, this means that the magical thinking underpinning uncertainty absorption – that is, the faith in the modeller over the model – lends itself to a kind of realist, positivist discourse. This is another contradiction of scientism in action – adding to those discussed by Whyte (1956). The idea that marketing researchers are conducting a scientific endeavour capable of providing objective facts is a powerful way to increase clients' confidence. It is something clients can believe in. Scientism is a kind of magic.

8

Marketing Outsight

The last chapter closed by arguing that the discourse of science, represented in talk and materiality, is a way for marketing organizations to start the process of uncertainty absorption. By projecting an image of themselves and marketing action using scientific references, marketing organizations can increase their clients' confidence in their work and, we might also assume, overcome some of the ambiguities of marketing discussed by Alvesson (1994; 2001). They imply that they possess a set of technical skills capable of uncovering information about consumers and markets that their clients lack.

Does this mean that Marketing Science has replaced Marketing Art as the way to bedazzle clients? Well, when we look at the way the research team works at Super we actually see that, while they present their activities using general scientism and specific scientism, their work also involves creativity and imagination alongside data science and computation. Specifically, as we will see, the need to embed clients' assumptions, interests, and expectations in their research requires Super to be more flexible than the scientistic presentation of their work suggests.

This switch from the discourse of Marketing Science to Marketing Art is clearly demonstrated in Super's facial coding product, Emotionality. As I entered the field, Super had recently launched this new product offering. Emotionality is promoted as a way to measure Kahneman's (2011) notion of System One thinking. Dan describes it to clients as a 'super high level predictive analysis' that exposes 'what people don't know and won't tell you'. In short, it is meant to reveal consumers' inner truths – ones that are perhaps even more true because the consumers do not know them themselves. In this way, Emotionality is framed as a method that removes the mediation imposed on traditional marketing research through research participants (who must tell you what they think, something that is difficult when they don't know what they think). Instead, computers do the work – or at least that is what Super wants its clients to think.

The problem is that computational analysis presents the research team with too much data but not enough information. It creates what I call *surplus research* and *empty signifiers*. When we look at the ways that members of the research team mediate Emotionality studies, we see them engage interpretative practices, such as chartism (Preda, 2007), which push the surplus research and computational analysis to the background while, at the same time, give meaning to empty signifiers produced through computational analysis. This is not a matter of 'fattening out', as Ariztia (2015) describes the practice of insight from an ethnography of advertising in Chile. It is a matter of pushing things out of sight. It is a process I call marketing outsight.

To illustrate the practice of marketing outsight, in this chapter I dive into the methodology and technical infrastructure that underpins Emotionality. Here, we will see how the introduction of computer analysis has supported the adoption of facial coding in marketing. But, looking at the ways that Emotionality research is interpreted in the research team, and presented to Super's clients, we will see that computation, big data, and machine learning is replaced by simple interpretations of charts and storytelling.

Getting into Emotionality

At the start of my work at Super, Dan asked me to write a literature review about facial coding data. This is a form of data analysis in which a computer processes an algorithm to assess which emotions are displayed on a consumer's face. The company had begun selling a research product using this method, but members of the research team were aware of controversies about the data and how to interpret it. 'It's just a matter of time before we present to a client who wrote their dissertation about it and knows more about it than us', Dan says to me. In other words, he knows what his team do not know, and this makes him anxious.

I was somewhat sceptical about facial coding data at this point too. As I entered the field, I assumed it was another passing fad, following in the footsteps of neuromarketing a few years prior (Schneider and Woolgar, 2012; Schwarzkopf, 2015b). Indeed, facial coding is an incredibly old method for analysing emotions that dates back to Charles Darwin's (1872) book on the topic – yes, that Charles Darwin (Cluley, 2022).

Inspired, in part, by the observations he made of his children, Darwin viewed emotions as distinct psychological states that are expressed outwardly unlike cognitions and attitudes. He believed that the way all species express their emotions is universal. To support this, he exposed pictures and wood engravings of human and animal faces to research participants and asked them which emotions they saw. His findings were disseminated in a best-selling book.

Here, though, Darwin omitted some images and replaced others with more cost-efficient wood engravings. Researchers have subsequently uncovered instances in which Darwin would add lines or remove details in his published work to support his claims. This controversy meant that Darwin's thinking had only been utilized to limited extents in cognisant fields such as anthropology and psychology up to the late 1970s. As far as I can tell, it was first recommended for consumer research by Bettman (1979), the former editor of the prestigious *Journal of Consumer Research*, nearly 30 years ago. But, despite Bettman's endorsement, facial coding failed to gain acceptance in marketing until the mid-2010s.

By this point, facial coding had become 'a common tool in market research' (McDuff and el Kaliouby, 2017: 148). Indeed, McDuff et al tell us that many well-known brands and large advertisers 'use this methodology to test their content, including MARS, Kellogg's, Unilever and CBS. Unilever now tests every ad the company develops with this technology (over 3000 ads annually)' (2015a: 516). Before paying to distribute an advert, following Hopkins' (1923) experimental logic, these brands measure consumers' emotional responses to their advertising using facial coding methods. What changed? Why has facial coding been adopted after so long in the wilderness?

On the ground, one key difference I suspected is the introduction of facial coding through computers. This is the main thrust of Super's sales pitch for Emotionality. Super argues that, through computational analysis, Emotionality is able to measure System One reactions. For the facial coding data product, Super recruits a sample of viewers from the client's target audience using an over-the-counter sample provider, anonymized here as Aloha. Aloha maintains a panel of qualified research participants. That is to say, it has a list of people who have signed up to receive invitations to participate in market research studies. Aloha verifies their identities and manages their data. Aloha sends out requests for companies such as Super to the people in its panel and mediates payments between them. Aloha takes a percentage of these payments as a handling fee.

Although I was unable to establish what this exact percentage was, Dan told me that participants are offered around a US$2 incentive to take part in an Emotionality study (the rate varies depending on the country and the specificity of the target audience). He was unsure of the exact amount as this was handled by the admin team. The incentive is a digital payment that can be used to make online purchases or traded into cash, for a fee paid by the participant to Aloha.

From the research participant's perspective, the research process is primarily conducted by Aloha's system. It invites them to participate, hosts the survey, and makes the incentive payments. Typically, there is no direct human contact between Aloha and research participants. Indeed, depending on the study design, the participants may not be informed who the client is nor be informed of Super's role in the research process.

In exchange for the digital payment from Aloha, participants consent to watch a test advert on an internet-connected computer with a webcam recording them. They must install a third-party app on their device that displays the advert and records their responses. This app is designed and managed by a Silicon Valley based start-up anonymized here as Analytico. Analytico has a formal partnership with Super. After watching the test advert, respondents' videos are automatically uploaded to Analytico's data cloud via the app. At this point, respondents are forwarded to the online Emotionality survey delivered by Aloha's system. It examines the participant's brand perception, purchase intention, and self-reported emotional responses using the Element of Emotionality. Once complete, Aloha transfers results of the Emotionality surveys to Super's database.

At the same time, Analytico processes the videos of respondents watching the test advert. It uses its proprietary image recognition algorithm to analyse each frame in each of the respondents' videos using Action Units. Action Units are standardized movements on specific regions of a face that, once coded, can be combined to infer emotions, concentration, and other forms of non-verbal communication through the Facial Action Coding Scheme (FACS).

FACS was developed by Ekman and Friesen (1978). It is a protocol designed to allow human coders to identify *universal emotional expressions* of happiness/joy, sadness, surprise, fear anger, disgust, and contempt (Ekman, 1993). The FACS system formalizes how human coders can evaluate, explain, and document their judgements. As Ekman and Friesen (2003: 20) put it: 'It is not enough to determine what emotions are read from facial expressions. It is also crucial to discover whether the interpretations of the observers are correct or not.' This is because the face is not always a reliable way of reading emotions. Individual facial expressions, for example, may indicative multiple emotions at the same time. This is particularly true of smiles. While they are part of the facial expression of happiness, they 'often occur when a person is not happy' (Ekman and Friesen, 2003: 101). Moreover, the face does not always tell the truth. It 'conveys both true and false emotion messages. There are uncontrolled, involuntary, true expressions and also qualified, modulated, or false expressions, with lies of omission through innovation and lies of commission through simulation' (Ekman and Friesen, 2003: 20).

Despite these words of caution from its developers, Analytico's algorithm uses FACS to make a prediction about the likely presence of the universal emotional expressions in each frame in each respondent's videos. These are then aggregated into time-series charts for each universally accepted emotion. Once completed, the results are transferred to Super's database along with a link to Analytico's own online results platform. Here, members of the research team can review aggregate time-series plots for each emotional response. They can view these charts in sync with a copy of the original advert. They can also view images of individual respondents watching the advert.

Although Analytico's algorithm is not public access, the main benefit of its approach is set out in the computer science literature. Here, we are told that computers can execute a FACS analysis much more quickly than human coders. It is estimated that, while it normally takes a human coder up to six hours to code one minute of video, the same minute of video can be processed by a computer within seconds (McDuff et al, 2015b). McDuff and el Kaliouby (2017: 150) tells us that they were able reduce over 50 years of 'direct coding time' to 72 hours of computational processing.

This increases the quantity of data that can be analysed. For example, McDuff et al (2014; 2015a) analyse 3,268 webcam videos with participants watching one of three adverts. McDuff et al (2015b) analyse 12,230 webcam videos with 1,223 participants watching 10 of 170 advertisements. McDuff and el Kaliouby (2017) analyse 2,186,207 videos from 500,170 unique participants.

There are, however, trade-offs at work here. Not all web-users have or are willing to use a webcam to record their faces and this may introduce self-selection bias. In one study, 16,366 web users visited the study website but only 7,562 had a webcam and only 5,268 were willing to be recorded. Even if people are willing to be recorded, they do not necessarily produce information-rich videos. Another study reports that only 17 per cent of frames in useable videos demonstrate any emotional expression. This creates problems for the accuracy of the predictive algorithm. McDuff et al (2014: 638) explain that 'a large number of the false positive and false negatives occur when the viewers are relatively inexpressive'. In addition, poor quality recordings, respondents' physical characteristics such as eye-glasses and facial hair, as well as features in the room where they are being recorded such as low lighting can affect a computer's ability to identify a face in an image and to code it accurately. In McDuff et al (2015a), only 3,268 of 5,268 videos were useable. In other words, while computers can process a large quantity of data, they need to in order produce any meaningful findings.

The appeal of facial coding as deployed at Super, then, appears to be that it can provide access to large amounts of data. The implication is that, through this, it is possible to reveal patterns of behaviour not visible with smaller datasets. In this way, it is an appeal based on Marketing Science. It reveals consumers' inner truths. It does so thanks to the translation of FACS and Action Units into computational algorithms and the installation of a technical infrastructure that can process machine-readable images of people watching adverts. However, this translation has its own limitations. The data might not be particularly revelatory. Indeed, the best computers can do is offer a prediction of the likely presence of an emotion. They cannot describe its actual presence (for more see Cluley, 2022).

Chartism

In practice, the research team ignore these issues and clients have yet to challenge them. Rather, when analysing Emotionality data, the research team concentrate on the time-series plots produced by Analytico. These are abstracted as the source of inner truth. They are treated as meaningful objects.

Interestingly, though, they are read not as predictions of the likely expression of emotions but are treated as descriptions of their presence. This might seem a nuanced distinction, but it is the same as the difference between my guess at the week's lottery numbers, or tomorrow's weather, and a recording of the actual lottery numbers or the actual weather. This suggests that the important thing in this action is not what the computation of Analytico's algorithm says but that the research team can say the data is based on a computational algorithm.

Analysis of Emotionality research is executed, primarily, by Becky at her desk in the research team's neighbourhood (see Figure 8.1). Becky drinks coffee and listens to music over a pair of headphones while she works. Most days, new studies are added to her board during the daily huddle and completed studies are archived. She typically completes a Deck for around four studies each day.

In her words, Becky's analysis involves creating a 'story'. This may have been a reflection of Becky's background in the humanities and her identity at work. She frequently leaves postmodern literature on her desk. Her copy of David Foster Wallace's *Infinite Jest* was particularly hard to miss. However, as we have seen in Greg's description of the analysis of a Big Picture Project in Chapter 6, the idea of telling a story is one which appears often when the research team describes what they do. Indeed, it has developed as a common way for marketing researchers, in general, to frame their activities (Cluley et al, 2020). It marks a notable shift in register away from the discourse of Marketing Science towards Marketing Art.

Figure 8.1: My view of the research team neighbourhood

Note: From left to right: Becky, Joanne, Andy.

Becky begins her storytelling with a 'smile track'. This is a one-dimensional time-series chart visualizing the aggregate level of happiness expressed by respondents. She looks for notable movements in the chart – either up or down. These moments then become key elements of her story. If, for example, the line on a smile track moves up, Becky looks at the test advert to see what could explain this movement. Is something funny happening? Is a new character introduced? Is there some text that appears on the screen?

Becky then combines the movement of the smile track with the scene in the test advert to establish her narrative. In so doing, she engages in a practice known in financial markets as chartism (Preda, 2007). This is a way of making sense of financial markets based on the shapes displayed on valuation charts. Like chartists in the financial sector, Becky works on the basis that the shape of the smile track is inherently meaningful. Her attention is captured by movements of a line up and down. Sharp angles have their own meaning, gradual slopes tell her something different. These shapes become the characters and events in her story. She seeks to explain their causes and motivations as well as their interactions.

In some cases, though, the smile track does not offer any notable movements and no meaningful shapes emerge. When this happens, Becky must manufacture them. She looks for other ways of creating shapes on a smile track. Her first technique is to divide a smile track into different demographic categories. She can then look at a smile track for men, women, young people, dog owners, and so on. This is facilitated by a function in Analytico's dashboard. Here, Becky not only looks to see if the individual smile tracks for these groups have any notable movements, she also looks to see if there are any noticeable differences between the groups. She can start her analysis from the observation that, for example, 'Men find the joke funny' or that 'Men find the joke funnier than women'. In both cases, she continues with the chartist practice of looking for meaning in the shape of the line graph.

If dividing an aggregate smile track into its component smile tracks fails to create any noticeable visual patterns that she can narrate, Becky's next technique is to compare the smile track for a test advert to other smile tracks. She can, for example, look to see if there are noticeable differences between an aggregate smile track for all adverts compared to the test advert, or for aggregate smile tracks for specific product categories. This allows her to make claims such as 'The advert provokes greater levels of happiness than other ads' or 'The opening scene provokes more happiness than the average car advert'.

Finally, Becky can look to see if there are noticeable differences between smile tracks for different groups of respondents and the test ad. Here, she can start her analysis with claims such as 'The advert provokes greater levels of happiness for men than the average advert' or 'The opening scene makes men happier than the average car advert'. Comparison cases are chosen by intuition. She has learned some typical explanations. Becky has learned, for example, that 'most Indian consumers smile more' and 'people just don't get excited about banks'.

Having identified a key moment from the shape of a smile track, Becky's job is to explain it. She engages in what we might call, paraphrasing Moeran (2005), post-evidencing. Just as Moeran tells us that the presentation team at Asatsu decide on their creative work and then develop a post-rationalization of their choice, Becky intuitively selects an explanation for movements on the smile track and then interrogates the data for evidence to support her claims. This might push her outside of the data collected for the study to Super's other datasets or online information searches.

Verbatims

Emotionality surveys offer respondents an open text box to explain their answers. The Deck for Emotionality requires Becky to include 'verbatims' from this data. That is, direct quotations from respondents drawn from the open text responses. According to Dan, these are meant to represent an unmediated 'voice of the consumer'. Becky can access a list of these response via Super's database. However, she reports that showing the voice of the consumer is one of the hardest parts of her work. This is evidenced in the following fieldnotes:

> I ask Becky how things are going. She looks stressed. We are sat at our desks in the Research Team neighbourhood. She asks me, rhetorically, if I can script a deck for her. I haven't picked up on her attitude, I offer to help and she laughs. 'It's alright, I've just got to get this done', she tells me. She sips her coffee and explains her issue. She brings up a spreadsheet of text. She tells me this is the qualitative data she has to use for her verbatims. There are a lot of blank entries or one-word answers. Becky explains that viewers are not given extra incentives to offer meaningful qualitative data and they can complete the surveys without offering any. Apparently, if they made this mandatory it would increase the number of incomplete responses and, consequently, increase the costs of data collection. I ask why she has to use this data. She says that the clients expect to see the 'voice of the consumer'. 'Does this make them trust the data?', I ask. Becky says, 'it might. But it shouldn't'. She explains that it is common for respondents to complain about the 'boring survey' or reveal that they 'have already seen this advert in another study'. In other words, the qualitative data actually reveals weaknesses in the data. Becky says that 'there's no reason for people to leave long answers, so I don't trust them when they do'.

The paucity of the qualitative data means that Becky often has to revisit her initial interpretation of a chart to find an event and explanation that can be supported with a verbatim. Alternatively, she exploits the ambiguity of short answers. When a respondent offers a single word or description of something from the advert, she is able to recruit this as evidence for her story. For example, while speaking through her analysis in the fieldnote, Becky shows me the advert and the smile track. It suggests that audience express happiness when a brand-related cartoon character appears on screen. One of the qualitative answers says the name of the cartoon character. Becky uses this to support her claim that audiences experience happiness when they see the cartoon character. She adds the name of the character as a verbatim to the Deck.

Becky's problem when telling a story based on Emotionality studies is, then, that the data tells her too little. It does not give her clear instructions or answers. It produces empty signifiers – in this case, the shapes on a chart. In response, Becky has to add things to the data, she must give it meaning using her imagination and intuition. This is illustrated in her engagement with the qualitative data generated in a study and her chartism with the smile track. She looks for meaning in shapes created through computational analysis and imposes her story on the voice of the consumer.

At the same time, there is too much data. There is surplus research generated by the computational analysis. This, of course, is the benefit promoted to clients but it causes an issue in action. Not only does Becky have data for hundreds of respondents, but each respondent's data can be broken down into millisecond responses. These are, in many ways, meaningless as people do not change their emotions that quickly and are, really, a product of the computational method. To deal with this information overload, Becky narrows her analysis down to aggregate smile tracks and looks to reduce them further to key moments. In so doing, she ignores much of the data that has been facilitated by the computational infrastructure described earlier. Indeed, Becky has access to a range of emotional expressions including *surprise, concentration, shock, anger,* and *dislike,* each of which had their own time-series 'tracks' available in Analytico's dashboard. However, she only turns to these as a last resort. She rarely talks about their absence.

Becky explains that this approach allows her to complete studies quickly and complete the cards assigned to her in the daily huddles. In other words, it helps her to work profitably. It also helps her to tell a story that clients want to hear. Becky says that 'most other emotions don't really produce anything interesting' and that 'most brands don't want to think that the ad they have spent months designing and tens of thousands of dollars producing makes consumers angry'.

Giving meaning to data, in other words, not only means concentrating on, and amplifying, some aspects of the data. It also involves ignoring or hiding other data that have been collected. Although these interpretative activities are described as marketing and consumer insight – they operate as much by pushing things out of sight. Insight, in other words, depends on marketing outsights.

Computationality

Emotionality shows us how scientism, in particular the specific scientism of data science, both creates problems within marketing research practice but also opens up spaces of possibility where marketing researchers can engage in the kinds of editing steps March and Simon (1958) characterize as uncertainty absorption. Traditionally, emotions have been quantified through self-report measures. These ask research participants to score their own emotional responses to marketing communications, usually via Likert-type scales. Emotionality is different as it shifts the work of quantification away from the people experiencing the emotions. Respondents simply have to react naturally and a computer can analyse the emotions they are expressing for them.

Super emphasizes this computationality of the data when promoting it to clients – as does the technical infrastructure underpinning its claims in computer science research. The idea is that humans, including consumers and researchers, have been removed from the measurement process altogether. In their place, quantification is performed by a computational infrastructure of webcam videos, image processing, predictive algorithms, and dashboards. Once a research participant has agreed to be involved, all they do is watch an advert. The rest of the process is automated. The benefit of this is that it is possible to sample much larger datasets and to do so much quicker and cheaper than similar processes involving human coding. This, in turn, offers researchers access to large quantities of data and the promise of unlocking insights and inner truths they could not see otherwise.

But, while an advantage in theory, surplus research creates problems in practice. Market researchers work to develop simplified models that meet their clients' assumptions, needs, and interests – they do not need as much data to do this and need more flexibility to give meaning to it. In short, the computationality of a research method such as Emotionality both builds clients' confidence in their work and necessitates that the research team works through marketing outsights to reduce the surplus but meaningless data into simple models. The computational science of data lets them tell convincing stories by pushing much out of sight. It hides their art.

9

Artistic Qualification

Having seen how scientific discourse and artefacts displayed at Super create a space for the research team to conduct marketing outsight, in this chapter we will look in more detail at the techniques of interpretation through which the research team tell stories. In a client presentation, Joanne describes the research team's work as being focused on 'giving meaning to data'. This marks another surprising revelation from the field as it suggests that the research team, and their clients, understand their work as a process that goes beyond and adds something to the data they have collected. For me, it marks an acknowledgement that their work is structured around the discourse of Marketing Art.

My central claim is, then, that despite the computational techniques, data science, and scientific themes displayed to clients, the ways that marketing researchers engage with all this data is far from scientific. Rather, interpretation is a process I call artistic qualification. It involves the use of intuition and imagination to pick the right story and assign meaning to particular elements of a dataset. Through this, the research team is able to offer simplified accounts of consumers and markets that combine clients' interests and expectations alongside Super's own business needs. They mix their understandings of clients with concerns relating to their careers, the demands placed on them by their organization, as well as industry and cultural trends. In short, while scientism, particularly the specific scientism of computationality, helps to build clients' confidence, it is through these more artistic activities that market researchers take the next step in uncertainty absorption.

In this sense, artistic qualification has more in common with postmodernism than positivism. But it is not a matter of making things up. There are symbolic tools that the research team use to ensure their artistic interpretations absorb uncertainty by relating to the data and to their audiences. This is where, in other words, marketing science turns into marketing science fiction.

We will observe the process of artistic qualification at work in this chapter through the concepts of 'the stat' and 'the headline'. The stat is a key number that the research team want their clients to focus on from a research project. The stat gains significance in relation to a short, qualifying description, known as the headline. We will see how these analytic tools are used in a meeting between members of the research team, sales team, and an academic researcher. The focus of this meeting is a Big Picture Project called the 'Online Content Survey'. Thanks to the collective nature of this discussion, it shows us the interpretation of data in action. It is an episode when marketing researchers collectively decide on the key findings from a dataset.

The Online Content Survey

The Online Content Survey is a Big Picture Project initiated by the sales team. It is a survey of online publishers who use Super's ad network concerning the future of the industry. Online publishers are organizations who run online newspapers, magazines, and such like. They offer advertising spaces on their webpages which brands can purchase programmatically through Super's ad network. When this happens, the publisher pays Super a commission fee and Super can collect data on the viewers' responses to the adverts.

The sales team hopes to use the results of the Online Content Survey to win new blue-chip accounts in North America – where Super has recently opened an international office. Another ad network provider, anonymized here as North Advertising Online, has garnered much attention in the trade press for a similar survey earlier in the year. It emphasized the growth opportunities for ad networks. Super's sales team hopes that Super's expertise in research will allow them to produce a more compelling study that will not only attract as much in the industry press, if not more attention, but also support Super's brand position. In other words, the aim of the study is to emphasize the importance of programmatic advertising and emotional targeting. The sales team has paid to present the results of the study in a keynote presentation at a North American advertising industry conference.

The Online Content Survey has been designed by Andy from the research team and an academic consumer psychologist employed at a leading North American business school – anonymized here as Professor Ivy League. Dan had delegated the design and execution of the survey to Andy to support his professional development. Participants are not offered any financial incentive to take part in the study. Instead, they have been offered access to the results in exchange for their participation. As such, while most of the survey focuses on online advertising and the importance of emotional responses – and this is both Super's and Professor Ivy League's main concern – it also covers broader issues. This ensures that the survey can offer something of value to potential participants.

I was unable to clarify exactly how Professor Ivy League started working with Super. From what I could tell, the Online Content Survey was his main collaboration. Dan tells me that, as far as he understand it, Professor Ivy League had studied at university with some of Super's American employees. However, at this point, both parties clearly feel that they have entered a mutually beneficial relationship. Super has facilitated access to research participants from its client list, while Professor Ivy League has agreed to analyse the data for Super without charge. Super can use this analysis for promotional purposes. Professor Ivy League holds the study data and can publish the results in academic journals. He can also highlight the partnership with Super in these publications.

This is a powerful rhetorical move in marketing scholarship as there is an implicit (sometimes explicit) premium placed on 'industry relevance' by many journal editors. Having industry practitioners publish in their journals is a mark of prestige. Indeed, before the meeting, Dan had asked me to review a working paper written by Professor Ivy League. I was intrigued as it utilized latent class regression – a data science method not commonly used in marketing scholarship. Shortly after my ethnographic observations, this paper was published in a leading academic marketing journal.

The purpose of the meeting is to table read the survey results in preparation for the conference. It follows an earlier table read between members of the sales team and Professor Ivy League. The interpretation of the results has become urgent as the online advertising conference is scheduled in a few weeks.

The analysis has been delayed as it has proved harder to recruit participants than originally hoped. Andy had initially sent email invitations to clients specified by the sales team. The aim was to get at least 100 responses. But uptake was slow. In response, Andy asked Dan for help. Dan raised the issue with the senior leadership team. He did not want to use up the research team's resources on a study for the sales team as it was not profitable. The senior leadership team suggested that the sales team use the invitation to the survey as an opportunity to contact their clients. They saw this as a win-win. The research team would get the data they needed and the sales team would get a chance to talk to their customers.

But this solution did not work. The sales team felt belittled by the idea of data-gathering and considered this the research team's job. They also said that they were concerned about contacting their clients. The team's director, Ross, said it was 'better to let sleeping dogs lie'. In other words, asking online publishers on their network to consider the future of the industry was risky. It might encourage them to consider their relationship with Super. So, the task of motivating the sales team fell down the organization's hierarchy to Andy. He faced an uphill struggle and continually raises the issue with Dan in the research team's huddles. After several extensions to the survey window, Andy has only managed to recruit 86 respondents.

To make matters worse, the publishers who agreed to participate are the wrong kind of publishers. The sales team had hoped that the leading, blue-chip publishers on Super's ad network would complete the survey – especially legacy publishers that North American clients would recognize. These, unfortunately, are precisely the group who refused to participate. As we will see, part of the meeting involves a discussion of this problem and possible solutions.

The need to appeal to a specific, North American audience not only informed the assessment of the data, it influenced the collaboration with Professor Ivy League. Prior to the meeting with Professor Ivy League, I asked Dan why they were partnering with an American business school, when previous collaborations with local European schools had been successful. Dan explains to me that Super resourced the study as part of its campaign to win business in North America. He says: 'American brands don't care about our work with anyone else. They have all done MBAs and, most likely, couldn't get into Ivy League Business School! So, when they hear it mentioned, they instantly take notice.' Super had permission to advertise the collaboration with Professor Ivy League's employer on its promotional materials.

'User friendly ad formats saving the internet!'

The meeting is chaired by Sarah, a mid-level executive in the sales team based in Super's North American office. Other attendees are Rosa, a mid-level executive in the sales team based in the European head office; Dan; Professor Ivy League; and me. The meeting takes place online using a video-conferencing application.

Interestingly, because of Professor Ivy League's involvement, we are using a different video-conferencing platform to the one used for internal meetings. As we arrive, Dan leans over to me and whispers that Super pay for a specific video-conferencing application that is more stable than the freeware application they use internally. This is normally reserved for external presentations to clients as Super do not want to risk the freeware system freezing. This would not help them to build the sense of computationality in the eyes of prospective clients. Much like Moeran's observations about the use of special rooms in marketing action, discussed in Chapter 2, this gives the meeting an air of importance. Before signing into the meeting, I have to download a copy of the video-conferencing application.

Rosa, Dan, and I sign in via our laptops while sitting in Super's European head office. Dan and I are sat opposite each other on an open-plan desk in the research team's neighbourhood. Rosa is located across the second floor, open-plan office in the sales team's neighbourhood. Sarah is located in Super's North American office. Professor Ivy League is in his academic office at a North American university. As we sign into the video-conferencing call, he explains that he had just got back into his office from teaching a class and asks for a few moments to gather his thoughts before we formally start the discussion.

My guess is that all of us are in our thirties. Everyone is dressed in casual clothes. Professor Ivy League is the smartest. He appears to be standing at his desk and, through his webcam, we can see he is wearing a business shirt and has his hair neatly styled. He most resembles the style of an advertising agent described by Alvesson (1994). The sun is shining into his office. The background shows us a whiteboard with a to-do list written on it. Dan, Rosa, and I wear shirts and jeans. Our backgrounds show Super's head office, albeit it from different angles so that people walking behind us jump from one background to another. Sarah sits so close to her webcam that only her head is visible. Throughout the meeting she tends to sit with her head in her hands. The room behind her is dark. It is clearly nighttime where Sarah is.

Sarah starts the meeting. She explains that the aim is to 'pull out key stats' from the Online Content Survey. We are here, she continues, to 'mine the gold from a rich set of data for PR purposes'. She then invites us to introduce ourselves, which we do in turn.

Sarah provides the context for the meeting. She says that she and Professor Ivy League have already met to discuss potentially interesting findings and that she left Professor Ivy League with a list of analyses to run on the survey questions. In so doing, it is clear that Sarah is setting the agenda and putting herself and Professor Ivy League to the centre of the meeting.

Pre-meetings, or early table reads as I call them here, are a powerful opportunity to shape action. They allow people to develop scripts so that, in the actual meeting, they can present a united front. They can serve as a kind of rehearsal space where participants workshop ideas and prepare for the discussions in the actual meeting. They allow people to consider potential issues and rebuttals to their plans and ensure that any support work, approvals, or research has already been done so that there are fewer obstacles to getting their way in the actual meeting.

In this regard, Sarah makes the point that, prior to our current table read, she had also spoken with Bella, the chief executive officer, about the key messages Super wants to get out from the survey. Sarah emphasizes that Bella and the senior leadership team see this survey as a key part of Super's push into North America. They hope that the presentation at the industry conference will significantly raise the profile of Super's ad network – although she mentions at this point that Bella has raised some concerns about whether Super should 'surface the data' given the sampling issues described earlier.

Data

At this point, the conversation turns to the issue of data quality. It is worth emphasizing here that the concerns with the data from the survey are not abstract nor academic. It is not a question of the validity of the sample nor the power of the analysis. Rather, the concerns reflect Super's business interests. Super's push into North America is intended to recruit the legacy publishers that are typically based in the United States in the hope that these blue-chip accounts will grant the company more clout when speaking to other potential clients for its ad network.

As we have seen in Chapter 2, Moeran (2005) emphasizes the symbolic power of blue-chip accounts. In keeping with Moeran's (2005) thoughts, the senior leadership team believe that the symbolic power of blue-chip clients will be a valuable resource to break the North American market, and possibly beyond. The problem with the sample, then, is not that it lacks statistical power nor that it is not representative of a wider population. The problem is that it is not skewed towards the kinds of participants that match the senior leadership team's needs. Super want to be able to tell legacy publishers that the survey represents what other legacy publishers think – another Keynesian beauty contest. But there are no legacy publishers in the sample.

Sarah tells us that, as a raw number, the sample size is sufficient, even though it has fallen short of the target number of responses, because it compares with the similar survey published by North Advertising Online. She says that, while the aim was to get at least 100 respondents, the number is no longer an issue as Super have 'got more respondents than Northern Advertising Online did for their publisher survey'.

But, Sarah emphasizes, there is a problem with the publishers they have sampled. The first item for discussion in the meeting is, therefore, to agree on a way to frame the sample given the fact that blue-chip participants are missing. Sarah says that 'we need to get a good response to any questions about the sample because the first question at the conference will be "Who are your publishers?"'. She asks if 'there are any big publishers in the sample that clients would recognize?'.

Dan says no and suggests that, when asked which clients are in the sample, Sarah could say she cannot divulge this information for privacy and ethics reasons. He suggests that they could list the publishers on the network and leave the audience to 'guess which ones might be in the sample'. Sarah says this is fine in the presentation but that, in informal meetings afterwards, she will need to give more details.

She asks if there is a way to 'spin' the sample to give the impression that the sample includes blue-chip publishers. For example, Sarah asks, do we 'have organization-level data on the sample? If so, we could speak about the total revenue, number of employees or the reach of respondents'. These would be powerful, Rosa adds, because they would imply that there are blue-chip publishers in the sample.

Dan explains that the sample 'trends to companies which only employ their CEO!'. So, we dismiss the idea of emphasizing the size of the companies in the sample. At this, Rosa tells us that, in actual fact, many of the publishers with the largest audiences are not blue-chip publishers at all. Instead, they are often new publishers who tend to be based in emerging markets. 'They have huge audiences', she says. Rosa asks Dan if these are the kinds of publishers that have taken part in the survey. Dan responds, 'It's possible. If so, we can pull something together about the size of the audience for the sample. It's not going to be massively robust. I'll speak to Andy.'

With this resolution, Sarah brings this segment of the meeting to a close. She confirms that Dan will ask Andy to run some analysis on the total audience reach for respondents in the sample and that she will update Bella about this. 'At the end of the day', Sarah says, 'it's up to Bella to decide if the sample is okay'.

Analysis

We turn to the data itself. Sarah invites Professor Ivy League to speak through the analysis he has conducted following their earlier meeting – saying she is 'looking forward to finding out what we have got'. Professor Ivy League shares his screen and opens an SPSS output (see Figure 9.1). This is a proprietary statistics package sold by IBM. It is popular among academic researchers but not used at Super.

Professor Ivy League's SPSS output displays descriptive statistics for each advertising-related question on the survey and a number of cross-tabulations

Figure 9.1: Screenshot from the Online Content Survey meeting

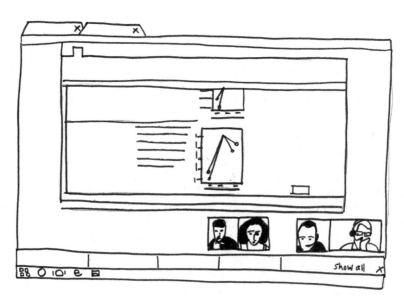

comparing the results between two questions at a time. These are all formatted as line graphs so that we can see, at a glance, differences in responses for different categories of respondents. This is, of course, another example of chartism – as discussed in Chapter 8. Sarah suggests that we scan through all the results and 'come back to headlines and takeaway points once we have seen the complete picture'.

Professor Ivy League begins slowly scrolling through this output. Despite Sarah's request for us to look through all the data before we discuss the key findings, he says that, in his opinion, the most obvious finding is that on average brand managers at online publishers predict the digital advertising market to increase annually by 10 per cent. 'That's a good news story', he states.

Sarah interrupts, saying she is 'actually disappointed' with that result. She says 'an increase of 10% is quite low. That's definitely not a stat we can run with'. She explains that, as online publishers' business models depend on advertising revenue and that as online advertising is meant to be an important area for growth, the idea that publishers only see the market growing by 10 per cent might be received negatively. Even if it turns out to be true and provides a solid footing for the industry, Sarah continues, 'that's not something to shout about on stage. This is meant to be a high growth industry!'. She then describes standing on stage at the conference saying that the market is predicted to increase by 10 per cent. 'No', she says, 'I can't do that. 10% won't cut through'.

After this disappointment, the meeting changes tone. It becomes much more pessimistic. Perhaps there is no gold to mine. Professor Ivy League continues to scroll through the descriptive statistics and highlights the other questions Sarah and he had decided to focus on in their earlier table read meeting. But each time, the results are underwhelming.

Sarah and Rosa shake their heads. 'I'm surprised by that' and 'That's too low!', they say. 'Why is that so low?' and 'Is this data right?', they ask.

As we move through the results, it becomes clear that Rosa and Sarah have a story in mind. Their disappointment is due to the emerging realization that the data may not let them tell it. They want to be able to talk about the unstoppable growth of the programmatic advertising industry in general and, perhaps more importantly, they want to argue that growth will be driven by emotionally engaging content. The data support this claim but not strongly enough. The stats are not large enough.

Dan asks Professor Ivy League to stop scrolling through the results when we get to a question about the drivers of industry growth. He notes that '52 per cent of publishers strongly agree that creative advertising quality is key to sustained growth in the online advertising industry. That's the biggest number we've found so far!'. Rosa responds that this 'might be a potential stat'. Sarah agrees, asking 'Does this mean that publishers are very concerned about quality of content? There could be a story about user friendly ad formats saving the internet. That could be our headline.'

Rosa questions if '52 per cent is high enough? It still feels kind of low, we were hoping for a higher number. It's a bit close to half, half empty, not half full and all'. Sarah asks Professor Ivy League if we can 'lump together' those who responded they are 'very concerned' about creative advertising with those who answered they are 'somewhat concerned'. He presses buttons on his mouse and refreshes the SPSS output. The new total is 90 per cent. This works. Sarah concludes: 'That's better than 52 per cent and it fits quite nicely with what we're saying. That 90 per cent number is really nice. … Maybe it's too nice!'.

At this point, Sarah seems to be imagining herself on stage at the conference. She says: 'That is a really nice stat which shows publishers think less interruptive formats are better. That's a really easy-to-understand stat and it's a big number. Do we lead with a stat or lead with the headline? Stat would be better, right? Yes.' Rosa agrees. They should open the presentation with the stat. It will get the audience's attention.

This prompts a new discussion topic in the meeting. Having decided on the headline and the stat, we now discuss how to strengthen the claim. Dan says that Sarah needs to be ready to answer any questions about why they combined the data. Given that nearly half the support for the claim is based on respondents who are 'somewhat concerned' with the statement, Dan suggests that the idea of 'saving the internet' might fall down under scrutiny. He states, 'If someone told me that I'd be sceptical.' However, Sarah, no doubt feeling the pressure of the conference spotlight already shining on her, seems frustrated. 'I'm not sure we have much of a choice, we have to present the survey and we don't have a better headline.'

Sarah asks Professor Ivy League and I what we think. I offer a diplomatic answer. 'As long as you report it …', I say, but tail off. Rosa interrupts saying: 'It would be really nice to beef up the position. Can we cut the data that really supports it?' In response, we begin to look through the survey questions for related items that support the claim that user-friendly ads will save the internet. However, the time allotted for the meeting is running out. Sarah sums up our progress saying: 'If we have to cut the data to make the data stronger that's okay.' She repeats her earlier phrase: 'We came here to mine the gold. If you break things out, we can pull out whatever looks best and just add them together.'

At this, the meeting ends. Sarah says that Professor Ivy League and her will continue to 'cut' the data around the headline to see if they can strengthen the stats. She thanks us all for our contributions and we sign out of the online meeting. As I close the video-conference app on my laptop, Dan looks around his screens and asks me what I thought about the meeting. Almost before I can answer, Ross, the sales team director, interrupts and asks Dan how the meeting went. They walk to the kitchen.

Interpretative tools

The Online Content Survey meeting provides us with an illustration of the ways that marketing researchers work with data – although we have to acknowledge that this research is explicitly designed for 'PR purposes'. It has been sponsored by Super in an effort to recruit new clients. But the project is still meant to offer some interesting and believable findings that showcase Super's research competence and ad network. It is, therefore, not straightforward puff. Indeed, the research has been designed with a leading academic consumer psychology researcher. Their institution is co-sponsoring the research and findings from the study have been published in leading academic journals.

That said, perhaps because everyone involved is aware of Super's business interest, in this meeting we can clearly see how the interpretation of data integrates external concerns and interests. It is conditioned by what the researchers want to say, think they can say, and what they think the audience wants to hear - it is a Keynesian beauty contest. These conditions are, in fact, interdependent. What they want to say and what they can say depends on what they think the audience wants to hear. For example, while the original 10 per cent growth stat was positive and may have been true, it was not acceptable because Sarah thought that it would not make a significant impact on clients.

Then there is the data itself. In this case, the data is a sample of 86 clients who had completed a questionnaire about the future of online advertising. The researchers have to focus on particular elements of the dataset. It conditions what they can say. Here, as the meeting progressed, Super's business imperative led the discussion to data that related to user experience.

In this regard, analysis and interpretation in action is more difficult than both the discourse of Marketing Science and Marketing Art suggest. It is not simply a question of reporting what the data says – as the discourse of Marketing Science implies. Equally, it is not simply a matter of saying whatever they want and manufacturing data to fit the story – as the artistic interpretation of marketing work would have us think. Rather, interpretation is a bricolage. It is an assortment of different things.

The interpretation is also driven explicitly by the need to communicate through particular media. The fact that Sarah was going to stand on stage and face in-person questions at an industry event is folded into the interpretation. But this is not all. The interpretation needed to fit into a 'headline' and a 'stat' format. Although they were not explicitly defined in the meeting, nor elsewhere at Super, these were key concepts that appeared repeatedly in the action at Super. They shaped not only how the researchers communicated with their clients but also what the researchers felt they could say. They are, in essence, the tools used at Super to create simple models of a dataset and to help pick the right story. They are so embedded at Super that they form the core elements in the design of the research product Decks. Each Deck requires the research team to include visualizations of the data that highlight the key stat and to include a headline as the title of each slide.

A headline is, essentially, a short statement that summarizes a key point of Super's story. In the Online Content Survey analysis, the headline we settled on was that 'user friendly ads will save the internet'. As in this example, headlines do not allow for nuance. They are direct and pointed. They have a matter-of-factness to them. The format pushes researchers to make bold claims. They must be easy for clients to understand but, ideally, invite the audience to want to find out more. That is, they must be linked to the data but call for further elaboration and storytelling.

The stat is a single number – almost always a percentage – that serves as evidence for the headline. In this case, the stat was 90 per cent. The preference for percentages reveals something about the conditions that limit analysis and interpretation. First, non-experts can give meaning to percentages. Researchers and clients alike do not need to understand the technicalities or methodology, even the underlying domain the data concerns, but can, simply, look for large numbers. Second, percentages demand an explanation. A percentage on its own tells us very little. We need to know what a percentage is a percentage of. Percentages are, in this sense, conversation starters. Third, percentages can be summarized in short sentences. They, too, have a matter-of-factness. Here, they are different to other statistical tests such as a t-test or a z-score or a regression coefficient which not only demand more statistical understanding but also require additional statistical information to make sense. Percentages have a tendency towards headlines. Finally, percentages are directly comparable across contexts and applications. They are easy to translate.

The headline and the stat work in a symbiotic relationship. How do we know 'user friendly ads will save the internet'? We know this because 90 per cent of people say so. Why is 90 per cent a meaningful number? It is big enough to have meaning because it is the number of online publishers who think user experience will save the internet.

The analytic tools of the stat and the headline serve two important functions. They operate as heuristics that allow Super to tell stories. They provide a way into the data. They also provide a simple piece of information for clients. They provide a simple statement about the world, about consumers, and about markets that can inform clients' decisions. They do not provide concrete directions nor recommendations for action. They do not lead Super to instruct clients to do something for a guaranteed result. Rather, they help them to make a suggestion, a nudge, a hint about a good course of action. In the case of the Online Content Survey, the stat and headline support Super's brand position.

It is important to note, as well, that the stat and the headline do not allow Super to imagine any results it wants. They constrain what can be said. They limit Super to the data. There might be a headline Super wants to use but, if it lacks the stat to support it, it will not make the claim. Super might cut the data to fabricate a stat but, even here, it is concerned about whether clients will accept it. In this sense, the process of analysis and interpretation proceeds iteratively between the headlines Super would like to be true and the data it has collected.

In the Online Content Survey table read, there is a story, if not a headline, that is implied at the start of the meeting. This remains unstated until we begin to look at the data. We begin, explicitly, looking for a stat. But, in reality, we are looking for both a stat and an associated headline. The two must work together. Both must fit the story. This process involves intuition and imagination. Indeed, Sarah asks us to picture her on the conference stage as she decides which stat and headline will work. As such, it is fair to say that telling a story and giving meaning to data is a more artistic than scientific practice.

Artistic qualification and uncertainty absorption

What we can see in the Online Content Survey meeting is that interpretation is neither captured by scientific nor artistic ideas. It is a creative process in which researchers give meaning to data. I call this artistic qualification because it is a process of qualifying – or assigning qualities to – data (Callon et al, 2002). It involves three core elements: what the researchers want to say; what the data allows them to say; and what they think their clients will accept.

The results of artistic qualification are conditioned by the way market researchers report to their clients. The stat and the headline encourage them to make simple statements that can be supported numerically. These statements have a fact-like quality to them. They can be stated with a matter-of-fact style such as 'User friendly ad formats will save the internet'. Grounding these claims quantitively through the stat, the interpretations developed by the research team have a further element of scientism but we should not mistake this for science. Rather, it is the very license afforded to them by scientism to work creatively with their data that allows the researchers to make these matter-of-fact claims.

10

The Art of Data

We have seen how Super uses space, material objects, talk, and symbolism to present its activities through general and specific scientism. It uses the social legitimacy of science to encourage its clients to trust it and, through this, facilitates uncertainty absorption. Yet, as we have also seen, when interpreting data, the research team at Super do not consider themselves engaging in scientific practices. Instead, they talk about themselves as 'giving meaning to data' and 'telling stories'. This is because uncertainty absorption is not about the application of scientific methods. It involves artistic qualification, as illustrated in the last two chapters.

This more creative practice is not hidden from clients – but its appearance is managed. In this chapter, I will focus on a second use of space, material objects, talk, and symbolism that occurs at Super that connects its activities to the discourse of Marketing Art. Just as Super designs dedicated spaces to perform for clients through scientism and present its research using scientific references, Super displays its good taste, productive cultural consumption, norm of newness, fun, personal relations, and anti-bureaucratic nature through its spaces and talk.

Again, though, no one involved in these performances believes that marketing researchers are artists in the strict sense of the term. As Alvesson (1994) suggests, this would undermine their value. Following their engagement with scientism, they legitimize their activities by embedding them in the social legitimacy of art. I coin the term 'artism' to refer to this action. It is the mirror of scientism as it involves aping the language, methods, and ethos of art without being artistic.

To illustrate the nature of artism at Super, the chapter describes the ways that artistic imagery and objects appear in Super's head office. I then explore how artistic practices influence the ways that the research team present their work to their clients. Here, we have the opportunity to return to the Luxury Car Social Media Playbook discussed in Chapter 6. I was able to attend the final client presentation for this Big Picture Project. Exploring the staging and scripting of this presentation helps us to see uncertainty absorption in action. We have already seen how the design of this Big Picture Project was shaped by Super's understanding of the relationships between the two clients – Stormer, a luxury car brand, and Splash, its creative agency. Super's sales team was keen to maintain their working relationship with both parties. But they knew that Stormer had commissioned the research because it wanted to 'give Splash a kicking'. To present these contradictory stories, Super engage in the kind of theatrical staging discussed by Rosen (1985) in his classic ethnography. It aligns competing interests, like the leaders at Spiro's, by developing sociality between its clients and members of the research team.

Spaces of artism

The location of the head office is suggestive of creative practice. As detailed in Chapters 4 and 5, the building is located in an up-and-coming creative quarter of a large European capital city. The streets around the building are covered in street art – indeed, one is likely to bump into guided street art tours when coming in and out of the building. The neighbouring buildings house record stores, independent clothing labels, coffee shops, and restaurants. There is an art and design school nearby. In spirit, the area is a million miles away from the business quarter of the city – even though, in reality, it is only a few subway stops. There is an artistic attitude in the air.

So, too, when we step into Super's head office we find a different atmosphere than the typical corporate environment. Walking into the head office, you are met by the reception. In place of the bright strip lighting, plastic desks, touchscreens, promotional displays, and cold aluminum elevators typical of corporate entrances, Super's reception is dark, cosy, and homely. As you enter from the street through a large double door, to your right there is a large wooden conference table. This serves as the reception desk. A female in her twenties, in casual yet fashionable clothes, sits behind the desk, with a laptop and telephone to work with. There are exposed wooden floorboards that have been stained dark brown. The walls are exposed bricks. Natural light is limited by the street-facing windows and is augmented by mood lamps. There is a dark blue display case housing industry prizes awarded to Super next to the reception desk, towards the front entrance, and an L-shaped dark blue sofa in the corner.

Travelling to Super's head office, then, one gets a sense of moving into fashionable space. One walks past artworks and artists as one approaches the building. Once inside, the space has the feeling of an apartment. It is defined, as much, by what it lacks. There is no artificial light – the kind we find in the Lab. There is no formal welcoming system. There are no visitor cards.

Anti-bureaucratic things

From the reception, you are met with two options. If you head through a door on the left, you are taken down a flight of stairs to the basement and the Lab – discussed in Chapter 7. However, if you take the door to the right, you are led up a flight of stairs to the main offices. These are complex, with open workspaces, private meeting rooms, and social spaces. We have seen how some of these spaces display scientism in our earlier discussion of the coding team's neighbourhood. We have also seen how the spaces are organized to support productive activities at Super. We have seen, for instance, how the kitchen is designed to encourage attendance and as a space for meetings and huddles.

Perhaps unsurprisingly, given the findings of previous ethnographic research, Super's working spaces also include a number of other objects. Some symbolize anti-bureaucracy and seem to be on display to show that Super is not your typical mechanistic bureaucracy. Walking through the open-plan office on the second floor of the head office building, for example, one sees a surf board leaning against the glass wall of a meeting room. In the basement, out of view of the Lab, there is a sensory deprivation chill out room. This is a space with no external windows. Inside, there is a single lamp and two loungers. Ambient music and white noise play on a constant loop and incense is sprayed into the space by an electronic diffuser. Also in the basement, there is a social space with games and comfortable seating (see Figure 10.1). Few of these objects are used or even spoken about in everyday activities.

There are also playful objects in the head office that, although not directly related to productive activities, do seem to support them in some way. For example, between the desks and the kitchen in the second floor of the open-plan office, there is a row of clocks set to the different time zones of Super's international branches and a video wall with real-time video links to Super's other offices. The walls and doors around the office are plastered with news clippings, printed memes, and posters. These typically make self-deprecating references to Super's staff and teams (see Figure 10.2). They are changed by the creative team depending on the priorities and activities in the building. They highlight brand news such as 'We won a Tiger Award', short-term mission statements such as 'It's Time to Crack Brazil', and social events such as the 'Don't Miss the Super Chilli Cook-Off'.

Staff are allowed to personalize their individual workspaces and teams have the freedom to accessorize their neighbourhoods. In so doing, the office spaces express a anti-bureaucratic theme. People decorate their desks with toys, books, food, and personal items. One team member in the admin team has large, bright red, shiny helium balloons tied to her workstation and chair. Teams hang memes and photographs around their neighbourhoods.

Figure 10.1: The social area outside the Lab

Figure 10.2: A team message board on the wall of the open-plan office

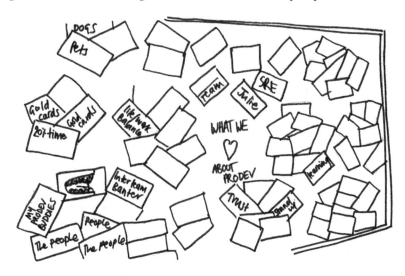

The office spaces are also adorned with objects selected by the creative team as part of their spatial branding. There are objects that give the offices a homely feel such as large Swiss cheese plants and Yuka trees. The walls of the office space house artworks produced by the creative team (see Figure 10.3).

Toys, dolls, and action figures are ubiquitous throughout the building. These objects bring street art, hip-hop culture, graphic novels, sci-fi movies, and

Figure 10.3: Artwork produced by the creative team in a meeting room

meme culture into the building – in short, they suggest cultural consumption. This is reflected in fieldnotes recorded after a meeting in the Study:

> This afternoon I tour the building on my own. I am interested to see which books they had on display in the Study – a meeting room on the first floor. I have already been in there for a meeting and asked Dan why there were so many philosophy books on the large mahogany sideboard with that sits opposite the door. Dan told me that 'The Founders put them there'. Initially, I just assumed that this is a space for the Founders to store old books. But on closer inspection it is clear that these things have been carefully placed and arranged. The sideboard is a display. Books are turned outward to show their front cover and there are a number of action figures carefully arranged on the shelves. Looking across the shelves, I see philosophy books by Wittgenstein, Bataille, Plato, Walter Benjamin, and Barthes. Another shelf is mainly pop business books like The Long Tail and The Big Short; there are copies of the academic journal New Media and Society, marketing textbooks and books about social media. On one shelf a Nietzsche book sits facing the room alongside a copy of YouTube and Video Marketing. I wonder if these combinations represent Super's brand.

As the fieldnote suggests, the objects and books on the sideboard in the Study are not organized haphazardly (see Figure 10.4). Each book is labelled with a 'Super library' shelf mark and placed in order on the correct shelf. As discussed in Chapter 3, such non-work objects have traditionally been

Figure 10.4: The sideboard in the Study

interpreted as a way to symbolize a marketing organization as being distinct from the more mechanistic bureaucracies typical of their clients. The same is true at Super. As the creative director explains in an ethnographic interview, the open-plan offices are a 'physical manifestation of the brand, we want to inspire our clients with what we can do but they can't'. The offices, he continues, have been designed to be 'fun and serious'.

In this regard, the head office guides clients on a dramatic journey through Super as an organization and as a building. It takes them from the basement where they see Super's pitch in the Lab, to the open-plan offices. Here, the space is staged for productive work such as conference calls and meetings. When they visit the building, clients can socialize with Super's teams in the kitchen and can observe the action in the office as a spectacle. This occurred regularly with many clients taking significant time to stop and watch Super's teams at work. The journey ends in the Townhall. This is Super's designated social space and is where the research team present their research to their clients.

The Townhall

The idea that the office spaces are there to be consumed by clients influences the design of a second presentation space in Super's head office. Just as the Lab is explicitly designed around Super's pitches to potential clients, there is a dedicated space for presenting research results to clients. It is called the Townhall.

The Townhall is a large meeting room on the top floor of Super's head office (see Figure 10.5). It is a rectangular open-plan room with exposed wooden floorboards, a mix of exposed bricks and whitewashed walls, and an exposed ceiling with strip, spot, and mood lights. It brings to mind a New York loft or contemporary art gallery rather than a corporate meeting room.

The entrance to the Townhall lies at one end of the rectangular space. It has its own bathroom next to the entrance. There also is a bar at the entrance side of the room. It has a coffee machine, fridges stocked with soda and beer, and a candy dispensing machine. The shelves behind the bar house tumblers, shot glasses, and bottles of spirits. There are also assorted popular culture artefacts centring on a science-fiction theme on the shelves. These include a replica of Darth Vader's helmet as well as Lego and Dr Who figures.

There are original art pieces on the walls. These are street-art inspired and mix hip-hop culture, technology, and classic styles. One prominent picture, for example, is a Dutch Golden Age style portrait of a famous hip hop artist, wearing both 17th-century clothes, and modern street wear. The hip-hop artist is holding an iPhone in his hand. It was produced by the creative team.

At the other end of the room, opposite the entrance and the bar, there is a large retractable screen that, when set up, nearly covers the entire wall. There is also a computer tower and monitor tucked in the corner beside the screen. In between, the Townhall is occupied by an assortment of rugs and leather sofas that can be moved around as needed. On one wall, there is a

Figure 10.5: The Townhall viewed from its entrance

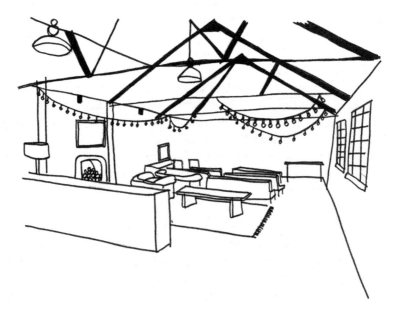

fireplace filled with real logs. Above this, there is a computer screen playing a video recording of a roaring fire on a permanent loop.

Unlike the Lab, people freely move in and out of the Townhall. There is an online booking system to claim the space but Super's teams often use it for impromptu meetings without a formal booking. Indeed, I used it as a convenient space to conduct interviews during the ethnographic observations. Even when presentations were taking place, it was common for people to come and go. The entrance at the back of the room means that people can move in and out without drawing attention to themselves.

Presentations in the Townhall follow a similar structure. It contrasts sharply with the structure of a pitch in the Lab. It is almost as if this is suggested by the physical arrangement of the space in the Townhall (see Figure 10.6). First, a narrator introduces the meeting. They then give way to a team of presenters who improvise alongside some slides or other visual artefacts such as videos. This progresses to an open dialogue between the audience members. When this happens, presenters act like stagehands. They support conversations between members of the audience by, for example, calling up relevant slides or searching online for information.

This presentation structure is illustrated in a pitch by a virtual reality (VR) supplier. In a research team huddle, Dan asked if I would attend this pitch as the research team delegate and added a card for this task to my board. Later that day, as the meeting was about to begin, I received an electronic reminder on my laptop. It prompted me to leave the research team's neighbourhood and head upstairs to the Townhall. I prepared a coffee for myself in the kitchen on my way. Fieldnotes document the meeting:

Figure 10.6: A presentation in the Townhall

> I walk into the Townhall. There is an audience of about 10 people from different teams sat on sofas. These have been moved to face the fireplace. The presenter, anonymized here as Pete, is a man in his mid-thirties with horn-rimmed spectacles and stubble. Pete sits in front of us on an office chair. He has slides loaded into the computer screen above the fireplace. He is wearing a casual shirt, chinos and training shoes. I take a seat next to Steffy who is visiting from Super's Asia Office. I had earlier introduced myself to her in the Kitchen. Pete begins the presentation informally, 'Okay guys, shall we make a start? If anyone else wants to join us, they can jump in'. Pete then gives a brief overview of the history of VR technology and high-profile applications for VR in marketing companies. As he does, he continually asks for input from us. He leans back in his chair. The atmosphere is similar to an academic seminar. Pete asks us questions and asks us to ask him questions.

A successful performance in the Townhall is, then, not intended to deliver information. It aims to 'get people talking' – as Dan puts it. In fact, for research team presentations, clients have access to research reports in advance of presentations, in the form of a Deck. They may have also had the opportunity to view rehearsals of the presentation. What they do not have is an opportunity to come together as a group. The audience for a research team presentation in the Townhall might include board-level executives, marketing and brand managers from the client, as well as their advertising agency, media buying agency, and other suppliers. Although these stakeholders might work together regularly, it is rare for them to meet in the same room. Moreover, while in their work they are stratified by function and power, it is rare for them to meet as equals. A presentation by the research team is an event where they can interact in person and become one as the audience. It is an opportunity to increase their sociality – as Rosen (1985) calls it in his classic ethnographic study, discussed in Chapter 2.

On this point, the Townhall is a qualitatively different space when contrasted against the Lab. While the scientific and impersonal theme of Lab is continued into the coding team's neighbourhood, the theme shifts as one moves further into Super's offices. The desks and neighbourhoods take a more personal feel and there are more cultural artefacts on display. This theme culminates in the Townhall. The space has a relaxed feel. In the Townhall, we find artwork, sofas, and rugs. In the Lab, there are operating tables, DNA strings, and telescopes.

The kinds of interactions suggested by the space are also very different to those suggested in the Lab. The Lab imposes a division between presenters and audiences. The Townhall removes the distinctions. It encourages socializing, breaking bread together, and conversation. Put simply, the Lab feels like a space to deliver a scripted message, while the Townhall feels like a space for an unplanned event or happening. It does so by referencing artist imagery and artistic practices in its physical design, just as the Lab apes the spaces of science.

If the Lab represents scientism in action, the Townhall is its opposite. To reflect this, I describe it as a space themed around artism. Artism not only involves including artwork and artistic practices in a space, just as scientism includes general and specific scientific references in the design of a space. It also emphasizes cultural consumption and suggests sociality and spontaneity. It replaces objective and impersonal arrangements with subjective and personal ones.

Signs of artism

Artism is expressed in the ways that Super talks about its research to clients. To illustrate this, we can consider the presentation of the Luxury Car Social Media Playbook to Stormer and Splash – a Big Picture Project discussed in Chapter 6. Prior to the final presentation in the Townhall, the presentation had been rehearsed in front of Super's sales team and research team. It had also been rehearsed separately to the client, Stormer, and its creative agency, Splash. After each rehearsal, Greg and Dan discussed the performance and made amendments.

Following the rehearsal to Splash, for example, Greg suggested that there might be a problem with the content. The performance felt 'weird' and the audience had been 'too quiet'. The next day, however, a second rehearsal for Splash was deemed to be more successful because 'they were way more talkative, they picked some holes in the methods'.

With these rehearsals completed, and Greg having modified the presentation, we had to wait for the full performance. As I heard these conversations, it dawned on me that the presentation was not really meant to communicate novel research findings. It was designed with a theatricality and dramatic arc – like a play.

The opening scene

The presentation takes place during a day-long visit by Stormer and Splash to Super's head office. This visit includes presentations from each of Super's teams. The research team's presentation takes place before lunch, following a presentation by the coding team about Super's ad network in the Lab. It is the centrepiece of the day.

Before the presentation, Dan, Greg, and I work in the research team's neighbourhood. Greg is visibly nervous. Although he normally wears smart, modish clothes, today it looks as if he has made even more of an effort. He is wearing a pristine shirt and chinos. Dan is much more relaxed and is in his normal active wear. Also as normal, he has his dog with him. At 11am,

Dan tells us to get ready for the presentation and we walk upstairs to the Townhall – dog in tow.

As we enter the room, we are met by eight people from Stormer's marketing team and Splash's account team. Some are helping themselves to drinks and candy from the bar, others sit on the leather sofas facing the wall-mounted projector screen. A member of the IT team is sitting at the far end of the room, tucked in behind the computer by the screen. Also sitting at the far end of the room is Sophie, a mid-level executive from the sales team. She is acting as a guide for the day. She takes the visitors from one area of the building to another, ensures that Super's teams are ready to present and that the visitors are comfortable.

Dan and Greg walk to the far end of the room by the screen. Dan takes a seat on the sofa positioned directly in front of the screen with his dog. Greg walks to a chair in front of the screen that is facing the audience. I position myself on a sofa at the back of the room.

Dan and Greg already know the audience members from their earlier rehearsals. Introductions are not needed. Sophie starts the presentation by inviting everyone to take a seat 'wherever you feel comfortable'. Before introducing the presentation, she asks if she can dim the lights. As no one in the audience objects, she turns the spotlights off, leaving a few mood lights on. She introduces the presentation as follows:

> I hope you've enjoyed the morning in the Lab. Finally, we've got out of the cold and the Wi-Fi dead zone! Now we've moving on to the main event of the day – the bespoke research we've worked on for you, looking at trends in your competitor set over the last 12 months. This has been work done by Greg and the Research and Insight Team. They are going to take you through some of the most interesting findings. Please feel very free to ask questions and give us your opinions throughout as well. I'll hand you over to Greg.

The presentation formally begins. Greg stands up and begins to speak without notes. He first reviews the methodology and offers a high-level overview of the data. As discussed in Chapter 6, he explains that he has analysed 5,000 videos from Stormer's competitor set over the last 12 months and highlights that his analysis is based on Super's database of Emotionality studies. At this point, I begin to notice differences and omissions between the way Greg is describing his work here and his earlier explanation in the table read. In particular, I note he does not mention how the data was sourced. There is no reference to external data providers. Instead, he only references Super's own research database.

Greg talks about the total number of views and shares and the share rates for each brand in Stormer's competitor set. Greg points out that the metrics are all 'trending upwards' but, he emphasizes, three brands account for over 50 per cent of the total views and total shares in the competitor set. Greg suggests that the sector is investing more in paid distribution – that is, paying social media platforms to force audiences to watch their ads. In his words, the data shows that brands are 'putting a lot behind getting views and distribution'. Picking out Stormer's main competitor, Greg observes: 'It seems they've really gone big on distribution. They've really upped the amount they're spending. They're getting way more views. 11 million views last year and then 85 this year. So really going big there. They've also backed it up with high quality content, shareable content.'

Here, Greg steers away from discussing the content of the adverts. Technically, he does not have any evidence that Stormer's competitors are investing in paid distribution. The success of Stormer's competitors could be due to them having more engaging adverts that audiences are choosing to watch and share 'organically' within their social networks. But Greg frames the upward viewing trends as evidence of paid-for distribution. This reflects Dan's guidance. As we saw in Chapter 6, Dan warned Greg to steer clear of commenting on the content of adverts as this might alienate Splash – Stormer's creative agency.

Greg then presents an analysis of the 'most viewed and most shared advert from the competitor set'. This is a humorous advert, themed around Christmas. It was produced by one of Stormer's main competitors. I will anonymize it here as Christmas Ad. Greg plays Christmas Ad in its entirety on the large projection screen at the far end of the Townhall. As it plays, he takes a seat at the side of the screen. When the advert finishes playing, Greg stands up and says:

> You can see there is something completely different about this. It's not attached to a particular model or car. Not product focused at all. It's a piece of hero content that stands out against other car ads and does something completely different and reaches out from the normal audience. And they've put money behind that, and they've really supported it. Targeted it well.

Here, Greg not only continues with the theme of distribution, he also introduces a term that appears repeatedly in the presentation: 'hero content'. Shortly before the ethnographic visit, the idea of hero content had come into vogue in social media and digital marketing circles. It refers to branded content that engages audiences, even those not interested in the product, brand, or category. It is designed to generate a large number of views and shares. It should drive audiences to a brand's social media sites where it is supported by product-focused content and rational appeals. This 'functional' content should then interest actual and potential consumers by showing them how products work, highlighting their features and benefits, or offering technical support.

In the explanation of this advert's success, Greg frames the Christmas Aid advert as hero content. He briefly mentions that it stands out from other social media content produced by the competitor set but quickly focuses on distribution. He emphasizes that the competitor 'supported' the content by 'putting money behind it'. The implication is that Stormer's problems may not be caused by the quality of their content, which is Splash's responsibility, but, rather, by their failure to support their content. In short, this interpretation points the finger at Stormer and away from Splash. It also provides Stormer with something they can do differently, without making an explicit recommendation.

Greg then shows a new slide on the screen that visualizes the Elements of Emotionality survey study he designed for the Christmas Ad. This is a chart he designed himself. The slide displays a spider diagram that compares the average emotional responses for all ads in Super's database, all automotive ads in their database, and emotional responses from a sample of 200 respondents for the Christmas Ad. The spider diagram compares these in terms of key emotional responses from the Elements of Emotionality including Hilarity, Amazement, Warmth, Social Good, Zeitgeist. Greg speaks through the chart:

> On the outside of the diagram, we have all the emotional responses that we track. Here is just the UK norm in red and the automotive norm in blue. So, we can see where the Christmas Ad over-indexes and under-indexes. Automotive ads tend to over-index on amazement and exhilaration. Think of your typical car ads: they are very amazing, going through exhilaration, driving fast in nice cars on nice roads. It's exhilarating, amazing. But they under-index, you don't see too many car ads go through warm, happiness, nostalgia and hilarity. And that's what you can see on the righthand side, where we've plotted for Christmas Ad in black. You can see looking at hilarity, how far it over-indexes, doing something different that's not normal. Also, it covers a few of the other bases. But it's mainly that hilarity that gains it that cut through.

In this description, we see another example of interpretation through chartism – as described in Chapter 8. Greg bases his analysis and explanation on the visual differences between the Christmas Ad and other ads on the chart he has created. The shape of the spider diagram is taken to be inherently meaningful.

At this point, Dan interrupts the presentation. He rises up from his seat so that, while still sitting on the sofa, he can turn and face the rest of the audience. He asks: 'Does this ring true to you guys at all? Are you spending a little but less on distribution perhaps. Is that what's driving this? Or perhaps you've increased distribution but less so than your competitors?'

The head of marketing for Stormer, a middle-aged man in a sports jacket and shirt, responds: 'My sense is it's not terribly surprising. I think though that the reassuring thing is that we're still punching quite high. So that's not a bad thing. We know we've been crap at social media. So that's not surprising.'

This prompts Dan to offer his own interpretation of Greg's analysis. Following the comment from the head of marketing for Stormer, Dan says:

> What's interesting here is the different strategies that the brands have been using. That's what we wanted to show you guys … there's a lot to learn from your competitors. But what's really consistent across the strongest brands that we're seeing is you've got this combination of hero content, continuous support and the use of new technology to inspire audiences as well. There's loads of this kind of stuff from [competitor], which is great if you like them, if you're a fan of the page, and you're on the brand channel. But to get people to visit those channels then you need hero content. The point is, it's got to be very different to gain cut through versus other videos. It's got to be very, very emotive. You guys could potentially go for different emotional responses to get that cut through in a different way.

In this summary, Dan edits Greg's interpretation – a key step in uncertainty absorption. He does so by combining both artistic qualification and an appeal to scientism. First, Dan is influenced by what he wants to say. Specifically, his interpretation harmonizes with Super's brand position and its focus on emotions. It is content which makes an emotional appeal, he argues, that will gain cut through. Second, Dan claims that the success of the Christmas Ad can be explained by the different emotional responses it created in audiences. Finally, Dan's comment reflects what he thinks the audience believes.

In terms of scientism, Dan's interpretation not only picks out the idea of emotionality but he makes reference to data sources not presented to Stormer and Splash. He tells them that there is a consistency 'across the strongest brands that we're seeing'. In making this claim, Dan enacts uncertainty absorption. He implies that he has data to back up his claim, but he only presents his claim.

Case studies

Dan's interruption marks a change in the presentation. As he stops talking, he shifts his body back around to look at Greg. Greg returns to centre stage and moves from discussing broad trends to illustrate the key social media plays he has identified. A pattern emerges here. Greg plays an advert and then talks through the visualization of the Elements of Emotionality study for it before emphasizing a key lesson for Stormer. After playing six adverts, Greg summarizes the key social media plays:

> Provoke unusual emotional responses through stunts and feats of engineering. This suits the sector and provokes emotions such as amazingness. Don't worry about production values and celebrities. These don't guarantee any shares. Include social issues that can drive sharing through social motivations. Go beyond products to create hero content and then support that hero content with paid views. The content's not enough on its own. It has to be distributed well and widely. Go big or go home. So, with other brands spending loads and loads, upping their distribution, increase spend big to get your voice heard. Use continued support to keep the conversation going. Using product focused videos here and distributing them as widely as possible.

Again, as Greg draws this section of the presentation to a close, Dan intervenes inviting comments and questions and offering his interpretation of Greg's analysis. He once again shifts in his seat so that he is facing the audience. 'Okay any questions or comments', he asks. The head of marketing for Stormer responds, 'I was just thinking: is there an average across the data?' Dan now offers an interpretation of the social media play highlighted in Greg's presentation that relates them to Stormer's social media marketing. He says:

> I would say the videos you guys have supported might not have been the best choices. As Greg said, you've got nice videos. Product based, but funky. But some other videos that you guys are producing – which are really, really nice – are tending to not be supported. That's what's coming out here. By no means are there no good Stormer videos. They just kinds of got lost a little bit, just put on a brand channel. They've gained organically with organic shares, which is fine. But you guys could have used those videos more proactively.

This is an interesting summary as it is not based on the data presented by Greg. Instead, Dan makes an assessment about the quality of Stormer's content – arguing that they have some content which is 'really, really nice' but not supported sufficiently. In so doing, Dan makes a switch that meets the objective of the research he and Ross took from their interactions with Stormer and Splash. He argues that it is not simply the case that Stormer has been unsupportive. Rather, they have supported the wrong content. This opens a space for a discussion about how they could support the right content. In the process, Dan has steered the discussion away from Splash's creative output to Stormer's own decision-making processes. He says that Stormer have the right content – even though this is not proven by the data.

Spotting the right content

In the earlier two scenes to the presentation, Dan offers summaries of Greg's presentations. In both cases, he edits Greg's interpretation in a way that reflects the earlier discussion with the sales team about the relationship between Stormer and Splash and the business opportunities on offer to Super from both clients. Neither Dan nor Greg have made any negative assessment about the quality of Splash's creative work for Stormer. The first act of the presentation frames the discussion around distribution. The second act further frames it around which content Stormer has chosen to support through its paid-for distribution. Noticeably, in these interactions the delegates from Splash remain silent.

Now the presentation takes a new dramatic turn. Dan still faces the audience. Greg steps to the side of the stage. Attention shifts to Stormer and Splash. The head of marketing for Stormer responds to Dan's intervention about supporting the wrong content. He confesses:

> Maybe there's a need for education. We don't manage the budgets centrally. As a central marketing team, we balance budgets with across different markets but we don't control what it gets spent on. So maybe there's a bit of education that needs to be done in terms of what to support and what not to support in our branches. I think we're clear about our hero videos and what's a more rational, functional video.

In this response, we see the head of marketing accept Dan's interpretation. Implicitly, he agrees that they may have supported the wrong content. But, he explains, this is because they lack control over their branches. The solution he offers is to educate them about which hero content to support with paid distribution. In the process, the decision makers from Stormer begin to make a decision. Their uncertainty starts to be absorbed.

After a discussion about why this is the case with other delegates from Stormer, the head of marketing steers the discussion back to content by asking if there are any 'heavy hitters' in their content. It appears as if he has not heard the message he came to the meeting expecting to be told. The head of marketing states: 'In terms of our effectiveness, we're definitely, really good at functional content. But, nevertheless, there's no big heavy hitters from us, is there? I think that's where we need to put the emphasis.'

Dan replies that 'if you look at just pure numbers' Stormer do not have any heavy-hitting content. But marketing science fiction is not about looking only at what the numbers say. He again repeats his assertion that

Stormer have strong content that 'is really nice, that is heavy hitting'. But, Dan continues, the 'reason that hasn't surfaced is it's not enough to have really strong content. I think you guys are producing some strong content but distribution is not weighted in your favour'.

At this point, the assistant head of marketing for Stormer enters the conversation and begins to speak to the head of marketing. She highlights an example of a PR film that Stormer produced 'outside of any media plans and marketing budget' that performed well on their key social media metrics. It achieved 'a completion rate of 80 per cent on two million views, which is a very healthy sign'. This means that, of the two million views, the average viewer watched 80 per cent of the video. The assistant continues, 'it means if it was pushed, if we had put paid-for spend behind it, it could have gone to 25 million views, it didn't go to 25 million cause there wasn't enough money'. In this intervention, the assistant essentially accepts Dan's interpretation and repeats it back to the room. She is speaking to both Dan and the head of marketing.

Dan responds:

> That's exactly right. So we've looked at these videos retrospectively and we've picked out your best videos and put them through an Elements of Emotionality study. But is there something we can do to help you guys in those conversations with the territory teams or your media agency guys? We would definitely be happy to have the same conversation with them.

The head of marketing and assistant now speak directly to each other. The head says: 'It's definitely the hero space that's important for us cause all that stuff is just snapped up by all the right blogs.' The assistant confirms: 'and supporting hero also brings people into all channels for functional content'. At this point, Dan interrupts the conversation. It appears that he has sensed that Stormer have accepted the message. The narrative arc is complete, uncertainty is absorbed. The problem, they all seem to agree, is identifying the right hero content to support with paid distribution. Dan seizes on the opportunity to pitch the research team's products:

> I was going to say before, before they run, we can help you test if a video is hero content. We can actually do that before you launch them. We can help you decide if they're potential hero content or not because we can test, we can run a test called Virality EQ. It is a super high-level data analysis but it's visualized in a really simple, really top line, way. It will pull out the emotional responses that your content is provoking and tonnes of brand metrics. For a not huge amount of money, if you've got a video that you think will be good in certain

territories, we can test that video in those territories to create an argument to take to the territory teams to say let's back this video then it's not just your opinion but you're actually basing that decision on some data. We can definitely help you with that.

The head of marketing and assistant look at each other and nod. 'Okay', Dan says, 'Thank you very much for listening to our presentation'. At this, he makes a point of congratulating Greg for the presentation. Dan says: 'I just want to say to Greg, that was great work. It's not easy to present to a room with so much experience but I think Greg did a great job.' He leads a round of applause for Greg.

Stormer's head of marketing comments that he is 'really impressed with Greg's presentation'. He asks Greg about his background and how he experienced the presentation. 'Was this really your first big presentation?', he inquires. There follows a developmental conversation in which people seem to let their guard down. Although Splash's delegates remain silent, Stormer's head of marketing and his assistant offer words of support and encouragement to Greg. The head of marketing recounts a story about dealing with his nerves at the start of his career. He concludes by repeating that he was 'really impressed' with Greg. Interestingly, then, this final act shifts the presentation from the data to the presenter. It centres the analysis onto Greg. It is discussed as 'his presentation' and 'his research' and is linked to his personal story – much like we have seen marketing workers in more creative functions such as advertising like to think of their concepts as 'their ideas'.

At this, Sophie steps forwards and encourages the audience to applause again. 'Thanks everyone, now it's time for lunch.' Dan and Greg walk out of the Townhall. I join them as they walk past. 'That went well. Well done', Dan says to Greg as we walk down the stairs.

I was surprised by this final act of the presentation. It seems to mark a moment where the participants spoke authentically to each other – not as client and marketing organization but as individuals. There is an appreciation for Greg's work and a focus on his development. There is an air of empathy. Again, my sense was that this was encouraged by the homely atmosphere and sociality encouraged by the space and the sense of connection that the presentation team had built with the audience. The result is that the presentation ends on a note of sociality not computationality.

The dramaturgy of data

We can see in this presentation how marketing action is organized as marketing science fiction – that is, action that makes strategic appeals to science *and* art to fulfil the function of uncertainty absorption. Using scientism at the front end of their relationships with clients, and computationality in the collection and analysis of their data, the research team allow themselves to translate their research around their perceptions of the client's interests and assumptions. Having built confidence through scientism, they are able to engage in artistic qualifications that combine what they want to say, what their data allows them to say, and what they think their clients want to hear. As we see at the end of the presentation in the Townhall, this ends up with a moment of empathy between the clients and the research team.

11

Marketing Science Fiction

The book opened by asking if marketing is really a science. It is easy to think that it is in the age of data-driven marketing, consumer analytics, and neuromarketing. But, if marketing is increasingly approached as a science, should we not study it like a science? In other words, do we not need market science studies?

Marketing science studies – the approach I advocate – explores what people who claim to be doing marketing science do. This helps us to understand how they convince others that their work is scientific. It necessitates that we investigate marketing as something people share with a range of tools, techniques, and objects. To gain this appreciation, we must go to work with marketing workers in marketing organizations and not fall victim to industry hype.

When we do so, we can see that marketing organizations like to present their activities as a form of science as a response to the ambiguities of marketing as a form of knowledge work that lacks true professional status (Alvesson, 1994). That is, it helps to build their clients' confidence in their work. It also helps to satisfy the needs of their clients. It is too easy, and incorrect, to assume that the clients of marketing organizations are rational actors who want marketing organizations to do their marketing for them either because they are special artists or scientists.

Life would be simple for marketing organizations if this were true. If clients wanted creative advertising agencies to imagine fresh advertising campaigns or marketing research companies to report their findings, marketing action would be easy. But marketing action is based on a different idea of clients. It is based on the idea that clients need marketing organizations to help them to make decisions. They do not want marketing organizations to make decisions for them.

In short, clients turn to marketing organizations to absorb their uncertainties about their consumers and markets. On this point, Braverman, the foundational work sociologist whose thinking encouraged us to step into marketing work, emphasizes the importance of marketplace uncertainty in the historical emergence of marketing. He writes:

The overall purpose of all administrative controls, is, as in the case of production controls, the elimination of uncertainty and the exercise of constraint to achieve the desired result. Since markets must remain the prime area of uncertainty, the effort of the corporation is therefore to reduce the autonomous character of the demand for its products and to increase its induced character. For this purpose, the marketing organization becomes second in size only to the production organization in manufacturing corporations, and other types of corporations come into existence whose entire purpose and activity is marketing. (Braverman, 1974: 184)

Marketing organizations absorb uncertainty by providing creative expertise and scientific models of consumers and markets. The discourses of Marketing Art and Marketing Science are, in this sense, not ideals but tools. They are not templates for marketing action but ways of making sense of marketing action, ways of presenting marketing action, and ways of enabling marketing action.

On the ground, science and art exist in a dialectic relationship (Rosen, 1987). Just as Rosen (1985) tells us that the breakfast at Spiro's involves a social drama between equality and inequality, marketing action at Super seems to progress through the opposition of art and science. It is neither science nor art. But it has elements of both. It combines them into something new. Where a marketing organization emphasizes art, it tends to find science impressing itself on its action and vice versa.

So, at Super we have seen a marketing organization working on the assumption that its clients need to be supported. To help build their confidence, marketing workers present marketing action through scientism. They suggest that their activities are comparable with scientific practice. At Super, this involves using scientific references to imply a computationality to its work.

However, where they engage in scientific research, in this case computational science, marketing workers find that it forces them into creative practices. Computational science methods require marketing outsights. They encourage use of imagination, cultural consumption, and intuition to push the wealth of data to the background and make sense of the, otherwise abstract, research results. Here, marketing researchers hide surplus research and repress what they bring to the empty signifiers produced by computational analysis. Computational science calls for artistic qualification as researchers combine what they want to say, what their clients want to hear, and what the data suggests in short statements and simple percentages that give their interpretations a matter-of-factness.

Such work is not hidden from clients. Researchers are open about the ways they give meaning to data. They do so through meetings such as table reads and rehearsals in which marketing workers make explicit their clients' assumptions, interests, and expectations. They even invite their clients into these discussions. These more creative practices are displayed through artism as a marketing organization uses cultural consumption and creative techniques to build sociality with its clients.

Understood as a dialectic in which science turns to art, and art turns to science, means that marketing in action may be better understood as a marketing science fiction. Ironically, in this sense, marketing action might actually be more of a science than many think – just not a science that meets the ethos of science (Merton, 1938). For instance, Law and Williams tell us that 'scientists undertake a version of market research' as they assess the likely value of their discoveries to different groups and package their findings with these considerations in mind (1982: 537). We can expand this by saying that marketing workers and marketing organizations undertake a version of science to align their discoveries to different groups and package their findings with these considerations in mind. Like scientists, they recruit cultural references, delegate their work to non-humans, and seek to mobilize a network of actors who present their simple models as matters of fact (Latour, 1987).

A structural functional theory of marketing

Could we see this if we did not go to work with marketing workers? Or, to return to the question I posed in Chapter 2, is there a unique ethnographic theory of marketing?

My sense is that we can only understand marketing action, such as the action I observed at Super, by recognizing the importance of economic imperatives and material relations between marketing organizations and their clients – and between marketing organizations and their marketing workers. These relations are best seen from the frontline of marketing action. In particular, thinking about *marketing as work* encourages us to pay attention to the ways that marketing action supports the securing of profit by capital within a marketing organization. This is a topic rarely discussed in marketing theory and sociology. It is more common to think about the ways that marketing workers support the accumulation of capital by manipulating consumers. But it is the focus of one of the earliest classic ethnographic studies of marketing by Rosen (1985).

Appreciating the securing of profit by capital as a function of marketing work helps us to reframe the relationship between marketing and computational science. Computation draws on and supports the automation of marketing action such as the automated data-gathering processes we have seen at Super. It encourages marketing organizations to operate through the principles of scientific management such as the use of the board at Super. These standardize tasks around the most efficient way of working but also mean that marketing workers tend to work with a small number of interpretative tools such as chartism, marketing outsights, stats, and headlines. The result is that marketing organizations can claim the scientific advantages of big data (through the sheer volume of supposedly bias-free measurements, it uncovers inner truths of consumption), while simultaneously increasing the profitability of their work and their ability to absorb uncertainty.

The automation of marketing work, in turn, calls for new displays that can dazzle clients – of the kind emphasized by Moeran (2005). It requires marketing organizations to engage in specific scientism that materializes the immateriality of computer code and justify their work through scientific ideals. Through this, they can win accounts and service them as profitably as possible. This also provides them a license to engage in artistic qualifications as they tell stories about the data that interest their clients.

We might ask, here, whether marketing organizations turned to automation to increase profits, and then post-rationalized them to their clients through scientism or vice versa. We will never know which is the cause and which is the effect. However, my suspicion is that the profits came first. Indeed, I find it hard to believe that a for-profit research organization such as Super would promote a research product simply because of their scientific ideals without any consideration of their profitability. If they did, they would display their lack of seriousness in the same way that creative advertising workers cannot completely embrace the ideals of fun at work (Alvesson, 1994).

In this regard, exploring marketing action ethnographically also helps us to frame the turn to science as a response to the structural ambiguities of marketing work and the challenges it poses for marketing organizations and marketing workers. While they might still struggle to articulate a set protocol or specialized knowledge base, presenting themselves as a scientific operation helps to distinguish marketing organizations from their clients and legitimize their work in a way which complements, rather than undermines, the position of their clients. In short, understanding the structural relationships that animate marketing action is essential if we want to explain why marketing organizations work the way they do and vice versa. We cannot ignore the fact that most marketing is a profit-making endeavour nor the fact that most of the clients of marketing organizations are other marketers. These provoke responses in marketing action that may be taken-for-granted by marketing workers and, as a result, go unseen through other methods.

Ethnographic research is also a way to open up the black box of marketing. It shows how marketing works. It is only by participating in marketing action that we can appreciate the role that physical objects play in marketing work and the importance of display work. For instance, without going to work, we overlook the importance of Super's award-winning head office. We would perhaps think of it only in terms of its branding activities. We would not see that it is intentionally and continually designed to perform for staff and clients. We would not see that it includes a series of dedicated performance spaces that take clients on an immersive journey into the organization. Put simply, we would not see how much marketing action is directed into the realm of production rather than consumption.

Marketing and society

Without opening the black box of marketing action in this way, it is tempting to accept lazy criticisms of marketing. In this case, we have seen critics point to marketing – in particular data-driven marketing and targeted advertising – as a source of contemporary social ills. For critics, modern marketing is a weapon of math destruction (O'Neil, 2017) which encourages mass surveillance of consumers (Zuboff, 2019).

Put in broad strokes, this line of argument runs as follows: marketers have embraced computational technologies and digital media because they allow them to predict our behaviours and intervene in our actions. Marketers, social critics claim, exploit social media feeds and search results to create filter bubbles (Pariser, 2011). They shape the 'daily you' to the point where they can swing elections, bring down governments, and extinguish revolutions (Turow, 2012).

There is something to this analysis. Marketing activities do fund many digital technologies which, without marketing, would not turn a profit (Srnicek, 2017). They do allow brands to collect data about us and to use that data, in combination with digital technologies like social media, in an attempt to persuade us of the value of their products. But, when we go into marketing organizations which use this kind of digital data and engage in computation research, this image of a cybernetic marketing science is tempered by the presence of marketing science fiction. We see that all the big data and machine learning does not eliminate uncertainty. It does not make brands into evil geniuses.

If anything, opening up the marketing black box leads us to ask a different critical question than that which occupies many critics. Namely, why do brands bother? They are not able to control consumers as convincingly as the critics suggest. They still struggle to understand them. They hope that their online videos will be shared, they want to be heroes and win awards and win (or at least not lose) accounts. They still seek assurances that they are doing the right thing – or at least not doing something stupid.

If we return to Braverman (1974) and Whyte (1956), we can contextualize the ways that marketing organizations have embraced digital technologies as part of a longer story of scientism. Brands turn to digital media and computational science as a response to the overwhelming uncertainty they face – just as they have turned, previously, to engineering, experimental science, and cognitive science. They want to believe in marketing science fictions. They are not evil geniuses but driven by insecurity and uncertainty. The best they can hope for is that marketing organizations can help to absorb their uncertainties – not eliminate them. By opening the black box of marketing, we see that marketers are not shapers of society as much as they are shaped by it (Pollay, 1986). Here, marketing science studies is needed to put marketing science into perspective.

Getting out

Finally, to complete my aim of supporting ethnographic research through a thick description of my methods, I would like to talk about the challenges of getting out of the field. This is an issue which is almost never discussed in existing ethnographies of marketing. But it is both emotionally and practically difficult.

In my case, I felt ready to leave Super after six months onsite. As discussed in Chapter 5, the assembly line nature of the work became a grind. While other junior executives might have been willing to continue with the drudgery I was experiencing, perhaps offset by the opportunity to build a life in a large European capital city, commuting back to my home every weekend and living out of a suitcase was tiring. The work I was doing at Super was increasingly unfulfilling and repetitive.

However, I had not planned an official end date for my research. Here, I ignored Neyland's (2008: 149) advice that the exit 'should not be left to the end of an organizational ethnography'. Personally, I found Neyland's advice both practically and philosophically hard to follow. If I set an end date before entering the field, how could I guarantee I would see what the field could show me? What if I had not been surprised? What if my colleagues had not yet let their guards down and opened up their work for me to see and participate in? Would I not risk conducting a drive-thru or jet plane ethnography that Neyland, himself, warns against?

But, as a new teaching term began, I found it difficult to travel to Super's head office. For a few weeks, I attended the office less and tried to juggle my role at Super with my work as an academic. At the same time, another academic researcher had started a visit at Super. They were on a placement as part of a cultural studies course where they were taught by one of the founders. We shared a desk in the research team's neighbourhood and, as I was not coming into the office regularly, this researcher took over the desk space with their personal effects. I continued to sign into huddles when they took place online but found few cards were added to my board. In this sense, I felt that I was being exited by the field.

During the next few months, my role shifted from a participant in the action to being a (primarily digital) observer. I continued to attend online meetings and presentations, continued to monitor the team's emails, boards, and shared drives. I made occasional visits but felt like an outsider. I continued to perform some productive work in the months that followed. For example, at one point Dan emailed me to ask if I could help Greg with a coding task. In an online meeting, Greg explained that Super wanted to run some tests based on emotionally coding webpages on their ad network. He sent me a link to an online spreadsheet with weblinks and, over two days, we worked through these links and used a coding sheet to categorize the emotional content of over 2,000 webpages.

I arranged further ethnographic interviews to help solidify the research direction. In an interview with Andy, in particular, I had to spend some time explaining why I was not coming into the office anymore. He told me he wondered where I had been and that the team carried on without discussing my absence. I felt both pleased and hurt at this. I had worked alongside the team for several months, so part of me hoped I would be missed.

During these interviews, and as I began to describe my experiences to colleagues, I saw research themes emerge. I found that I was surprised by new elements of my observations and in new ways. Eventually, without notice, I was removed from the email list, board, and shared drives. I created an electronic archive of the materials I had collected and archived digital files in case I would lose access to them. I decided not to continue my engagement with Super any further.

That said, as I returned to work in a university my experience at Super impressed itself on my work. I tried to follow Dan's leadership style. Often, when struggling with some writing, I will think about the speed at which the research team scripted their research. In meetings where a senior academic from, for example, a political science department makes claims that business schools need to teach students how to code and should stop wasting our time with qualitative research, I think about how the image of business differs from its realities. When I read about the future of marketing in top academic journals, I wonder if their authors are not caught up in a machine dream.

It was at this point, having exited the field, that I began to think about writing about my experiences. Neyland (2008) suggests that it takes an average of eight years to complete an ethnography. I began by slicing my data into a series of papers, some of which have seen the light of day. A pandemic later, I 'fattened out' – to quote Ariztia's (2015) participant – my experiences. Here, I was glad that I had the advantages of modern technological infrastructure – such as online file storage, online email archives, and word processors and audio recorders. Through these technologies, I could return to my experiences and step back into Super even though I had exited the field.

Organizational ethnography, in particular ethnographies of marketing action, are not for everyone but they can help you think.

References

Adorno, T.W. and Horkheimer, M. (1944). *Dialectic of Enlightenment.* London: Verso.

Ahlberg, O., Coffin, J., and Hietanen, J. (2022). Bleak Signs of Our Times: Descent into Terminal Marketing. *Marketing Theory*, 22(4): 667–688.

Alvesson, M. (1994). Talking in Organizations: Managing Identity and Impressions in an Advertising Agency. *Organization Studies*, 15(4): 535–563.

Alvesson, M. (1998). Gender Relations and Identity at Work: A Case Study of Masculinities and Femininities in an Advertising Agency. *Human Relations*, 51(8): 969–1005.

Alvesson, M. (2001). Knowledge Work: Ambiguity, Image and Identity. *Human Relations*, 54(7): 863–886.

Argyris, C. and Schön, D.A. (1974). *Theory in Practice: Increasing Professional Effectiveness.* San Francisco: Jossey-Bass.

Ariztia, T. (2015). Unpacking Insight: How Consumers are Qualified by Advertising Agencies. *Journal of Consumer Culture*, 15(2): 143–162.

Arndt, J. (1985). On Making Marketing Science More Scientific: Role of Orientations, Paradigms, Metaphors, and Puzzle Solving. *Journal of Marketing*, 49(3): 11–23.

Arnould, E.J. and Cayla, J. (2015). Consumer Fetish: Commercial Ethnography and the Sovereign Consumer. *Organization Studies*, 36(10): 1361–1386.

Bartels, R. (1951). Can Marketing Be a Science? *Journal of Marketing*, 15(3): 319–328.

Barthes, R. (1977). *Image-music-text.* London: Macmillan.

Bass, F.M. (1993). The Future of Research in Marketing: Marketing Science. *Journal of Marketing Research*, 30(1): 1–6.

Bass, F.M. (2001). Some History of the TIMS/INFORMS College on Marketing as Related to the Development of Marketing Science. *Marketing Science*, 20(4): 360–363.

Bass, F.M., Buzzell, R.D., Greene, M.R., Lazer, W., Pessemier, E.A., Shawver, D.R., Schuchman, A., Theodore, C.A., and Wilson, G.W. (eds) (1961). *Mathematical Models and Methods in Marketing.* Homewood: Richard D. Irwin.

Bate, S.P. (1997). Whatever Happened to Organizational Anthropology? A Review of the Field of Organizational Ethnography and Anthropological Studies. *Human Relations*, 50(9): 1147–1175.

Becker, H.S. (1996). The Epistemology of Qualitative Research. *Ethnography and Human Development: Context and Meaning in Social Inquiry*, 27: 53–71.

Becker, H.S. (2007). *Telling About Society*. Chicago: University of Chicago Press.

Becker, H.S. (2008). *Tricks of the Trade: How to Think About Your Research While You're Doing It*. Chicago: University of Chicago Press.

Belk, R.W. and Pollay, R.W. (1985). Images of Ourselves: The Good Life in Twentieth Century Advertising. *Journal of Consumer Research*, 11(4): 887–897.

Bernbach, W. (2003). *Bill Bernbach Said …* . New York: DDB Worldwide Communications Group Incorporated.

Berners-Lee, M. (2020). *How Bad are Bananas? The Carbon Footprint of Everything*. London: Profile Books.

Bettman, J. (1979). *An Information Processing Theory of Consumer Choice*. Reading, MA: Addison-Wesley.

Bradshaw, A., McDonagh, P., Marshall, D., and Bradshaw, H. (2005). 'Exiled Music Herself, Pushed to the Edge of Existence': The Experience of Musicians Who Perform Background Music. *Consumption Markets & Culture*, 8(3): 219–239.

Braverman, H. (1974). *Labor and Monopoly Capital: The Degradation of Work in the Twentieth Century*. New York: Monthly Review Press.

Brown, S. (2007). Are We Nearly There Yet? On the Retro-dominant Logic of Marketing. *Marketing Theory*, 7(3): 291–300.

Brownlie, D. (1997). Beyond Ethnography: Towards Writerly Accounts of Organizing in Marketing. *European Journal of Marketing*, 31(3/4): 264–284.

Burrell, G. (2013). *Styles of Organizing: The Will to Form*. Oxford: Oxford University Press.

Burrell, G. and Morgan, G. (1979). *Sociological Paradigms and Organisational Analysis*. London: Routledge.

Buzzell, R.D. (1964) *Mathematical Models and Marketing Management*. Boston: Harvard University Press.

Callon, M. (1984). Some Elements of a Sociology of Translation: Domestication of the Scallops and the Fishermen of St Brieuc Bay. *The Sociological Review*, 32(S1): 196–233.

Callon, M. (1990). Techno-Economic Networks and Irreversibility. *The Sociological Review*, 38(S1): 132–161.

Callon, M. and Law, J. (2005). On Qualculation, Agency, and Otherness. *Environment and Planning D: Society and Space*, 23(5): 717–733.

Callon, M. and Muniesa, F. (2005). Economic Markets as Calculative Collective Devices. *Organization Studies*, 26(8): 1229–1250.

Callon, M., Méadel, C., and Rabeharisoa, V. (2002). The Economy of Qualities. *Economy and Society*, 31(2): 194–217.

Callon, M., Akrich, M., Dubuisson-Quellier, S., Grandclément, C., Hennion, A., Latour, B., Mallard, A., Méadel, C., Muniesa, F., and Rabeharisoa, V. (2013). *Sociologie des Agencements Marchands*. Paris: Presses des Mines.

Cluley, R. (2011). *Creative Production in the UK Music Industries* (Doctoral Dissertation, University of Leicester).

Cluley, R. (2013a). What Makes a Management Buzzword Buzz? *Organization Studies*, 34(1): 33–43.

Cluley, R. (2013b). Downloading Deviance: Symbolic Interactionism and Unauthorised File-sharing. *Marketing Theory*, 13(3): 263–274.

Cluley, R. (2016). The Depiction of Marketing and Marketers in the News Media. *European Journal of Marketing*, 50(5/6): 752–769.

Cluley, R. (2017). *Essentials of Advertising*. London: Kogan Page.

Cluley, R. (2018). The Construction of Marketing Measures: The Case of Viewability. *Marketing Theory*, 18(3): 287–305.

Cluley, R. (2020). The Politics of Consumer Data. *Marketing Theory*, 20(1): 45–63.

Cluley, R. (2022). Interesting Numbers: An Ethnographic Account of Quantification, Marketing Analytics and Facial Coding Data. *Marketing Theory*, 22(1): 3–20.

Cluley, R. (2023). An Ethnographic Study of Organizational Performances in Business Services: Space, Staging and Materiality. *Human Relations*, 76(11): 1802–1826.

Cluley, R. and Brown, S.D. (2015). The Dividualised Consumer: Sketching the New Mask of the Consumer. *Journal of Marketing Management*, 31(1–2): 107–122.

Cluley, R. and Green, W. (2019). Social Representations of Marketing Work: Advertising Workers and Social Media. *European Journal of Marketing*, 53(5): 830–847.

Cluley, R., Green, W., and Owen, R. (2020). The Changing Role of the Marketing Researcher in the Age of Digital Technology: Practitioner Perspectives on the Digitization of Marketing Research. *International Journal of Market Research*, 62(1): 27–42.

Cochoy, F. (2007). A Sociology of Market-things: On Tending the Garden of Choices in Mass Retailing. In Callon, M., Millo, Y., and Muniesa, F. (eds) *Market Devices*. Oxford: Blackwell Publishers/The Sociological Review, pp 109–129.

Cochoy, F. (2008). Calculation, Qualculation, Calqulation: Shopping Cart's Arithmetic, Equipped Cognition and Clustered Consumers. *Marketing Theory*, 8(1): 15–44.

Cochoy, F. (2009). Driving a Shopping Cart from STS to Business, and the Other Way Round: On the Introduction of Shopping Carts in American Grocery Stores (1936–1959). *Organization*, 16(1): 31–55.

Collins, H.M. and Evans, R. (2002). The Third Wave of Science Studies: Studies of Expertise and Experience. *Social Studies of Science*, 32(2): 235–296.

Cronin, A.M. (2004a). Currencies of Commercial Exchange: Advertising Agencies and the Promotional Imperative. *Journal of Consumer Culture*, 4(3): 339–360.

Cronin, A.M. (2004b). Regimes of Mediation: Advertising Practitioners as Cultural Intermediaries? *Consumption Markets & Culture*, 7(4): 349–369.

Darwin, C.R. (1872). *The Expression of the Emotions in Man and Animals*. London: John Murray.

Day, R.L. and Parsons, L.J. (1970). *Marketing Models: Quantitative Applications*. Scranton: Intext Educational Publishers.

de Waal Malefyt, T. (2017). Advertising Magic: The Paradox of Keeping-while-giving. *Anthropology Today*, 33(2): 19–23.

de Waal Malefyt, T. and Morais, R.J. (2010). Creativity, Brands, and the Ritual Process: Confrontation and Resolution in Advertising Agencies. *Culture and Organization*, 16(4): 333–347.

Deleuze, G. (1988) *Foucault*, trans S. Hand. Minneapolis: University of Minnesota Press.

Diaz Ruiz, C.A. (2013). Assembling Market Representations. *Marketing Theory*, 13(3): 245–261.

Ekman, P. (1993). Facial Expression and Emotion. *American Psychologist*, 48(4): 384–392.

Ekman, P. and Friesen, W. (1978). *Facial Action Coding System: A Technique for the Measurement of Facial Movement*. Palo Alto: Consulting Psychologists Press.

Ekman, P. and Friesen, W. (2003). *Unmasking the Face: A Guide to Recognising Emotions from Facial Expressions*. Los Altos: Malor Books.

Ewen, S. (1976). *Captains of Consciousness: Advertising and the Social Roots of the Consumer Culture*. New York: Basic Books.

Feldwick, P. (2015). *The Anatomy of Humbug: How to Think Differently about Advertising*. Kilworth Beauchamp: Troubador Publishing.

Fletcher, W. (2008). *Powers of Persuasion: The Inside Story of British Advertising 1951–2000*. Oxford: Oxford University Press.

Fox, N. and Alldred, P. (2017). *Sociology and the New Materialism: Theory, Research, Action*. Thousand Oaks: SAGE.

Franco, P., Canniford, R., and Phipps, M. (2022). Object-oriented Marketing Theory. *Marketing Theory*, 22(3): 401–420.

Frank, R.E., Kuehn, A.A., and Massy, W.F. (1962). *Quantitative Techniques in Marketing Analysis*. Homewood: Richard D. Irwin.

Frank, T. (1998). *The Conquest of Cool: Business Culture, Counterculture, and the Rise of Hip Consumerism*. Chicago: University of Chicago Press.

Geertz, C. (1973). *The Interpretation of Cultures*. New York: Basic Books.

Goffman, E. (1959). *The Presentation of Self in Everyday Life*. London: Penguin.

Goffman, E. (1961). *Asylums: Essays on the Social Situation of Mental Patients and Other Innates*. London: Doubleday.

Goulding, C. (2005). Grounded Theory, Ethnography and Phenomenology: A Comparative Analysis of Three Qualitative Strategies for Marketing Research. *European Journal of Marketing*, 39(3/4): 294–308.

Green, W. and Cluley, R. (2014). The Field of Radical Innovation: Making Sense of Organizational Cultures and Radical Innovation. *Industrial Marketing Management*, 43(8): 1343–1350.

Gurrieri, L. (2012). The Don Draper Complex: Consuming Work, Productive Leisure and Marketer Boundary Work. *Journal of Marketing Management*, 28(7–8): 784–808.

Hayek, F.A. (1942). Scientism and the Study of Society. Part I. *Economica*, 9(35): 267–291.

Hayek, F.A. (1975). The Pretence of Knowledge. *The Swedish Journal of Economics*, 77(4): 433–442.

Heath, T., Cluley, R., and O'Malley, L. (2017). Beating, Ditching and Hiding: Consumers' Everyday Resistance to Marketing. *Journal of Marketing Management*, 33(15–16): 1281–1303.

Hegarty, J. (2011). *Hegarty on Advertising: Turning Intelligence into Magic*. London: Thames & Hudson.

Herman, E.S. and Chomsky, N. (1988). *Manufacturing Consent: The Political Economy of the Mass Media*. London: Random House.

Hill, T., Canniford, R., and Mol, J. (2014). Non-representational Marketing Theory. *Marketing Theory*, 14(4): 377–394.

Hopkins, C.C. (1923). *Scientific Advertising*. New York: Bell.

Hutchinson, K.D. (1952). Marketing as a Science: An Appraisal. *Journal of Marketing*, 16(3): 286–293.

Jeffery, M. (2010). *Data-driven Marketing: The 15 Metrics Everyone in Marketing Should Know*. New York: John Wiley & Sons.

Kahneman, D. (2011). *Thinking, Fast and Slow*. London: Penguin.

Kelly, A., Lawlor, K., and O'Donohoe, S. (2005). Encoding Advertisements: The Creative Perspective. *Journal of Marketing Management*, 21(5–6): 505–528.

Kenny, K. and Euchler, G. (2012). Some Good Clean Fun: Humour, Control and Subversion in an Advertising Agency. *Gender, Work & Organization*, 19(3): 306–323.

Keynes, J.M. (1936). *The General Theory of Employment, Interest and Money*. London: Macmillan.

Kotler, P. (1971). *Marketing Decision Making: A Model Building Approach.* New York: Holt, Rinehart and Winston.

Kuhn, T.S. (1962). *The Structure of Scientific Revolutions.* Chicago: University of Chicago Press.

Latour, B. (1987). *Science in Action: How to Follow Scientists and Engineers through Society.* Cambridge, MA: Harvard University Press.

Latour, B. (1994). On Technical Mediation. *Common Knowledge,* 3(2): 29–64.

Latour, B. and Woolgar, S. (1979). *Laboratory Life: The Construction of Scientific Facts.* New York: Princeton University Press.

Law, J. and Williams, R.J. (1982) Putting Facts Together: A Study of Scientific Persuasion. *Social Studies of Science,* 12(4): 535–558.

Leiss, W., Kline, S., and Jhally, S. (1990). *Social Communication in Advertising: Persons, Products & Images of Well-Being.* New York: Psychology Press.

Lilien, G.L., Rangaswamy, A., and De Bruyn, A. (2013). *Principles of Marketing Engineering.* New York: DecisionPro.

MacKenzie, D. (2006). Is Economics Performative? Option Theory and the Construction of Derivatives Markets. *Journal of the History of Economic Thought,* 28(1): 29–55.

Mangham, I.L. (2005). Vita Contemplativa: The Drama of Organizational Life. *Organization Studies,* 26(6): 941–958.

March, J.G. and Simon, H.A. (1958) *Organizations.* New York: Wiley.

Marchand, R. (1985). *Advertising the American Dream.* Berkeley: University of California Press.

Marx, K. (1978). *Capital: Volume II.* London: Penguin UK.

McDuff, D. and el Kaliouby, R. (2017). Applications of Automated Facial Coding in Media Measurement. *IEEE Transactions on Affective Computing,* 8(2): 148–160.

McDuff, D., el Kaliouby, R., Senechal, T., Demirdjian, D., and Picard, R. (2014). Automatic Measurement of Ad Preferences from Facial Responses Gathered over the Internet. *Image and Vision Computing,* 32(10): 630–640.

McDuff, D., El Kaliouby, R., and Picard, R.W. (2012. Crowdsourcing Facial Responses to Online Videos. *IEEE Transactions on Affective Computing,* 3(4): 456–468.

McDuff, D., El Kaliouby, R., Cohn, J.F., and Picard, R.W. (2015b). Predicting Ad Liking and Purchase Intent: Large-scale Analysis of Facial Responses to Ads. *IEEE Transactions on Affective Computing,* 6(3): 223–235.

Merton, R.K. (1938). Science and the Social Order. *Philosophy of Science,* 5(3): 321–337.

Merton, R.K. (1948). The Self-fulfilling Prophecy. *The Antioch Review,* 8(2): 193–210.

Merton, R.K. (1957). *Social Theory and Social Structure.* New York: Free Press.

Merton, R.K. (1973). *The Sociology of Science: Theoretical and Empirical Investigations.* Chicago: University of Chicago Press.

Mills, C.W. (1951). *White Collar: The American Middle Classes*. Oxford: Oxford University Press.

Mirowski, P. (2002). *Machine Dreams: Economics Becomes a Cyborg Science*. Cambridge: Cambridge University Press.

Moeran, B. (2005). Tricks of the Trade: The Performance and Interpretation of Authenticity. *Journal of Management Studies*, 42(5): 901–922.

Moeran, B. (2006). *Ethnography at Work*. Oxford: Berg Publishers.

Moeran, B. (2007). A Dedicated Storytelling Organization: Advertising Talk in Japan. *Human Organization*, 66(2): 160–170.

Moeran, B. (2009). The Organization of Creativity in Japanese Advertising Production. *Human Relations*, 62(7): 963–985.

Morin, C. and Renvoisé, P. (2018). *The Persuasion Code: How Neuromarketing can Help You Persuade Anyone, Anywhere, Anytime*. New York: John Wiley & Sons.

Muniesa, F. (2014). *The Provoked Economy: Economic Reality and the Performative Turn*. London: Routledge.

Neslin, S.A. and Winer, R.S. (2014). The History of Marketing Science: Beginnings. In Winer, R.S. and Neslin, S.A. (eds) *History of Marketing Science*. London: World Scientific, pp 1–17.

Neyland, D. (2008). *Organizational Ethnography*. London: SAGE.

Nilsson, J. (2019). Know Your Customer: Client Captivation and the Epistemics of Market Research. *Marketing Theory*, 19(2): 149–168.

Nilsson, J. (2020). Producing Consumers: Market Researchers' Selection and Conception of Focus Group Participants. *Consumption Markets & Culture*, 23(4): 376–389.

Nilsson, J. (2021). Shaping Epistemic Distance: Producing and Withholding Knowledge in Market Research. *Journal of Cultural Economy*, 14(1): 101–116.

Nilsson, T. (2019). How Marketers Argue for Business: Exploring the Rhetorical Nature of Industrial Marketing Work. *Industrial Marketing Management*, 80: 233–241.

Nunan, D. and Di Domenico, M. (2019). Rethinking the Market Research Curriculum. *International Journal of Market Research*, 61(1): 22–32.

Nyilasy, G. and Reid, L.N. (2009). Agency Practitioner Theory of How Advertising Works. *Journal of Advertising*, 38(3): 81–96.

Ogilvy, D. (1963). *Confessions of an Advertising Man*. New York: Atheneum.

O'Neil, C. (2017). *Weapons of Math Destruction: How Big Data Increases Inequality and Threatens Democracy*. London: Crown.

Paas, L. (2019). Marketing Research Education in the Big Data Era. *International Journal of Market Research*, 61(3): 233–235.

Packard, V. (1957). *The Hidden Persuaders*. London: Penguin.

Pariser, E. (2011). *The Filter Bubble: What the Internet is Hiding from You*. London: Penguin.

Parsons, T. (1951). *The Social System*. London: Routledge.

Pickering, A. (2010). *The Cybernetic Brain: Sketches of Another Future.* Chicago: University of Chicago Press.

Piercy, N.F., Cravens, D.W., and Morgan, N.A. (1997). Sources of Effectiveness in the Business-to-business Sales Organization. *Journal of Marketing Practice: Applied Marketing Science*, 3(1): 45–71.

Pollay, R.W. (1986). The Distorted Mirror: Reflections on the Unintended Consequences of Advertising. *Journal of Marketing*, 50(2): 18–36.

Potter, J. and Wetherell, M. (1987). *Discourse and Social Psychology: Beyond Attitudes and Behaviour.* London: SAGE.

Preda, A. (2007). Where Do Analysts Come From? The Case of Financial Chartism. *The Sociological Review*, 55(S2): 40–64.

Prus, R.C. (1989). *Pursuing Customers: An Ethnography of Marketing Activities.* London: SAGE.

Quinn, L., Dibb, S., Simkin, L., Canhoto, A., and Analogbei, M. (2016). Troubled Waters: The Transformation of Marketing in a Digital World. *European Journal of Marketing*, 50(12): 2103–2133.

Renvoisé, P. and Morin, C. (2007). *Neuromarketing: Understanding the Buy Buttons in Your Customer's Brain.* New York: HarperCollins Leadership.

Rosen, M. (1985). Breakfast at Spiro's: Dramaturgy and Dominance. *Journal of Management*, 11(2): 31–48.

Rosen, M. (1987). Critical Administrative Scholarship, Praxis, and the Academic Workplace. *Journal of Management*, 13(3): 573–586.

Rothenberg, R. (Guest). (2016). Brands Can't Pass the Buck on Policing Media Issues. *Digiday.com*, 5 August. https://digiday.com/media/iab-chief-brands-cant-pass-buck-policing-media-issues/

Schneider, T. and Woolgar, S. (2012). Technologies of Ironic Revelation: Enacting Consumers in Neuromarkets. *Consumption Markets & Culture*, 15(2): 169–189.

Schwarzkopf, S. (2015a). Mobilizing the Depths of the Market: Motivation Research and the Making of the Disembedded Consumer. *Marketing Theory*, 15(1): 39–57.

Schwarzkopf, S. (2015b). Measurement Devices and the Psychophysiology of Consumer Behaviour: A Posthuman Genealogy of Neuromarketing. *BioSocieties*, 10(4): 465–482.

Sharp, B (2010). *How Brands Grow: What Marketers Don't Know.* Oxford: Oxford University Press.

Shugan, S.M. (2002). Marketing Science, Models, Monopoly Models, and Why We Need Them. *Marketing Science*, 21(3): 223–228.

Simon, H.A. (1979). Rational Decision Making in Business Organizations. *The American Economic Review*, 69(4): 493–513.

Simon, H.A. (1945). *Administrative Behavior.* New York: Free Press.

Skålén, P. and Hackley, C. (2011). Marketing-as-Practice: Introduction to the Special Issue. *Scandinavian Journal of Management*, 27(2): 189–195.

Smith, A. (2019). *Consumer Behaviour and Analytics*. London: Routledge.

Srnicek, N. (2017). *Platform Capitalism*. John Wiley & Sons.

Svensson, P. (2007). Producing Marketing: Towards a Social-phenomenology of Marketing Work. *Marketing Theory*, 7(3): 271–290.

Svensson, P. (2019). Critical Studies of Marketing Work. In *The SAGE Handbook of Consumer Culture*. London: SAGE, pp 351–364.

Tadajewski, M. (2014). Paradigm Debates and Marketing Theory, Thought and Practice: From the 1900s to the Present Day. *Journal of Historical Research in Marketing*, 6(3): 303–330.

Tadajewski, M. (2016). Focus Groups: History, Epistemology and Non-individualistic Consumer Research. *Consumption Markets & Culture*, 19(4): 319–345.

Tungate, M. (2007). *Adland: A Global History of Advertising*. London: Kogan Page.

Turow, J. (2012). *The Daily You: How the New Advertising Industry Is Defining Your Identity and Your Worth*. New Haven: Yale University Press.

Wang, J. (2010). *Brand New China: Advertising, Media, and Commercial Culture*. Cambridge, MA: Harvard University Press.

Watson, T.J. (2011). Ethnography, Reality, and Truth: The Vital Need for Studies of 'How Things Work' in Organizations and Management. *Journal of Management Studies*, 48(1): 202–217.

Weber, M. (1905). *The Protestant Ethic and the Spirit of Capitalism*. London: Unwin Hyman.

Wells Lawrence, M. (2003). *A Big Life in Advertising*. New York: Simon & Schuster.

Wernick, A. (1991). *Promotional Culture*. London: SAGE.

Whyte, W.H. (1956). *Organization Man*. New York: Simon & Schuster.

Wilkie, W.L. and Moore, E.S. (1999). Marketing's Contributions to Society. *Journal of Marketing*, 63(S1): 198–218.

Williamson, J. (1978). *Decoding Advertisements*. London: Marion Boyars.

Wymbs, C. (2011). Digital Marketing: The Time for a New 'Academic Major' Has Arrived. *Journal of Marketing Education*, 33(1): 93–106.

Zaltman, G. (1997). Rethinking Market Research: Putting People Back In. *Journal of Marketing Research*, 34(4): 424–437.

Zeithaml, V.A., Jaworski, B.J., Kohli, A.K., Tuli, K.R., Ulaga, W., and Zaltman, G. (2020). A Theories-in-use Approach to Building Marketing Theory. *Journal of Marketing*, 84(1): 32–51.

Zuboff, S. (2019). *The Age of Surveillance Capitalism: The Fight for a Human Future at the New Frontier of Power*. New York: Public Affairs.

Zwick, D. and Bradshaw, A. (2016). Biopolitical Marketing and Social Media Brand Communities. *Theory, Culture and Society*, 33(5): 91–115.

Zwick, D. and Denegri Knott, J. (2009). Manufacturing Customers: The Database as New Means of Production. *Journal of Consumer Culture*, 9(2): 221–247.

Index

products *see* Compare studies;
 Emotionality studies; Heartbeat studies;
 Virality studies
relationship with clients 96, 98, 168
 Luxury Car Social Media Playbook
 99–102, 107–108
research team 70–72
scientism 111–125
 general and specific 123–125
 signs of 119–123
 spaces of 111–119
scripting 89–90
staff relations 93–95
working day 81–84
 huddle time 84–88
surveillance capitalism 5–6
Svensson, P. 1, 59, 62

T

thick descriptions 57
translation 7, 10

U

uncertainty 98
uncertainty absorption 13, 104–107, 124,
 135, 167–168
 Luxury Car Social Media Playbook
 presentation 161, 163, 164
 Online Content Survey 147

V

verbatims 133–135
Virality EQ score 96–97
Virality studies 70, 87, 90, 120, 121–123

W

Wang, J. 17, 62, 63–64
Watson, T.J. 77
White Collar (Mills) 8
Whyte, W. 110–111

Z

Zuboff, S. 5–6